The Remains of War

Surviving the Other Concentration Camps of World War II

G. Pauline Kok-Schurgers

iUniverse, Inc.
Bloomington

The Remains of War
Surviving the Other Concentration Camps of World War II

iUniverse books may be ordered through booksellers or by contacting:

iUniverse
1663 Liberty Drive
Bloomington, IN 47403
www.iuniverse.com
1-800-Authors (1-800-288-4677)

Because of the dynamic nature of the Internet, any web addresses or links contained in this book may have changed since publication and may no longer be valid. The views expressed in this work are solely those of the author and do not necessarily reflect the views of the publisher, and the publisher hereby disclaims any responsibility for them.

Any people depicted in stock imagery provided by Thinkstock are models, and such images are being used for illustrative purposes only.

Certain stock imagery © Thinkstock.

ISBN: 978-1-4502-9671-7 (sc)
ISBN: 978-1-4502-9668-7 (dj)
ISBN: 978-1-4502-9667-0 (ebook)

Library of Congress Control Number: 2011902322

Printed in the United States of America

iUniverse rev. date: 03/28/2011

Overzichtskaart Noord Sumatra

STRAAT VAN MALAKKA

ATJEH

INDISCHE OCEAAN

RESIDENTIE SUMATRA'S OOSTKUST

RESIDENTIE TAPANOELI

PADANG

LAWAS

TOBA MEER

Sabang
Kota Radja
Sigli
Meureudoe
Lhokseumawe
Bireuen
Takengon
Laut Tawar
Talang
Meulaboh
Idi
Langsa
Tandjong Poera
Besitang
Pangkalan Brandan
Beliawan
Tebing Tinggi
Kisaran
Tandjoengbalai
Medan
Brnei
Deli rivier
Kota Tjane
Lawe Si Galiga
Kaban Djahe
Brastagi
Pematang Siantar
Prapat
Samosir
Balige
Toetoeng
Taroetoeng
Sibolga
Singkel
Tapaktoean
Goenoeng Sitoli
Bandar Poerba
Rantau Prapat
Goenoeng Toea
Padang Sidempoean
Asahan rivier
Bila rivier
Barumun rivier

autoweg
residentiegrens
rivier
spoorweg

0   100 km

For all of you we had to leave behind. You fought and lost your lives, but ultimately won over pain and evil. In my mind and memory, I will always touch you.

For Jacob, who had to suffer for my sake but understood the urgency.

For Paul and Natascha, Stella and Mark. I am present with you in the prayer that, now and always, a rainbow will shine on you and shadows will disappear.

And for Anna Mercx, without whom the Dutch translation of *The Remains of War* would not have been possible.

PREFACE

In 1942, Japan overpowered the Royal Dutch Marines in the Sea of Java and sent eight hundred men to an early grave. Soon after, the Dutch army in Indonesia surrendered to the Japanese, first in Java, and then in Sumatra, two of the largest islands of the Indonesian Archipelago.

The Japanese army then steadily conquered all of Sumatra, harnessing the hostility of a part of the local Indonesian population who had been carrying out anti-Dutch sabotage operations before the Japanese had even arrived. Atjeh, Sumatra's northernmost province, was a particularly difficult front, populated by secret guerilla troops just waiting to support the Japanese soldiers.

Once in charge, the Japanese army released many of the native Indonesian soldiers, but kept the European men as prisoners, putting them to work all over Sumatra. They were interned in camps, and forced to work in airfields, refineries, and harbors, constructing air-raid shelters.

The large majority of POWs who fell into Japanese hands in north and central Sumatra were concentrated in Belawan Harbor, the harbor in the capital of Medan. These men were then sent overseas to Burma, where they were forced to build the Burma-Siam Railroad.

More than four thousand men died and were buried there, most of them family men—fathers, grandfathers, and sons. And they died alone, as if abandoned and forgotten; until the end of World War II, their wives and mothers and children were not privy to where they had been, and often never learned when or how they died.

Meanwhile, Dutch women and children were kept in concentration camps, and what happened to them there has remained an untouched and rather forgotten subject. Harsh conditions, including savage Japanese soldiers who entertained themselves by humiliating, torturing, degrading, and ruthlessly killing these women and children, have been insufficiently documented.

Since 1945, numerous books, documentaries, and films have enlightened the world about the atrocities of World War II everywhere. Yet, remarkably, one group of people and one place on Earth remained unvisited. A few efforts made to film concentration camps during the Japanese occupation of Indonesia did not bring to light the true extent of injustice that took place among these innocent, defenseless women and children; they did not portray even a fraction of the misery—the hunger, the abuse, the sickness and disease, the separation of boys from their mothers, the dying. And that's not to mention the lifelong aftereffects: the bitterness forever left in victims' hearts, the inferiority complexes, and the thoughts of suicide.

That is just one reason why now, sixty-five years after Emperor Hirohito signed a document of surrender, I must write about my experience in these camps. There are many other reasons, of course, but the primary one is the realization that after my generation is gone, no witnesses will be left to open the history book that Japan would like to keep closed forever. Hirohito never admitted the countless murders of war victims, and, so far, Japan has denied any part of this dark past—and its loss would be unforgivable.

All of this is why I felt the need, after sixty-five years, to write down what I could not touch for so long. It is where I found the courage to unlock the caves of memories that would destroy parts of what I had won and gained personally in the years after the war.

In those sixty-five years, we survivors have had to fight to regain a sense of normalcy, and, even now, still carry the garbage of humiliation, abuse, and depression. Caged control and emotions have instilled permanent damage. Fear, panic, despair, and grief have created a warped people who have had to spend the rest of their days trying to deal with the change and disability caused by relentless cruelty, terror, and sadism.

Then children—unsuspecting, innocent boys and girls—we are now men and women with the seal of sadistic Japanese brutality forever stamped in our memories. And these are the true remains of war: the painful remembrances of what are still black pages in history.

Yet there will never be an end to them, unless we face them, accept them for what they are, and have peace. But then, perhaps, we were not created *to have* peace, but *to bring* peace.

CONTENTS

LANGSA—HOME

Langsa, Island of Sumatra, 1942

In the far distance, the soft droning of airplanes grew louder, just as the sirens started. On Dad's bike, which was far too big for me, I pushed the pedals harder, as people walking the street began to run in the same direction. They were silent, except for their bare feet, which flapped on the asphalt when they passed me. Some couldn't go fast, for they were pulling children in carriages or cradling babies on their backs. But the people wearing shoes, who were almost as swift as I was on my bike, were the most difficult to avoid. It was the second time this week that planes had sent us running for the bomb shelters housed on every street corner.

The now thunderous planes fed my fear as they passed overhead, the pain in my side growing. The bike took over, just as I reached the shelter at the end of the sloping road; it wobbled awkwardly and landed in the ditch, its back wheel catching my knees. I thought I could hear the pounding of my heart over the sirens as I crouched under the wheel and watched the planes fly over me. A red ball showed under each wing, and inside one, I could see the shadow of someone sitting in the cockpit. They were gone before I could see much more.

I abandoned the bike and dove through the shelter entrance into darkness and the damp stink of sweat and fear. The sounds were different here. There were no sirens. Only suppressed sobs, whispered assurances, and children weeping. My knees were burning and felt wet, but the darkness of the shelter felt good and safe—no one could see me and I could not see anyone. We were all anonymous and all the same; here, we were all afraid.

A long time later, once the sirens were silenced, we dared to leave the shelter. Outside, it was quiet, and the sun had lost much of her brightness; we

1

must have been inside for over an hour. As everyone hurried away, I noticed how many of us had been pressed together in that small space. Shelters were relatively small, not larger than an average bedroom, and also the ceiling was lower. Indonesian people, Dutch people, even some Chinese women; despite our disparate races, we had shared the same feeling of confinement, the same dank-smelling darkness, and the same desire for it all to be over.

I gratefully inhaled the fresh air, walking around the hill to look for Dad's bike, but it was not where I had left it. I decided to wait until the masses of people had let up to look further, and I leaned against the hill to examine my knees. They had been bleeding and were scraped up good and painful. It didn't worry me, though. I had had bleeding scrapes before and they always healed. I stood up stiffly when I saw the last people disappear in the distance.

After running twice around the shelter hill, I finally had to accept that the bike was gone. I sighed. Losing that bike was serious. Mom would be furious. Dad had used it to go to work each morning as the principal of the only Dutch grade school in Langsa.

Langsa was a little town on the island of Sumatra. Sumatra was one of the larger islands of Indonesia, which was at that time a colony of the Netherlands. The numerous Dutch who lived in Indonesia owned tea or rubber plantations, had jobs in the two oil refineries, or worked for the government or as teachers in the many Dutch schools. Also, Indonesian children went to Dutch schools and were taught the Dutch language. Likewise, most Dutch children learned to speak Indonesian because they were so close to the Indonesian servants in their families. So, all but a few children in Langsa were bilingual.

Having been born in Indonesia, I didn't know any other life, and I loved our small town. I loved my many friends, some of whom were half Indonesian, because their Dutch fathers had married Indonesian girls. I loved our servants, Sitah and Hassan, even more than I loved Mom and Dad. They were sweet and patient, they never raised their voices when we were bad, and they were always with us, not just when Mom or Dad, for whatever reason, couldn't be there. Sitah and Hassan were married and had their own rooms at the back of our house, where they slept, took baths, and prepared their meals. They cooked outside on a little wood fire between some bricks. Mom and Dad trusted them unconditionally, for they were devoted to us and treated me, my baby sisters Easabella and Emma-M, and my younger brother, Simon, as if we were their own.

Sitah was there mostly to take care of us children. Hassan was responsible for what went on in the house, but when he was done with his work, he would take Simon under his wing. At five, Simon was quiet and a bit shy, and seemed happy only when he was around Mom. Being the sole boy in our family, he was Mom's darling and she showed this often enough. Easabella and Emma-M were too young to notice, and I told myself I didn't care—I had Dad's attention and, even better, I had Peter, my best friend. I wished Peter were my brother.

Running around with bleeding knees looking for Dad's bike had tired me out, and I sank against the slope of the hill and closed my eyes. The wind felt cool and soothing over my face, and, for a moment, I pushed away my guilt over losing Dad's bike, only to replace it with disturbing thoughts of the last few weeks.

Mom and Dad and all their friends had become so nervous and irritable, and they always stopped talking when kids were around. Then the shelters had popped up everywhere and we were told to immediately head toward one when the sirens went off. The sirens could be heard all over the city, and every time they sounded, the Indonesians would mumble a streak of prayers, followed by curses to ward off danger and evil spirits. I had heard these chants so often that I could almost say them too, but Mom didn't like to hear it.

When the high-flying planes started coming over, Dad explained that the red painted ball under each wing was the Japanese flag. The newspapers were talking about the Japanese, too, publishing pictures of soldiers and articles warning of Japanese invasions.

Life had changed. Everything felt uncomfortable now. It was as if no one really knew what to expect. Uncertainty and fear had changed our little city.

The schools closed, too, but I liked that part. I had more time to roam those places Mom didn't want me to go. Sometimes, after Dad started going away at night, Mom would pace the floor, biting her nails. That made me suspicious. Mom was proud of her hands. They were large and slender, with beautiful, long, polished nails. I found her crying last week, trying to repair them.

The last two Sundays, we had also missed brunch with our neighbors, Uncle Cor and Aunt Maggie. They were good friends of Mom and Dad and had two sons, Kees and William. The Sunday brunches had started after Uncle Cor built a large pool in their backyard, and the boys had wanted me to come for swims. They didn't have to ask twice. We would race through the water, and usually Kees or William won, because they were awesome swimmers.

But when it came to running long-distance or climbing coconut trees, I had them both beaten. Hassan had taught me to climb a coconut tree with a strong rope looped around both my ankles. Using the thick horizontal grooves of the sloping tree, I could almost walk to the top, where my fingertips could touch the large green fruit hanging in clusters under the palm leaves. The boys could only go up halfway, after which they would slide down with red faces and lots of excuses. Then, when they weren't watching, I would drop a coconut on one of their heads. Of course, I had to pay for it when I came down; they always threw me in the pool.

Whenever the three of us played ball, I tried to interest Simon to join, but he never did. Simon was a sissy around the pool too. He didn't like to get wet. He never even wanted to join Easabella and Emma-M in their little baby tub, though he claimed it was because they peed in the water and the water made him cold.

Uncle Cor and Dad had met playing soccer on the same team, and once the pool had been built, it hadn't taken long for the adults to begin spending all their Sundays together around it, discussing everything from children's behavior to difficult situations among the locals.

Uncle Cor was an army officer and sometimes would not be there because he had duty, but Dad and the ladies would still play cards together or supervise games of Monopoly and Checkers, which Kees and William loved to play. Then after the games and laughter, we enjoyed the Sunday *ricetafel*, prepared by Sitah and Aunt Maggie's cook.

The two women were experts in Indonesian cooking, so watching them was fun. They used Indonesian spices over fresh, raw chicken thighs. They fried large plantains and changed them into sweet, brown delicacies. We watched the raw, large prawns die when Sitah slipped them into the boiling water, turning them instantly pink. The odor of fried, salty, sardine-sized fish filled the air all morning and made us hungry long before lunchtime.

These *ricetafel* dishes were cooked outside on little open fires between large bricks on the ground. The cooking area had always been swept spotless, and next to the darkly colored bricks would sit neatly split pieces of wood, exactly the size of the space between the warm, burned stones. The food was prepared in black *wadjangs* (woks) with wooden handles to protect hands from getting burned. The cooks would squat comfortably in front of their fire, stirring, when necessary, with long wooden spoons, or just watching the food bubble and become delicious.

Mom and Dad came from Holland, so they hadn't known about rice and spicy Indonesian dishes before Dad had come here to teach. Although they came to love the rice dishes, Mom and Dad still liked to eat potatoes, vegetables, and meat regularly. I, however, was born in Indonesia and had grown up on its food. Whenever Dutch food was on the menu, I tried to hide around mealtime and sneak to the back of the house, where I knew Sitah and Hassan would have their meal of rice with several side dishes. They would not only allow me to eat, but to do so with my hands. I had become skilled at forming a delicious clump of food between my fingers, which I would bring to my mouth, without losing one grain of rice. No spoon was needed; my thumb would push in the food. And no plate had to be washed afterward, since we used cups of palm leaves held together with a toothpick. The palm leaves would enhance the taste of the warm food and were thrown out when the meal was finished.

Our dinners were at noon instead of at night. At night, we had soup and sandwiches. Sitah and Hassan would eat before the family, because Hassan had to serve at the table when we had our meal. So by the time I came out of hiding, everyone had eaten. Mom would be angry and punish me for being late for dinner. She would tell me that dinnertime had passed so I could just be hungry the rest of the day. I made sure to look repentant, but knew, without seeing him, that there was a smile on Dad's face. He knew where I had been during mealtime. After dinner, the adults became sleepy, and us children had to stay in our rooms till Mom and Dad woke from their siesta.

Emma-M, Easabella, and Simon liked Indonesian food too. Every Sunday morning, they had furtively sneaked handfuls of *kriepiek* (shrimp crackers) from the large bowl when the adults weren't looking. (They were too busy watching Uncle Cor play his favorite accordion music.) Then after the music and games, we circled the large garden table and filled our plates. The rice would steam and the cooks would watch us all with broad smiles as we enjoyed their prepared delicacies. We could add hot peppers, if we could stand it, but only the adults enjoyed this. We children would pile pieces of *pisang goreng* (fried banana), salty fried fish, raw cucumber, boiled eggs, and fried chicken all around the rice, and sit somewhere in the shade. A large glass of cold lemonade would crown it all. This was my favorite meal.

But for the last couple weeks, no one had used the pool and there had been no Sunday brunches. There had been a lot of silence around the houses and gardens and among all the Dutch people.

Kees, William, and I waved when we saw one another, but didn't play or swim in the pool anymore. Mom and Aunt Maggie, who used to have coffee and conversation regularly, only spoke to each other shortly when they happened to be in the garden together.

Before Dad had been forced to close the school without being given a reason, he had explained to me that the Japanese armies were landing on the Indonesian islands and soon would also land on Sumatra. Right after that, Uncle Cor had left. That had been three weeks ago, and we hadn't seen him since. The newspapers had published frightening stories and pictures of Japanese parachutists, who had landed around the two airfields of the city of Palembang, and were fighting with KNIL (the Royal Dutch-Indonesian Army) soldiers for the two oil refineries there. Uncle Cor was in that army, and Aunt Maggie hadn't heard anything from him since two weeks ago, when he had mentioned a possible withdrawal of troops. He had told her he didn't know if he would be in the group that would go, and this had seemed to make Aunt Maggie very afraid. I heard her complain to Mom about her sleepless nights and the continuous questions of Kees and William, which she didn't know how to answer.

There was also silence among the local Indonesians. Some of the men looked angry and threatening. They congregated on corners and stopped talking when *blandas* (white people) passed them. I asked Hassan why they were acting so different from before, but he hadn't wanted to explain. He only warned me to stay away from them.

For a whole week now, we children had stayed inside, having been warned not to show ourselves on streets or in stores. Sitah and Hassan had done all the shopping and when they did, they had gone together instead of alone, as they'd used to. Even in the house, we had been ordered not to show ourselves in front of the windows. The curtains were closed at all times. Hassan had offered to build a fence around our garden so that at least we could play there. But Mom had refused. She said she'd rather keep us close by, where she could see us at all times. I had found it puzzling that Hassan had agreed without arguing; he too must have been afraid.

I wasn't even supposed to be on the streets, let alone with Dad's bike. But I'd needed to return the cartoon magazines I'd borrowed from Arthur, one of my classmates who received a new series of them from Holland each month. They were beautifully colored and the drawings were fabulous, and Arthur's mother had let me borrow them only under the condition that I would return them spotless and in time. I didn't dare keep those magazines any longer.

Now, Dad was gone. I couldn't even explain to him how I lost his bike. In fact, missing Dad had been the worst part of all that had happened over the last few weeks. The empty place at the dining table, and the corner of the living room where Mom had placed his recliner, covered with an unruffled, clean plaid, which reminded us each moment of his absence.

Evening came down around me. Getting up stiffly, I headed home. My knees hurt. The drying scabs opened and started to bleed again. I dreaded having to face Mom. Maybe she would feel sorry for me when she saw my knees, and not be so angry about my losing Dad's bike. She had not been herself since Dad was picked up last week. Even Simon had not been able to rid her of the worried frown on her face or restore the smile in her eyes.

Neither Mom nor Dad had prepared us for what had happened that day last week. I had woken up very early to the loud noises that filled our house: slamming gates and men shouting in a foreign language. I had run to the front door and opened it just in time to see Dad kiss Mom at the roadside. They stood by an idling truck.

A small man in uniform shouted something at Dad, poked a rifle into his back, and then pushed him around to the truck bed, where some other men, who I'd seen in town before, pulled him up. Then Dad turned and saw me. He waved and blew me a kiss, and he kept waving till the truck turned the corner.

My eyes followed until he was gone, and then I sank onto the steps of our front porch. Time seemed to stop as I watched the dust drift back onto the road. The road was empty and still; no one was on it and nothing moved.

Why had he left? I thought. *Why hadn't he at least said good-bye to us? And why hadn't he said anything last night?*

In the wake of the chilly night, dew sparkled where light touched it. The birds weren't even awake yet and the trees loomed as dark shapes against the paling sky. There was no sound until the front door creaked open behind me. Without turning, I knew that Simon was standing there. Mom still stood at the roadside. She looked frozen in place, watching the corner where the truck had disappeared with Dad. Then she turned and saw us. She was pale and her eyes were puffy.

She seemed to pull herself together then and walked toward us. She touched my head in passing, and then, picking up Simon, she said, "Get inside, Sofia. It is too cool out here and Daddy will be gone for awhile." She dropped Simon in his bed and locked herself in her bedroom, where I heard her cry and say things I couldn't understand.

Later at breakfast, she explained that Japanese soldiers had picked up all of the Dutch and other European men in town and that no one knew where they were going. In the meantime, the women would have to remain in their houses with their children until they received orders from the Japanese army, which must then be followed without questions or protest. She didn't speak anymore after that. She just turned around and called Sitah, asking her to feed Emma-M and help Easabella dress.

I looked at Mom, not fully believing her. Had she and Dad known this was going to happen? Was this what they had been whispering about the last few days? They must have known if the Japanese army had ordered it. And they seemed to have been prepared for the truck to arrive so very early in the morning. But if they knew, then why couldn't we say good-bye to Dad?

As I opened my mouth for more answers, Mom said, "Don't ask questions, Sofia. I either have no answers or I don't want to give them to you. Just believe that Dad could be back soon. That makes it a lot easier."

I felt cheated, like Mom was just saying that to make me feel better. Like she didn't trust me enough to share with me what she knew, or didn't think I was old enough. Simon was little, and Emma-M and Easabella were still babies, but I was nine years old. I could understand and take care of things. I kept looking at her, until she got up and disappeared into her bedroom once again. I knew that look she'd had on her face. It meant that Mom was going to have one of her "bad-nerve days."

When Mom had her bad-nerve days, I stayed far away from her. Before, I would take the little girls outside to play or go for a ride in my wagon, which was big enough for both of them. They would screech when I pulled them hard and fast, Easabella with slight fear, but Emma-M with loud laughter. Simon had never joined in. He preferred staying with Mom and moving around her silent and unnoticed.

But we couldn't go outside anymore, so I looked for a place to hide instead. There was nowhere to go but Sitah and Hassan's rooms at the back of our house. It was a safe place with gentle silence.

Whenever Dad had talked about the changes over the last few weeks, Mom had listened silently, but then often cried and became afraid. Dad had tried to calm her and had promised to find out more about the future of the Europeans in Indonesia. He had also promised to see if there was a possibility For Mom and us children to return to Holland. Then, just before he had been taken, he had locked up the documents and history books that he had collected since coming to Indonesia. He had loved to read about the early years, centuries before, when Dutch sailors had landed on the coasts of these beautiful islands and were welcomed by the friendly population.

Why had Dad secured his books and documents? Had he been worried about the rising interracial tension in their area, which he often discussed when talking to parents of his *Indo* students (students with mixed parents)? Or had he thought they would be stolen? Lately, groups of young Indonesian men would roam the streets, and Dad had said he'd heard mocking remarks from them about the *blandas*. Further, he'd said that some Dutch houses had been robbed. Had he thought they might also rob ours?

I think Dad had been worried about Mom. He knew all about how she got nervous whenever something unexpected or risky happened. Every time Dad was away, she worried till he was back. And now … Mom would not be able to deal with all this.

I had been sent off to Sitah whenever Mom and Dad had their serious discussions. Even Simon had not been allowed to stay, although he was Mom's darling. She seemed to like his affection and his quiet presence. He was always around her.

Simon was so different than I was, which was, perhaps, why I felt Mom loved him more than me. More than any of us. I loved playing with boys and didn't like a single girl I knew. My favorite games were *kastie* (a form of softball), marbles, and soccer, and sometimes I needed to fight. Though when I fought, I did so for Simon, who was often bothered by stronger boys because of his shyness, and because his red hair was an easy target for ridicule. He was small for his age and looked frail, and he didn't like to play with rough boys, so he was considered a pushover. He never stood up for himself. So I did it for him. I didn't mind doing it, but Mom hated it. She couldn't seem to bring herself to love me as she did Simon, even though I often had to fight for her one and only son.

Perhaps she was right. I wasn't a girl with girlish behavior and I was certainly not the lady she wanted me to be. I had no dolls, I preferred shorts over dresses, and I rarely had sandals on my feet as soon as school was out. I felt that Mom wanted me to be the girl I never could be. Perhaps she would have more luck with Easabella or Emma-M when they were older.

Regardless, Simon was sent off to be with Sitah, too, whenever Mom and Dad had their discussions. Sitah would pretend that everything was normal, but then I would see her whisper to Hassan, and once I heard her say that something was very wrong. Easabella and Emma-M were not sent off, however, because at two and three years old, they wouldn't understand Mom and Dad's serious conversations anyway.

Of course, I had eaten with Sitah and Hassan many times, but for Simon this was relatively rare. He would never miss the noon meal with Mom and Dad. He didn't want to disobey Mom or disappoint her, and he had told me so. Simon had his own thoughts about Mom. He loved her dearly and would not jeopardize her special affection for him.

But the few times that Simon had eaten with Sitah and Hassan, he had loved it. Going to visit them was exciting for him and having a meal served in a palm leaf made it extra special. To top it all off, Sitah would allow us to eat with our hands instead of a spoon. Then, Simon would even forget about Mom for awhile. Mom had never allowed us to eat with our hands, but somehow Simon still knew how. He had only never told her.

Sitah would make the familiar palm-leaf cup and fill it with boiled rice. She would add chicken and *kang-kung (*vegetables) to it, along with a bit of *ikan terie* (small fried fish) seasoned with mild pepper sauce. Then she would put it into our hands. It was so good that we would forget why we were eating outside, and Simon was wise enough not to tell Mom about it later.

I thought about all of this as I walked the long road home from the shelter, which was taking much longer than the ride there on Dad's bike. The shadows of the dying day had disappeared, as evening falls early in the tropics; dusk is often no longer than thirty minutes. It was almost totally dark, but the heat of the day had disappeared and a cool wind blew around me and soothed my sore knees. The cicadas sang loud and shrill but fell silent when I passed, only to continue again behind me. Here and there among the houses, an oil lamp radiated soft light. I tried to identify to which house each light belonged, until

I recognized the lantern in our own yard. I went around to the back of the house and was greeted by the delicious aromas of Sitah's cooking.

My eyes, now used to the dark shadows, found Sitah and Hassan sitting in front of the fire. They sat contently silent, almost as if they knew what the other was thinking. They were much more than servants to me, and even much more than guardians. Sitah and Hassan were my very best friends.

Hassan worked mostly in the house. He served meals with polished glasses and silver whenever we had guests. Mom had taught him to serve like an English butler and had bought him a beautiful white uniform. It had a long pair of white pants with a jacket that was always spotless. The jacket had copper buttons that shone like gold and ran from the very bottom up to the collar, which closed high against his neck. The sleeves were long with broad, decorated cuffs. When he moved among the guests in that uniform, topped by the black Muslim cap on his head, he looked like a prince. He was very proud of it. He washed and starched it himself and allowed Sitah to iron it under his watchful eyes.

When Hassan finished his daily work, he would go find Simon, who was usually playing games in whatever room Mom was. Simon would come alive then, because going outside with Hassan meant playing soccer, or flying one of his kites. Hassan kept many kites in his room, just so that he could teach Simon how to fly one perfectly whenever the wind was right. Hassan also made Simon laugh with his many stories, and he endlessly smoked long, thin cigarettes, which he rolled himself. He would blow the smoke around us, to chase away evil spirits.

His feet were calloused, with orange soles—orange, because he washed the soles of his feet once a week with the sap of betel nuts. He believed that doing this would cause his footprints to disappear immediately behind him, so that bad spirits couldn't find him. Hassan had once promised me sap from the betel nuts for my feet, but Sitah had said it wasn't the season for betel nuts.

Simon's eyes would fill with wonder whenever Hassan talked about spirits and about toads walking upright and about ants who invented fire, earning them the proud name of *semoet api* (fire ants). They had a fiery red color, Hassan would say, and when they bit your toes, your nails would start to burn. Simon never walked barefoot after hearing that story the first time.

Hassan would always sit close to the fire, eating his meal. His long fingers would pick among the rice, find what he wanted, roll it all into a neat ball, and then scoop it deftly into his mouth. He would do this over and over, using his thumb to push the food back into his mouth while making little grunts in reply to Sitah's soft words.

Meanwhile, Sitah's fingers would pop peanuts out of their shells. The peanuts Sitah and Hassan liked were bought in the shell. They were fried in a *wadjang* (wok) above the soft fire of the wood-burning oven. When they reached the right burned color, you could just push on the outer shell, which would pop open, causing the peanuts to fall into your hand. These fried peanuts tasted especially delicious around an open fire, which would also keep the mosquitoes away. Sitah, however, would aim the peanuts straight into her mouth, and she never missed. Then she would send the shells sailing into the fire, where they would flame violently before slinking into ash.

I loved Sitah. She had dark, wise eyes. When she laughed, her boobs shook happily, making Hassan smile. She took good care of Emma-M and Easabella, and when Simon's eyes became scared at Hassan's stories, Sitah would smack Hassan over the head and take Simon inside. Not quite six, Simon believed everything, and she knew this. Her lips were always red and juicy from the *sirih* (sweet tobacco) she chewed all day. I had to get used to that, but even then, had never let her kiss my face.

Now, they saw me walking up to them and made space for me between them. I slipped in and felt better.

Sitah saw my knees and clucked her tongue. "Sofia, when will you turn into a little lady?"

I leaned against her soft body. I felt safe and relaxed in the peace and closeness of these two, far away from the sirens and planes—at least for now. I told them about Dad's bike and my bleeding knees and wondered why I needed to be a lady. Mom and Sitah were always trying to make me into one, but Dad and Hassan didn't care.

"Let her be," Dad would tell Mom. "She doesn't need to be a lady for a long time."

Hassan liked me the way I was too. He never tried to change me. He showed me how to make a fire in a sandpit between two stones. He taught me how to climb coconut trees like monkeys do, fast and easy, and then how to turn the fruit free, making it drop with a dull thud. Usually, Hassan had already split the soft green bark by the time I'd slid down the tree, and when I was thirsty, nothing tasted better than the sweet juice that came straight from a hole in the top of the coconut.

He showed me that each coconut has three soft spots on top, which can be easily cut open, but said that only two needed to be opened to drink the juice. One hole would not work and three would be too many; the juice would run freely over your face and be wasted. Then he carefully pointed out which hole he was drinking from, so that I could use the other. When I asked him why we should use separate holes, he laughed and said we had different lips.

After we had drunk all the juice, he would split the nut in perfectly equal halves with a skilled, hard tap of his *parang* (large knife), after which we would

11

eat the soft fruit with our fingers, scratching it out in long, white ribbons and sliding it down our throats. Chewing, I learned, was unnecessary.

Hassan also showed me how to fly a kite and how to handle *alang-alang* (a narrow, tall grass with sharp sides), which could slice your skin to ribbons if you weren't careful. He taught me how to recognize the poisonous snakes from the harmless ones. He showed me how to kill scorpions before they could hit you with their poisonous tails, and he showed me how to kick a soccer ball with the side of your foot so that you wouldn't hurt your toes.

Sometimes, though, Hassan became moody. His eyes would become dark and staring, and he would refuse to talk. He wouldn't let Sitah out of his sight and carefully locked their room at night. This could go on for days.

I would know better than to try cheering him up. Hassan had been moody before, and Sitah had always warned me during those times not to bother him. She kept me away from him, explaining that he was *amok* (dangerously angry and confused), and would be so for awhile. She also told me that she would have to watch him carefully until he was better, to make sure he didn't become *mata-glap* (crazy). When I asked Sitah what Hassan did when he became *mata-glap,* she said that he would run through the street with a *parang* (large knife), screaming at people and threatening to harm anybody who came near. Hassan could then be dangerous. People would hide in the *kampong* (village) and only come out again when Hassan had been caught and locked up. Last year, Hassan had disappeared for more than two months, and when he'd come back, he'd seemed no different than before. He'd laughed with Simon and smoked his thin cigarettes, as usual. But he never talked about where he had been.

Hassan had told me something, though, when Mom and Dad had gone to the Dutch Club for their weekly bridge game. He had built a fire outside to keep us warm and drive away the nightly mosquitoes. Sitah had been putting Simon to bed, and the girls were already sleeping. Shadows moved over us, caused by the *kalongs* (bats) flying around, hunting for insects. I didn't like *kalongs.* Hassan had warned that they could sneak up on you soundlessly and then land in your hair, which, unless you chanted the magic mantra, would change you into a wicked witch.

Among the shadows, Hassan popped peanuts and filled my hands with them, and after he had peeled many, he stopped and stared into the playful flames. Apart from the occasional distant animal cry, the evening was silent.

I stood to add more wood to the fire and did not look at him while I asked, "What do you see, Hassan, in the fire flames?"

Hassan remained silent for so long that I thought he hadn't heard me. Then, finally, he said, "I look at the fire spirits, Sofia. There are a lot of them in there. When they dance, the flames go high; when they dream, the flames hide behind the coals." He smiled then and his voice became caressing as he went on. "Fire spirits are good spirits. They make you feel warm and protected. They come into your heart, so you feel loved and not lonely."

I looked at him then. "Were you lonely, Hassan, when you became *mata-glap*? Did no one love you then?" Hassan did not answer. Smoke from his cigarette circled his face and the firelight played with the shadows in his eyes.

Then he looked at me. "Each of us has a monkey on our chest, Sofia. Not many people are aware of him, but suddenly, one day, for some reason, he wakes up, looks around, and likes what he sees. He moves deeper inside you, and if you can't fight him, you'll have him there forever, breaking you up inside, piece by little piece."

The fire died down then, hiding Hassan in darkness. All I could see was the tip of his burning cigarette traveling up and down, somewhere between his fingers and his lips. Then Sitah came outside and put more wood on the fire, so Hassan never explained whether *mata-glap* felt like a loose monkey on his chest or whether he had broken apart piece by little piece.

By now, my knees had stopped burning. I felt comfortable leaning into Sitah, not thinking further than the moment. I could sit here till morning.

"Go inside, Sofia," Sitah said. "Mom will be worried. It is late, and she doesn't know where you are. Tell her about the bike. She will understand, because we all had to go to the shelters when we heard the sirens, and she knows how people become wild when afraid."

I hesitated.

"Go," Sitah continued. "She will not be angry. She has other things to worry about. She will have to look at your knees also."

Sitah was right. I had to face Mom.

Mom saw me coming and opened the door. "Where were you, Sofia? It is so dark outside, and late. Did you find a shelter when the sirens sounded?"

Her eyes were red; she had been crying again. I told her about the sirens, the shelter in town, and the lost bike.

She didn't say anything for awhile and then, when she did speak, she very much surprised me. "Someone else must have needed the bike more than we did, Sofia. Dad probably doesn't need it anymore anyway."

It was not like Mom to be so calm about something like this. And what was that supposed to mean anyway? Had she heard from Dad? Had somebody told her that Dad would come back soon? Something must have happened.

I looked at her with a thousand questions, knowing I would receive no answers. Mom's lips were firmly closed and she wouldn't look at me. She treated my knees without a word. Why was she so in control? Couldn't she talk about what had really happened last week when the Japanese soldiers had picked up Dad? Why could she not trust me enough to share what was worrying her so much?

My knees were brown now. Mom had washed them with something foamy and then dipped iodine solution all over them. It burned something awful, but apart from my trembling legs, I didn't show how much they hurt. Fighting back tears, I tried to stop the trembling.

"You are a tough kid, Sofia," she said. "I know that. But sometimes it doesn't hurt to cry."

Looking at Mom, I still did my very best not to cry, and went to bed. But when I awoke in the middle of the night, I found my face wet with tears.

The next day Hassan disappeared.

Sitah cried quietly all morning and explained that Hassan had left to check on his old father in Atjeh. Atjeh was far away, in the northernmost province of Sumatra. Its capital was Kota Radja. But, according to Sitah, he had to go, because the Japanese had landed soldiers in the area, and everybody was afraid. It would take Hassan a long time to find his father. He would have to take the train and then perhaps one of the busses, if they were running. Then he'd have to travel the rest of the way on foot, which could take several days, depending on how far north his father lived.

Atjeh was not a friendly part of Sumatra. The locals there were very much anti-Dutch, to the point that lots of Dutch residents had already moved out because it had become dangerous. The young Indonesian men there were helping the Japanese intruders as soon as KNIL soldiers had been forced to surrender. I wondered if we would ever see Hassan again.

"Things will never be the same," Sitah said, sobbing.

Sitah became very quiet after that. I missed her laugh, and from then on, I tried to help her with her work, hoping to make her happier. I also watched the little girls for her, so that she could do some of Hassan's work.

I never had to watch Simon because he was always with Mom. He'd wander from room to room, looking until he found her. Then he would lean against her or wrap his little arms around her legs, like he wanted to warm her. Simon could do things like that and Mom loved him for it. For instance, he could kiss her lips without disturbing her makeup. I always messed up her makeup, and therefore was only allowed to kiss her cheeks.

Whenever Mom went to Aunt Maggie's next door, Simon went with her. Mom had to be careful, because it was forbidden to leave one's house, but we had many shrubs and low trees in the garden, and with Simon's hand in hers, Mom managed to cross both gardens to visit her friend. Aunt Maggie had still not heard from Uncle Cor and desperately needed a visit from a friend.

Sometimes Aunt Maggie also crossed the gardens and would stay awhile with Mom. They would drink coffee and share their worries about their husbands. Then Mom would expect me to watch Easabella and Emma-M, so that I couldn't listen to their conversations.

I didn't mind watching the girls. They really were not babies anymore. They could talk and understand simple things. They did not pee in their pants anymore, and they could eat by themselves. Emma-M looked like me, with dark, wavy hair, and Easa looked more like Simon. They had both red, curly hair; but while Easa's was thick and darker, Simon's was flaming like a carrot. We all had brown eyes, except Simon. His were gray. Perhaps he was not really one of us. Perhaps he had been adopted because Dad had been disappointed that I was a girl. Or maybe they had just found Simon on the doorstep one day. That thought pleased me.

I liked Simon, but that was not enough. I was supposed to love him because he was my brother. He was too perfect, though, and never bad. Mom never had to spank him, which he often told me. He almost never lied and if he did, he made very, very sure he couldn't be caught. Yet, he always made sure I got caught. I would call him names like "carrot top" or "lighthouse," and he would run to tell Mom. By the time Mom would whistle for me to come pronto, I made sure I was long gone.

But Emma-M and Easa were small and sweet; they made everyone happy. Mom, at first, was upset when Emma-M came so close after Easabella, and they were both babies, but she got used to them, and Sitah helped by devoting most of her time to them. Although Emma-M was thirteen months younger than Easabella, she could almost do as much as her sister.

Not long after Dad was taken away, Mom returned from a visit at Aunt Maggie's and was completely different, more like she was before Dad had left. She had lost the empty look on her face and really saw us again.

"Gather the little girls, Sofia," she said, with her dress tight in Simon's fist. "Then come inside. I have something to tell you."

I picked up my baby sisters, one under each arm. As I walked them inside, they squealed and kicked until Mom snapped, "Stop that, Sofia! Things are serious enough!"

Then she explained how we were to go to the Simon Fraay Hotel the next day to get instructions from some Japanese officers. The message had been announced on the radio that morning. It must have been why she suddenly seemed so different, so focused. I was excited. Simon Fraay was the largest hotel in Langsa. I had never been inside before, but I had seen the servants in white uniforms standing at all of its doors, and had always wondered whether they were real or just statues. Now I could see them up close!

Mom said each of us would need to pack a carryall, with clothes and things that we would need away from home. There was a chance we'd have to spend the night, she said, if the Japanese officers didn't make it there in time. Sitah packed a suitcase for the girls, but Simon and I packed our own. She said we could take as much as we wanted, as long as we could carry it all.

Mom couldn't decide what clothes to pack. I wondered why she was so worried. We would be back home soon, wouldn't we? She did decide to take along some of her jewelry and the money she had in the house, though, since Sitah would be alone and, as she said, "lately, there were a lot of scumballs roaming the streets."

Simon wanted to know what scumballs were, but, for once, Mom had no time for him. "Never mind, Simon," she said. "Pack your bag!"

So Simon did. He packed his bag so heavy that he couldn't lift it, and so moped around the rest of the day, trying to decide what to leave. He must have packed and emptied his bag a half-dozen times after that.

Packing was not a problem for me. All I wanted were a few books and all of my marbles. I loved my books, because I could take the place of the hero in the story, or the winner, or the one most needed, and imagine a whole different life for myself. And I was proud of my marble collection. I had many, Some of them were really beautiful. Most of them I had won from friends and classmates, and a few I had traded for (those I treasured the most). They could be beautiful, with deep centers and flowing colors; some were milky, some were flaming, and some had a center like an owl's eye. Most of them were rollers, which were ordinary marbles with ordinary colors and little glass decorations. Then there were the hitters, which were special. They were used to hit a certain marble as a target and so needed to roll perfectly straight. The more stable the hitter was, the more sure you were that you'd hit your target. Those, for sure, I would never leave behind.

The next day, the streets filled with children, Dutch women, and quite a few Indonesian women who had married Dutch men. Their husbands also had left or had served in the KNIL. We all walked the same direction, lugging bags and suitcases. Our common destination was the Simon Fraay Hotel.

For us kids, it was a big adventure. It was like we were forming a parade. The sun was out and we would soon be eating in the largest hotel in town. Many kids ran excitedly between the mothers, chasing one another. Though if any child lost sight of his or her mother, she would be difficult to find again, since all the streets were filled with running children and lugging ladies; there were perhaps more than five hundred people.

Sitah carried Emma-M in a *slendang* (a shawl-type baby carrier) on her back, and tried to talk Easabella into walking. Easa was whining because she wanted to be carried too. Simon was holding onto Mom's dress again and carrying his own bag, though sometimes he just dragged it. With every step, the marbles in my pockets jingled, pulling my shorts down so that I had to hold them up with my free hand. Sitah had warned me that the marbles would tear through my pockets, but I wasn't going to leave them behind just so the scumbags could steal them. The bag over my shoulder was filled with more marbles, and with books.

Finally at the hotel, we gathered on the lawns, and for the rest of the day, these large, wide-open, green fields filled with more women and children from all directions. We had found our own space and seated ourselves gratefully. Lugging our bags in the hot sun had been harder than we'd expected—the road seemed longer and the carryalls seemed heavier.

After we were settled, Sitah kissed each of us and I wondered why she had tears in her eyes. Then she walked away, but turned around at the gate and motioned for me to come see her. I ran, suddenly afraid of what she would say.

She pulled me against her. "Watch over the babies, Sofia, and be good to Simon. If you have to stay here tonight, come to the gate tomorrow at nine o'clock. I'll be there." Then she kissed me again and turned to leave.

As I watched her go, I realized that today was not an adventure. Something bad was going to happen, and I had a feeling we would not like it. Though standing in the sun, I felt cold.

I walked back into the throng of bags and families and found my little group—Mom, the girls, and Simon. I sat behind Mom, leaning my back against hers, and wondered what Sitah had meant. The sun felt hot on my face now, and some little kids around us started crying and asking for water. Most mothers had brought drinking water and snacks, but most of it had been consumed on the long walk, and what was left was gone in no time.

After everyone had arrived and struggled to find a place on the grass, the noise died down. The shouting and calling ended, and younger kids fell asleep under the warm afternoon sun. The older kids, however, seemed only to feel the fear in their mothers rise, as the masses of people became almost silent.

The waiting had begun.

SIMON FRAAY HOTEL

Langsa, March 1942

Two Japanese officers arrived late that afternoon, in spotless decorated uniforms and shiny black boots. They had closed faces with narrow eyes. I studied them, wondering if they had difficulty seeing, because their pupils were barely visible. Chinese people were a familiar sight in Indonesia; they owned many local stores and had kids who went to school with us. Dad had told us that Japanese people were very much the same as Chinese, but looking at these officers, I couldn't understand how. I found them very different. They didn't smile like the Chinese tradesmen, but had stern, unfriendly expressions. They were also smaller.

As we watched the strangers, everything quieted. Even the children went silent. Then one officer shouted something in a rough, foreign language, which a tall Chinese man then translated into Indonesian. My family knew the Chinese man well enough for me to know that he didn't speak fluent Japanese, but had only picked up some of it while working as a cook on several Japanese ships. He looked uncomfortable standing next to the officer, but he did well enough that we could follow his translation.

We heard that we would not go home anymore, and that the gates around the hotel yards would remain closed. We would be assigned rooms at the hotel and were to obey all orders and adhere to all changes from there on out. Hotel servants would be assigned to help the women go home the next day to pack clothes and necessities for their families. The Dutch flag on top of the hotel would come down, and the Japanese flag would be hoisted. This was not a surprise, however, as all of the red, white, and blue flags that waved over Indonesia since the first Dutch sailors had landed on its shore centuries ago had come down wherever the Japanese army landed.

Finally, we were told that if a Japanese soldier or officer passed us, we were to stand still and bow—and not doing so would result in punishment. The Chinese translator took a step back after he had translated this last order and told us that we would learn later exactly what punishment would be dished out. As we listened, we slowly took in how frightfully our lives would change. We gradually understood that we were prisoners. We had lost our freedom to come and go and do as we pleased, gaining in its place a grave sense of danger and uncertainty.

I stared at the Japanese man in front of us, as the translator introduced him as an officer of the Japanese Imperial Army. He then told us that we were now considered prisoners of the officer's commander, the emperor of Japan, whose name was *Tenno Heiko*, meaning the God Emperor.

I looked at Mom. Easabella and Simon leaned into her. I remembered Sitah's tears and strange last words, and moved closer to Mom and the kids. I felt cold again in the still burning sun.

The next announcement that came was that we were to wait to be assigned our rooms. When it came our turn, since there were five in our family, we were lucky enough to get a room to ourselves; smaller families had to share a room. Boys older than twelve were given a camping bed in one of the large meeting rooms, though they seemed to think this was cool—as if they were being shown respect because they were older.

In the days that followed, our room became dear to us. By closing the door, we could shut out the ugliness of the unfriendly Japanese guards and their rifles, some of which even had bayonets.

Right now, the guards kept busy supervising the *koelies* (laborers), who were building a barbed-wire fence around the gardens. The laborers were Indonesian, some of whom had served Dutch families before being forced to work for the Japanese soldiers. The *koelies* were poked with a rifle as soon as they leaned back to rest a few moments. Watching them reminded me of Hassan, and for the first time, I was happy that he had left Langsa to find his father.

The *koelies* were gentle, discreet people. They were dedicated to the families they served and, in turn, were always treated with respect by their families. Trained by their mistresses, the servants in Dutch family houses were also paid a higher salary than any other type of servant. Some families had so many servants that their mistresses didn't have to do anything. They cleaned house, served meals, polished silver, welcomed guests, and sometimes helped in the kitchen, where the cook would ready dishes to take to the dining room on large, decorated trays. He would do this in a proud and silent way, watching everything around him. In our house, Hassan would ready the tea and cookies by four each day, which was about the time Mom and Dad awoke from their siestas. Meanwhile, Sitah would give us children baths and clean clothes, so that we would be neat before joining our parents for tea. Other servants never came into the house, but tended the garden or handled the garbage or ran errands, such as going to the *toko* (store) when the cook needed something unexpected. But most servants were considered part of the family and lived in rooms at the back of the house.

As announced, the day after we were assigned rooms, the women were escorted to their homes to collect as much as they could carry back. Mom had found Sitah when she went, and they had quickly filled a few suitcases. Sitah helped Mom carry them back to the hotel and then promised to come to the gates as often as she could to bring any other needed items.

Life at the Simon Fraay then settled into some semblance of a routine, though the little girls didn't play much; they just sucked their thumbs or took long naps. Simon, as usual, was constantly silent and watched Mom, trailing after her as soon as she left the room.

The Chinese translator was put to work as a cook in the hotel kitchen until he was needed to translate for the officers. He often misinterpreted, for which he was rewarded with kicks or smacks of the rifle, so that he learned to scream every time he wasn't sure of a message. He had confused us with that at first, but he had also befuddled the Japanese officers, who, as a result, had forgotten to hit him.

The women, after recovering from the shock of losing their independence, split into groups to take care of the washing, cooking, cleaning, sweeping, gardening, and babysitting. The officers had retained the original hotel staff, and had instructed the hotel owner not to accept any more paying visitors, since the entire hotel would be used to house prisoners. With such a large number of people, the women had to help. They washed clothes in the laundry spaces, or did their own cooking in a separate scullery. They kept their rooms clean and tidy, and took turns watching one another's children, especially when their mothers were outside sweeping the terraces or doing garden work. They cut flowers for the hotel's dining tables, which now were used only by us. The work kept the mothers busy and made the days go faster.

When the work was done, they spent the afternoons outside sitting in garden chairs under the hotel's wide sun parasols, though, of course, there was no afternoon tea with cookies. Still, they loaned their books to one another, and exchanged life stories and jokes. And, most of all, they shared plans for what to do when this was all over. Then, I heard in their voices what I was sure they could also hear in each other's—a longing for the return to normalcy and an uncertainty for the future. When they looked at their children, their eyes often filled with tears, which no one tried to hide. And when they had nothing left to discuss, silence would surround them. It was a comfortable silence, though, in which everyone seemed to think the same things, wondering what tomorrow would bring, when they would see home again, and where their husbands might be.

Siesta from two to four was required quiet time, and curfew was at eight. No one was allowed to be outside the hotel fence, ever. We were counted two times a day—before breakfast at eight in the morning, and in the evening after supper.

Our days were spent waiting for something to happen. Listening to the radio in the hotel lobby was forbidden, and the few small radios owned by some remained carefully hidden. Deep in the night, while the children slept, women would gather around those radios and listen to newscasts in hopes of hearing Japanese plans regarding their husbands and the thousands of Dutch people in Indonesia. If there was news, it would soon be shared with others, but nothing was offered that gave hope.

Another way to get news from beyond the Simon Fraay was to buy newspapers from the locals, but this had to be done in secret. We learned that smuggling in goods from the locals was possible, but only when you were fast and crafty, and had worthwhile things to trade. Of course, the locals were uneasy about doing this, because when caught, they were beaten; the Japanese soldiers who tirelessly circled the barbed-wire fence, seemed to like hitting those people, and when they did, they hit hard. Still, the hotel property was fairly large, so when the soldiers were on one end, exchanging goods happened on the other.

Occasionally, Sitah brought us things she thought we would miss or need. She was careful and sometimes even had a chance to speak a few words with Mom. One morning, she had thrown five sleeping mats over the fence just before the Japanese soldier caught sight of her. She was gone before he had reached her, and Mom had quickly left, mats under her arm, before he'd had a chance to see her face.

That same evening, Mom took me aside and spoke softly. "Go to the gate every day, Sofia, and wait for Sitah. She promised to come. Watch the guards, and do not let them see you talk to Sitah. You could put her in danger."

I wondered why, but didn't ask.

Mom went on. "Pretend you are playing. Sitah knows I hid jewelry at home. She knows where to find it and will bring it this week. Tell her to be very careful!" And with that, Mom had started to cry, and Simon moved into her lap.

Sitah didn't show up that day or the next, but she came the day after in the early evening.

I had waited for her a long time and almost did not expect her. She looked uneasy, glancing frequently at the guard as she walked slowly along the fence. I took my marbles out and crouched to play with them on the ground.

Sitah came carefully closer, and when she was close enough to hear me, I aimed one of my marbles under the wire, and said, "Be careful, Sitah, the guard is watching you. If you have Mom's jewelry, just drop it next to my marble at the fence and I will make it disappear."

I then walked toward the fence to get my marble, and the soldier watching us began to walk in our direction. As Sitah walked past, I saw something small drop next to my marble. She did not say anything, but kept walking along the fence and then away from the approaching soldier. I reached under the fence and, as with a snake's strike, swiped the small parcel together with my marble, dropped the parcel into my pocket and pretended to continued playing. The guard softly passed me, burning the back of my head with his suspicious eyes. The next time I looked up, Sitah was gone, but the soldier wasn't. He stood still, just watching me.

The parcel in my pocket felt hard, as I stood and walked slowly toward our room. It was almost dark now and not difficult to find the softly lighted window behind which I knew Mom was waiting. I had difficulty swallowing. My mouth felt dry and I could taste fear. Although the evening was balmy, I shivered.

When Mom opened the parcel, she found her most treasured garnet bracelet with the matching earrings. Dad had given them to her when they'd been married for ten years. Her eyes filled with tears, but she said nothing. I wondered if she was remembering the evening Dad had given those jewels to her.

It had been a beautiful evening. They had celebrated with wine and presents, and I had watched them from my seat on the swing, hidden in the shadows of the large tree in our front yard. Mom had given Dad a black, sleek fountain pen with a note that only Dad read. He had been surprised and wonderfully happy, because she had remembered that he had wanted the pen when they had seen it in a Chinese store the month before.

Then he had taken a flat, slender jewelry box out of his pocket and put it in one of her hands, folding her other over the box. "Beautiful jewels for a beautiful lady," he had said with his best smile. "They are the color of aged red wine." Mom's eyes filled with tears but she didn't say anything, just as now.

Sitting on the floor with my back against the door, I watched her and wondered if she grieved that evening not so long ago, when everything was normal and they had been so happy, or if the tears came from hearing again his caressing words and feeling his warm embrace. Dad loved to embrace Mom, and if he were here now, I knew he would do just that and kiss away her tears.

Mom got up, wiped her face, and disappeared into the bathroom. When she came out, she seemed her usual self again, and she hid the little bag of garnets deep inside the torn lining of her handbag.

Then she looked at me and whispered, "Sweet, brave Sitah. Did the Japanese guard see her, Sofia?"

I shook my head but couldn't speak. I felt weak and hollow. I still saw Sitah coming closer, hesitant but unafraid. I still heard the soft footsteps of the suspicious guard and felt the fear that came with thinking he could hit Sitah and shout at her.

Many servants tried tirelessly to bring necessities and valuables to their *nonjas* (mistresses), hidden in their *slendangs* (carrying shawls), *kabajas* (dress shirts), and even their *kondés* (hair knots). Their hands were empty when they walked the same sandy path that the guards had covered hundreds of times on watch rounds. The servants would walk slowly so as not to make the guards suspicious, but then from nowhere would appear a parcel, which would be cleverly shoved under the fence for a child to snatch up and run with. Some guards allowed talking; they didn't understand the Indonesian language anyway, but parcels were taken away if they could get their hands on them.

But after awhile, many locals, after having been pushed and shoved, and finally beaten and kicked, stopped coming. Others came only at night, hoping for a better chance to escape the soldiers; such it became with Sitah.

It was dusk the last time we saw her, just before the lights went on and you couldn't trust your eyes. We hadn't seen her for a few days and then, suddenly, she was there, slowly moving along the fence. Her hands were empty, but we could see her full *slendang*.

By now, the guards had become weary of watching us kids. We were too fast and noisy for them, and had quickly learned the best ways to fool them. But at this time of the day, they didn't have to watch too closely. Not expecting her visit, Simon jumped for joy, pointing her direction. "Look Mommy, Sitah!"

"Shhht, Simon," Mom said, putting her hand over his mouth, but it was too late. The guard had heard and started to saunter closer.

Dressed as always in a *sarong* (a wraparound skirt) and a *kabaja* (a dress shirt with long sleeves), Sitah loosened her *slendang* and quickly dropped the whole bundle next to the barbed wire. She then hurried away on her beautiful, open slippers, but in her haste, stumbled and lost one. She kept walking fast with one bare foot.

I dragged Sitah's bundle under the fence and handed it to Mom, who shoved Simon out of her lap and hurried away, but the guard, who had almost reached Sitah, started screaming and waving his rifle at her.

Things seemed to slow down around me. I gripped the wire hard and didn't feel the barbs going into my hands. Sitah turned and waited, standing straight and proud. The guard passed me fast, waving his rifle with the bayonet at Sitah. Sitah's face was calm and her eyes watched him come closer. She didn't move when he pointed his bayonet against her chest, just under her throat. But when it came down and almost pierced her foot, she cried out and nearly fell. She bent down under the soldier's strange, harsh, Japanese words and cradled her injured foot, blood coming through her toes and fingers.

I felt light and airy, yet I couldn't move. She whimpered softly, and I couldn't understand the words of the soldier, who still raged and poked his bayonet around Sitah and kicked at her legs. She lifted her face, pale in the middle of her black shiny hair. I could not see her eyes now, for the night had closed in. She then straightened up and, with a sense of total control and without hurry, whipped handfuls of sand in the soldier's face.

She looked at me and spoke softly. "Good-bye, Sofia, I'll go home now. Do not look for me anymore." Then she turned and went away, out of my life, taking with her part of the goodness and joy in me, leaving an empty spot to be replaced with something cold and numb and nameless. Love melted into sorrow and turned part of my heart into stone. Only then did I become conscious of the pain in my hands, caused by the wire barbs I had been holding this entire time.

The Japanese soldier raged and screamed, clawing at his face and eyes full of sand, then hitting the fence with his rifle. He kicked Sitah's little slipper, so that it sailed up and against the fence. With that, the grip that had held me to the fence broke. As tears ran down my face, I bent and pulled Sitah's slipper under the fence, tearing the skin on my arm. Then running somewhere off into the dark, my mind followed her, away and out of our lives.

"Good-bye, Sitah!" I called. "I love you, Sitah! I will always love you, Sitah! Good-bye!"

Something broke in me then, and I screamed as hard as I could, silencing the day's last few birds in an attempt to rid myself of a pain borne of powerlessness, and the memory of Sitah's bleeding toes.

Not long after, when Mom washed my ripped arm and bleeding fingers, I welcomed the pain. I knew that she couldn't wash away the dirt of this night and the memory of something beautiful. Something irreplaceable that was lost forever. Something I would never find again.

"What happened at the fence, Sofia?" Mom asked.

"Sitah said good-bye. She will not be back." And that is all I ever told Mom about what had happened.

Simon cried himself to sleep that night. He couldn't forgive himself for calling out her name when he saw her.

The next day when I awoke, there was a strange pattern across my right cheek; I had slept on Sitah's sandal, and all the little multicolored beads had left an imprint in my skin. I liked it there, and was sorry to see it fade. Mom didn't ask how I got the sandal. She just cleaned it for me.

All day, I couldn't get Sitah's visit out of my mind, so I talked to Peter about it. Peter was my very best friend. His father was an Indonesian KNIL sergeant and his mother was Dutch. Peter was small for his age, but he didn't care that I was a girl and not a boy. I didn't know his father very well, because he was often away on patrol with the army. His mother, small like Peter, always spoke with a soft voice and tried to make me happy whenever I visited by showing me her daughter Sonja's extensive doll collection. Sonja was Peter's younger sister and looked very much like a doll too.

The weeks went by, each day the same. The women suffered from boredom and, as there was still no news about their husbands, many sleepless nights. They wrote endless letters to their husbands for whom they had no address and for which they had no stamps. They became irritable and often quarreled.

It was very different for us kids. We roamed free, sharing secrets and games. I had never had so many friends living so close by and so immediately available. We had no rules. And when we chose teams to play soccer or *kastie* (a form of softball), boys and girls were considered equal, although the strong kids were always chosen first.

Everybody in Langsa knew about *kastie*. Next to soccer, it was the most chosen game when there were enough players. Two leaders were picked, who then took turns choosing members for their teams.

We'd choose a field to play in, in which we would place three stakes—one close by and two farther outfield, but at equal distances from the base. Then one team would spread out in the field, while the other team lined up behind a baseline, taking turns to try to hit the ball that was thrown at them from the pitcher on the field team. Using a strong, round club, you'd try to hit the ball as far away as possible, and then run to the closest stake. And if you hit the ball far enough, you might have time to reach the second pole and maybe even the third.

The goal of the other team was to catch the ball as quickly as possible and return it to base before the runner could reach the next pole. Each team would gather points, and, of course, the team with the most points won. So the leaders choosing teams would look for hard, precise hitters and fast runners.

Hotel Simon Fraay had beautiful grassy terrains to play *kastie* on, and the Japanese soldiers would often watch us, seemingly trying to understand the game. But they would laugh and cheer when they saw others doing so, pretending they knew about the game.

When it was too hot to play *kastie,* we had marbles. We all had marbles. Some had more marbles or prettier marbles than others, but every boy and girl had them and knew the games.

Peter and I were both experts in marbling, so we couldn't decide who was best. We shared marbles, too, and our favorites were always hitters. My favorite was a glorious gold one with dark spots, like dancing shadows hidden inside, and it came alive under the light. When using it, I always won. Peter's hitter was fabulous though. I had never seen one like it. It was multicolored, but transparent, with a dark liquid center. Peter thought his hitter had a black, evil heart, and he used it because he said evil usually won over good and gold. He must have been right, because I tried to win over Peter's black-heart hitter many times, but never could. I tried to talk him into trading, but he said no. I even tried to buy it from him, first for one hundred marbles, then for money, and then for one hundred marbles plus money, but Peter still said no. So Peter kept his black heart and I my gold, but there was nothing I wanted more than that marble.

Our favorite game was always played on a smooth, clay surface around a ring about ten feet in diameter, with twelve marbles arranged in a cross in the center. A line would be drawn four yards below the ring. From there, each player would shoot a marble as close as possible to the cross without touching it. The owner of the closest marble would start the game, the next closest would go second, and so on. For the game itself, the goal was to use a slightly larger hitter to shoot as many marbles from the cross as possible, so that both the hitter and the marbles that were hit would roll outside the ring.

To form the cross, all players would have to enter marbles. When there were three players, each player would enter four marbles, and when there were four players, each would enter three marbles. Each arm of the cross had three marbles, and then in the center would be a round stone or rubber seed, which was slightly larger than the marbles and had no value.

The player had to remain behind the ring line, and if he or she touched the line, he or she would be disqualified; he or she'd have to leave his or her marbles in the ring and not play anymore. The marbles that were shot out of the ring became the shooter's property and enabled him or her to go again. If the shooter couldn't knock a marble from the cross outside the ring, he or she would lose a turn. If a marble was knocked out of the ring, but the player's hitter stayed inside the ring, another player was allowed to try to shoot the hitter out, in which case, he or she would own the hitter.

The only way to shoot a marble outside the ring was to use a method called "knuckling." It goes like this: the knuckle of the forefinger rests on the ground while holding the marble above the first joint of the thumb. The top of the thumb is held down by the middle finger. When ready, the player releases the thumb with just the right speed and accuracy in the direction of the target. Any player who touched the ring with his or her hand or knuckle when shooting would again be disqualified and lose his hitter.

It was an easy game, and you could win or lose a lot in a short time. I had won most of my marbles in matches, and my collection was now extensive. Last year, I'd had them separated in Dad's socks according to size, color, and value, but I won so many that Dad ran out of old socks, and I had to sell half of them. Then I won them all back again, so Hassan gave me some of his socks.

Karel de Boer bought marbles from me all the time. He was one year older, but we were in the same class in school after he'd repeated the last grade. Since he was older, he was bigger and stronger, and he would turn mean and ugly when he lost his marbles. He had a big mouth, too, and told me what dogs and cats did when they were horny, and what people did when the bedroom door was closed. Dad had warned me not to play with Karel, calling him *pienter boesoek* (bad), but then Karel never played with girls anyway. He always said he thought girls were sissies and not worth his time. That's why my selling marbles to Karel always happened at night, when his friends wouldn't see him sneaking around our house.

A few weeks ago, during school recess, I had given him ten first-class marbles, which he lost. He promised to come by later that afternoon to pay for them, since he had no money with him at school. But when he showed up that night to pay, he tried to cheat me, claiming the marbles were not worth the price I'd asked. After I kicked him hard in the shins, he punched me and threw the money in the sand. I didn't care—the money had been right, and that had been the end of it. Bruises were temporary.

Dad joked whenever I came home with bruises, but Mom always complained.

"Girls do not fight, Sofia," she'd say. "When are you going to behave like a lady?"

I would have liked to have been born a boy. Boys were allowed to do more, required to help less, and could keep their names when they got married. Not being a boy, though, never held me back. No game was too wild, and my feet were hard enough to play soccer without shoes, like the Indo boys did. Toes could make cracking sounds when they kicked a soccer ball without shoes, unless you played every day and kicked really hard—and my toes never cracked.

Peter and I were together almost every day, and I loved him more than my brother. We spent our time making a plan of escape to go see what had happened to my family's house—namely, my toys, Dad's books, and Sitah, who perhaps still lived there. We couldn't try to visit Peter's house, because it was outside Langsa. We'd have to cross parts of the city to get there, and that would be too dangerous. He'd lived there with his mother, his older sister, and his father, who had left the same time as Uncle Cor to join his garrison. Peter had to be taken to school each day on the bike carrier of one of his cousins.

Each morning, we would watch the Japanese soldiers making their rounds outside the hotel and work out the details of our plan: in the morning, right after we were counted, we would make ourselves very thin to slip under the wire fence and then cross the sandy path the soldiers walked daily, in order to reach the ditch running along the main road. We planned to follow that ditch all the way to our house to remain hidden from the main road.

The only problem was that the guard was always patrolling the path. So for three days, we watched the guard and timed his rounds. After that, we stole some *goenie bags* (jute bags used for raw rice) to solve the problem of *alang-alang*. Alang-alang was a tall, wavy grass with knife-sharp edges, and it grew in the ditches. It would cut our skin to ribbons if we crawled through it. The jute bags would protect us if we cut them into strips, which we then wrapped around our arms and legs. We might have problems breathing, too, if the bags smelled from the dusty rice; the chaff of the rice grain could even clog our noses. But we decided to tackle that problem only if and when we faced it. Finally, we collected coconut bark to pad our hands and knees, since we would need to crawl most of the way. Since the hotel cooks prepared many dishes with coconut milk, there was always coconut bark around the garbage containers, waiting to be picked up each day by trucks. Once preparations were finished, we planned to leave early the next morning. We were nervous but determined.

The next day, as soon as the dew had dried and after we all had been counted, Sonja, Peter's sister, helped wrap the jute bandages around us till we looked like caterpillars ready to hatch from big, brown cocoons. Finding the right place to make these preparations wasn't easy, until Peter thought of the best place of all. We kids had learned on one of our many roaming trips around the hotel that the garbage truck arrived very early each morning and stopped in front of the *goedang* (junk room) to pick up all of the hotel's garbage containers. Once they had driven away, no one entered the *goedang* again until after lunch. So it would be free for us to use all morning.

Changing from kids into formless, unrecognizable lumps was not easy. Sonja had to cover every piece of skin, even on our necks and faces, and she had to stop often to let us get used to the crawly, itchy feeling of the jute on our bare skin. We kept sneezing and scratching, and getting ready took longer than we'd planned, which made us nervous. But finally, Sonja decided that we looked safe and she let us go.

We moved slowly from the *goedang* toward the fence, Peter first, and I behind him. At first, it was clumsy and awkward, but we got used to the steady crawling even before we had reached the fence—that is, until, between the jute strips around our eyes, we saw the guard coming. He sauntered slowly, with his gun on his back. He seemed at ease, not anticipating any trouble. We sank down and remained motionless. I hoped he would not notice two brown patches amid the tall grass and want to investigate. I broke out in such a violent sweat, then, that I was sure he would sense my fear. What would he do if he saw us? Would he use his gun or, even worse, his bayonet, to rip off our disguises? Then, would he beat us?

I closed my eyes, but opened them again when I heard Peter moving forward. He had almost reached the fence, so I hurried after him. The rest of the trek went smoothly. We crawled underneath the fence onto the path and crossed it. Once in the ditch, we waited again. We had to move slowly so as not to bring our jute coverings into disarray, and stopped a second time to let the guard pass. We sat motionless, listening to his footsteps. By now, the sun was hot, and insects had started to land on the jute, searching for the smallest exposure of skin. I started to doubt our plan and wondered if we could make it all the way to my house, but we had gone too far to turn around.

Finally, the soldier's footsteps grew quieter. By now, I realized he'd have no reason to be extra alert, since no one before us had tried what we were attempting. And from the looks of him, I had been right. He hadn't seemed the least bit suspicious when he passed us. Still, even after we couldn't see him, we waited a few minutes. He might hear us, or just decide to turn around when we were least expecting it. But he didn't. And when we were sure he was out of earshot, we quickly slipped farther along the ditch.

The going was slow and tedious. We were hot and itchy, and stopped often to rest and wipe away the stink of the rough jute material, which scraped your skin with even the slightest movement of your arms or legs.

Once the hotel was out of sight, we dared stick our heads up to look out over the road and fields, and we had to be ready to duck again instantly, in case we saw anyone. But there was nothing. No traffic, no people, not even a wandering dog.

I looked at Peter. The jute over his face had come down, and his eyes looked far away, and his face was closed. Whenever he looked like that, I knew he wouldn't talk. He was thinking about something, and he had told me once that talking stopped his thinking. I wondered if Peter was thinking about what we were seeing, or, rather, what we weren't seeing.

A distant rooster crowed and a truck rumbled toward us. We ducked. Then hidden in the dust left by the truck, we crawled out and walked the road a little ways, jittery and ready to jump back down at the slightest sign of life. We slid back into the ditch as soon as we had turned the corner onto my street. Not far away now, I could see my house. I swallowed, and my throat hurt. We moved closer.

Once next to the driveway, under the cover of the large waringin tree in the front yard, we crawled out and bent our legs, sitting close to the ground. The jute bandages had shifted here and there, showing parts of our faces, but no one was around to see us, not even in cars on the road. In fact, the only noise on the silent street came from inside my house.

Two *grobaks* (two-wheeled, flat carts) stood at the front door, filled halfway with my family's stuff. A couple of large oxen, tied to the waringin tree, stood lazily whipping their tails at the flies. I could see clusters of the black flies on their eyelids as they turned their heads and stupidly stared at us.

We moved closer to the windows on the side of the house. Hidden by dense rhododendron bushes, I stretched to see what was happening inside. People were moving around, and every now and then, I saw one of them pass by a window. These were no Japanese soldiers; they were Indonesians, and some of them I knew. One of them was Aunt Maggie's gardener. They shouted and laughed, and, regularly, something would sail out the front door and land in the *grobak.* They were ransacking our house. All that we had once treasured was now strewn carelessly around the yard. Dad's books were in and around the *grobak,* some of their spines cracked or broken as if they'd been stepped on. The contents of his broken ink jar had spilled, staining the veranda steps. Emma-M's little bed stood next to the front steps filled with baby clothes and stuffed animals.

One of the playroom windows was broken and I moved toward it. I stretched my head up and looked in. The lamp over the little table where I used to do my homework was broken and pieces of its glass crunched under shoes. Then more shouting, more laughing, some loud calls, and a warning, and out the door came Simon's little bike, soaring out in a big curve. It missed the *grobak* and crashed against the side. I was sad that Simon would not be riding it anymore.

I pulled Peter's arm and we moved to the back of the house, where Sitah and Hassan had lived. There was no one and nothing left; only dark rooms and a musty odor. Cold ash was caked between the cooking stones. An old shirt of Hassan's, crumpled over the clothesline, waved gently in the wind. We slipped through the rooms, taking in the void, the absence of what once was, and I felt that they had been empty for weeks.

After that, we left in a hurry. Again, the road was abandoned with only occasional sounds of a bird chirping or a dog barking in the distance. My mind was racing and my heart bursting with feelings. Perhaps only now did I realize how deep a loss we had suffered over the last weeks. The loss of freedom and carefree living; the loss of people I really loved—Dad, Sitah, and Hassan; the loss of our house and everything in it, which Mom and Dad had collected since they'd been married. Everything had changed, and the years and the times past would not be back.

Seeing the ruinous destruction of Dad's books and our belongings, feeling the slight touch of Hassan's shirt in the wind against my cheek, and smelling the dark, lonely emptiness of Sitah's rooms broke open in me a well of hopelessness, along with feelings I had no names for. I had never felt despair before now. I had not been ready for this, and I did not know what to do with it.

The trip back to the hotel was not as cumbersome as the trip to the house had been. In the ditch, we were able to follow the trail that our bodies had made before, which meant we had fewer problems with the *alang-alang*, since most of it was still smashed down. When we reached the hotel fence, we saw just the back of the guard disappearing around the bend, so we moved quickly, safely crossing the path and slipping back under the fence.

We had been away almost three hours, and the first thing I wanted was water, both to drink and to cool off and clean up in. It was close to lunchtime now, but we needed baths more than lunch. So once inside, I disappeared into the bathroom. My face was hot, and my arms and legs itched and burned from the rough jute. I petted the *alang-alang* cuts, where the jute bandages had slipped. Some of them were bleeding.

In the bath, the cold water felt icy and clean. It flowed from the *gajong* (water can) high above my head, and slipped over my shoulders, which were warm and dirty. I couldn't stop drinking from the same cool, clean water. I grabbed the soap, rubbed it deep into my rough, painful skin, and slid my body along the wall's cool tiles. Something trickled into my mouth and tasted salty. I shivered.

"Sofia!" Mom's alarmed voice rang out from behind the door as she rattled the handle. I had locked it on purpose. "Sofia, are you in there?"

Too miserable to answer, I let her continue to rattle and call.

"Sofie, answer me, please. Are you all right?" Easabella cried behind the door. She cried a lot lately and had started to wet her bed again.

I sat up, still shivering. "I'm okay, Mom. I'll be right out."

A few minutes later, as soon as I opened the door, she saw the *alang-alang* cuts on my face. "What did you do, Sophie? Where have you been?"

I picked up Easabella. She was wet and needed a change. "I went back to our house with Peter." I buried my face in Easa's red curls and felt the shaking return.

Mom just looked at me with wide eyes. She seemed afraid to ask more.

"They robbed it empty," I said. "There is nothing left!" Then I pushed

Easabella into Mom's arms and rushed outside to escape her eyes, her questions, and her grief. I had enough of my own.

Rumor had started that the European men were still in Langsa, but soon would be transported to somewhere else. No one knew where the rumor came from and no one could confirm it, but it spread like wildfire and held tremendous power over the camp, perhaps because it gave us hope again. The women especially were excited and filled with anxious questions: What could this mean? Would the men pass the Simon Fraay during their transport? Would Dad be among them? If so, would we be able to see and talk to him again and even all spend time together? Would we then hear what Japan was planning for us?

Newspaper clippings that had been smuggled in were immediately circulated among the women, and radio announcements, listened to in deep secrecy were repeated in whispers around the camp, keeping hopes high. The rumor progressed to that of the men being transported to the harbor of Belawan, to perhaps be shipped out, and then it progressed to reality.

The men were not transported by truck, however, the way they had been picked up. They came marching, guarded by screaming, stocky Japanese soldiers wearing spotless uniforms and holding rifles with bayonets. They came marching in rows of four past the hotel, where all of us, women and children alike, stretched as tall as we could behind the barbed wire to catch a glimpse of someone long cherished and so very missed. Likewise, the men's faces turned toward us, longing to see their wives and children. Men who saw their wives waved and called, and some came dangerously close to the fence, reaching out in hopes of touching them. Whenever a man marched too close, he was immediately punished with vicious rifle blows, punctures of the bayonet, or, if he was lucky, just a rough shove back into line. By now, women had started to call out for their husbands and to cry.

As we looked for Dad among all of the marching men who were dressed alike, Mom advised us, "Look for Dad. You know he has black hair and most likely a red beard. It should be easy."

And that it was. We spotted him at the end, looking just as Mom had said, with his shocking dark hair and reddish stubble. Simon, Mom, and I stood pressed to the wire, Easabella on Mom's back and Emma-M high on mine. Then Mom bent far over the fence, and Dad saw her quickly.

We felt great and proud that we had picked him out of the mass of men and that he looked good despite his crumpled clothes and unshaven face. We reached out as far as we could to just touch him. The little girls started to cry, Simon shouted, and Mom and I reached further. For a moment Mom and Dad's hands touched, and, as little as it was, gave them both momentary glowing smiles.

Dad shouted, "Hang on, we'll get through! This will not last too long. I love you! I love all of you!"

Mom cried, "Follow him, Sofia, as long as you can see him!"

The long rows of men marched on, and Mom's last words followed me as I ran along the fence next to Dad, jumping high every few yards to see his face turned toward me. I waved and shouted, "Bye, Daddy! We love you, Daddy! We'll write you. Don't forget us, Daddy! Good-bye!"

And then the fence held me back. I had not been able to see him anymore anyway; dust and tears had been blocking my view.

Though often hungry and always watched by Japanese soldiers, we children kept our cool. We organized our days to be as exciting as possible. We had formed a close-knit group, most days roaming the hotel grounds like wolves. We went through garbage pails to find "treasures."

We liked to pester the Japanese soldiers, but whenever meeting one, we had to bow and show respect. So we bowed often, all twelve to fourteen of us. We'd be running along the fence and then stop abruptly when we passed the guard, bowing deep and screaming, "*Kiotske-Kiotske!* (Bow down and show your respect!)"

Karel de Boer had perfected the art of blowing a big fart just then, before we ran away, laughing so hard we could not hear the guard's furious screams as he chased us, running along the outside of the fence. We did not do that too often, but often enough.

Karel de Boer pronounced himself the leader of the pack, and enjoyed teasing and badgering other kids, especially when they were younger or weaker. So Peter and I depended on each other to face him. Peter was a lot smaller than Karel and often took a detour just to avoid meeting him. But when we were together, Karel wouldn't pester us.

None of us kids liked Karel, but we respected his strength and his big mouth. In fact, during the months at the Simon Fraay, I managed to collect from him a nice variety of rolling curse words, to the great annoyance of Mom. Whenever she heard me use one, she would call me in, and, when I was lucky, she would wash my mouth out with soap, skillfully avoiding my teeth. But when she was really upset, she would slap my mouth hard with the back of her hand. The taste of the blood was as bad as the pain, though, so she hardly ever caught me saying one of Karel's priceless words. Still, Peter and I, when we were alone together, would spend many hours using these words and making up fantastic stories.

Peter and I looked alike too, with brown eyes and dark hair. Mine was even cut short, so I only had to comb it when I got out of bed. Mom didn't like it, but Dad didn't mind; he had always taken me to his barber, and after we'd both gotten our hair cut, we'd stop for ice cream, which we'd eat sitting somewhere together in the shade. Thinking about those hours with Dad, when I had him for me alone, brought tears to my eyes.

The prisoner population of the Simon Fraay usually awoke when the *koempoelan* bell (gathering bell) sent its loud ringing into the quiet morning, summoning everyone to the gathering place—the largest field—to be counted at eight o'clock. This morning, however, the bell sounded an hour early, and nobody was prepared. This had not happened before, and it gave me an uneasy feeling. Something had to be wrong.

Healthy or sick, adult or child, morning or night, when the *koempoelan* bell sounded, it meant we had to get to the gathering place within a half hour. You stopped whatever you were doing and ran to the field, and if you were late, punishment would follow, hard and swift. So it was terrifying that, this morning, nobody was ready. Women were still dressing their little ones, and most older children were not even out of bed.

We had learned quickly that the Japanese officers had many rules, and that most of them we didn't understand until we broke them and were punished. We had gotten used to their angry kicks and shoves, and some women, if offending a soldier who was in a particularly nasty mood, had even been beaten. At the gathering place, the women had to keep their children quiet. When they cried or spoke, soldiers would not hit the children, but would shove or slap their mothers. We had also quickly learned the Japanese words that were shouted the most and the loudest. *Tenko* meant "gather," and *kirei* or *kiotske* meant "bow and greet." By now, we could all bow and greet like jackknives—legs stiff, upper body coming forward with a jerk, arms immobile along your body—because not doing it right would earn you a kick against the back of your outstretched knees, sending you forward with such force that at least two or three others in front of you would shoot forward as well. And this, in turn, would trigger more shouting, pushing, kicking, and waving of guns.

An Indonesian gardener who tended the flowerbeds at the hotel had told us one day that he had worked in Japan and learned that Japanese people were very different. He said that even Japanese soldiers and guards bowed, as it was mandatory, and that by doing so, they were not honoring their officer, but their Godly Emperor, the Tenno Heiko of Dai Nippon. Japanese soldiers obeyed their Godly Emperor unconditionally and thought it an honor to fight and die for him.

This morning, I ran toward the grassy *koempoelan* square, my hands cradled under Easabella's bottom, and Simon was dragging his feet beside me. Easa was wet again, but there hadn't been enough time to get her washed and changed. Others were running half-dressed or still in nightclothes to the field, where we found two Japanese officers waiting for us.

Arriving and standing next to Mom, who had already been there with Emma-M and was looking for us, I peered at the furious man standing on a wooden box. He screamed, as usual, in his harsh language, the Chinese translator next to him looking uncomfortable, almost scared, I thought. He translated that we were late and had shown disrespect for the *Tenno Heiko*.

Easa jumped on my back each time he smacked the butt of his rifle against the box. I looked at her. Easabella was always pale, but today her little face looked slightly bluish, and her hands seemed uncomfortable and nervous as they squeezed my neck. I let her slide off my back to ready both of us to bow at the *kirei* order. Two hours later we still stood and waited.

The sun gained strength and stood high in the sky, yet we remained on the grass square, by now exhausted, thirsty, and thoroughly fed-up. We were hungry, too, as no one had had breakfast yet. The children began to whine.

The Chinese cook had been sent back to the kitchen, for there was nothing left to translate. We were just counted and recounted, and screamed at. Not everyone was present yet, they said, but no one was missing. So the counting started again, accompanied by more shouting and pushing. The oldest boys were then removed from their families and set apart in a scared, silent group.

Finally, when the Japanese officer seemed bored of pestering us, he called back the cook to translate, and the show began. The message that followed was alarming: Tomorrow, the boys twelve and older would leave for an all-male camp. The day after, the rest of us would be loaded into trucks and taken out of Langsa, destination unknown.

There was no further explanation. Though the mothers of the older boys were nervous and had many questions, they were not answered. The Japanese officers left us with only the warning to be in time for the *koempoelan* the next morning. And with them, any hope of an end to this confinement disappeared, and a heavy silence descended. The group of boys seemed especially quiet, and some moved back to be close to their mothers.

For nearly three months now, we had been unwilling guests of the Hotel Simon Fraay, but our future had never seemed as uncertain as it did now. Where would we be taken the day after tomorrow? Somewhere outside Langsa? And wherever it was, would it be in the neighborhood of the all-male camp—or not? Would Dad and all the other husbands be at the all-male camp as well?

For the rest of the day, the Simon Fraay Hotel was in total chaos. Mothers were crying for their big boys, who would be leaving them in the morning. And the boys seemed not really sure what to feel.

Late that afternoon, I sat with Peter on the front steps outside the main lobby and, in my own mind, tried to answer his question: who had invited the Japanese army to Indonesia and given them the right to take our freedom and break up our families? Neither of us said much; we knew neither of us had answers. But we did know that Max van Wyk would leave us, so Peter and I went to see him.

Tall, lanky Max looked and acted older than twelve. He knew a lot, didn't talk much, and rarely laughed. Peter knew him better than I did, since their parents had been neighbors. Dad had taught him in school, though, and had often mentioned Max's great talent for drawing and painting. His drawings were sometimes displayed in the school halls, and I had always looked at them and admired the older boy with such a beautiful talent from a distance.

Max could build beautiful things out of nothing, just with his hands. Last year, he had built his sister Silvie a merry-go-round from djati wood. He had painted it in bright colors and filled the little platforms with animals: tigers, elephants, deer, and panthers. Silvie never let any one play with it without her being right there. So we usually just watched Silvie turn it around and around, fascinated by its beauty. Silvie adored Max.

Max was alone, sitting on the steps in front of his room, bouncing a ball between his knees. We sat a step below him, but did not know what to say.

"Hi, Max," Peter said. "What are you doing?"

"Nothing." Max kept bouncing his ball. His departure tomorrow, so unexpected and so soon, had already created a distance between us.

The sun wasn't hot anymore, and the last daylight colored the sky. It was noisy around us, as mothers were hustling to ready their boys for their trip, while, off and on, wiping away tears and stifling cries.

Max, Peter, and I didn't speak much. Each of us was lost in our own thoughts, and I think none of us wanted to speak for fear of breaking the magic of our togetherness. Right here, we were friends with the same uncertainty, the same fears, the same longings, just waiting together in the final hour of daylight for the shadows of the evening to melt us into darkness.

And so it was that we said good-bye to Max, clustered together and touching each other only with our eyes, but feeling the instinctual tears well up inside us. And as I had with Dad and Hassan and Sitah, I let Max go.

Early the next morning, trucks rolled in. They were large, lumbering trucks, with the driver's cabins separated from the beds. Each bed was open— just a loading space enclosed by horizontal boards about four feet high, to prevent its contents from falling out. They had no tops to protect us from rain, insects, sun, or wind. And they were dirty. When the gates came clattering down for loading, we saw the dirty cargo spaces, littered with pieces of cardboard and half-rotten bananas, which some people slipped on. The last cargo must have been fruit and no one had thought to clean the mess.

It was cloudy, and the sun had difficulty coming through the heavy sky. Mothers held their boys until the soldiers separated them, and we all stood powerless and scared and quiet. Everything had been said and everyone was spent.

Even the children were silent. Easabella and Emma-M sucked their thumbs and stood leaning into me. Simon had his small arms around Mom's legs. Watching the departing trucks and the mothers hugging themselves, I thought about the next day, when the rest of us would leave. I wondered what the Godly Emperor would decide next and if we, too, would be separated from Mom.

The next day came soon enough. Mom and I packed the little we had in suitcases, which did not take much time. We rolled up the five thin sleeping pads that Sitah had brought us; they were not heavy, but very strong. We had marked them, as we had done the luggage. When the trucks arrived, everyone's luggage was loaded onto them, piled high and covered by a tarp to guard against possible rain or blowing. I watched our baggage being loaded and worried that we might never find it again.

Then we had to wait for the other trucks to arrive—the "people trucks," and the waiting seemed endless. Everyone became hot and restless. The adults were irritable, and the kids fidgety and quarrelsome. Little ones cried without reason. I decided to take Easabella and Emma-M to see Mies Miedema.

Mies Miedema fascinated me. I hadn't known her before the Simon Fraay, and met her one day when I found her playing a game with Easa, Emma-M, and her own daughter. She was very tall and walked with giant steps. Her large hands were gentle when she handled her baby daughter, who was pale and sickly, and could only smile or cry. The baby had no name; Mies said that God would give her one and did not explain.

Emma-M and Easabella liked to play with the baby's sister, Phaedra, who was two years older than Easabella. Mies loved our two little girls. She joined them when they played with Phaedra and taught them songs and little dance steps. Whenever she looked at me with her gray eyes, I looked away, embarrassed by the warm feeling she'd start up in me. When she looked at me, she really, really saw me, and I loved her touch when she stroked my head.

Phaedra, too, was tall, but quite thin. Mies explained that Phaedra had grown too fast in too short a time, and needed a special diet, which being at the hotel had not helped. Mies believed that God would help, though, and that he would do what was necessary in his own good time.

I didn't know too much about God. I knew he lived somewhere above the clouds, and that he was happy when you were good, but punished you when you were bad. And I knew he was master over a lot of things: the sun and stars, the moon and wind, rain and birds, animals and people. Phaedra had a book full of Bible stories. The stories were nice, but often also scary. Mies said that they were all meaningful, though, and that she would explain them to me some day.

Finally, the trucks arrived. They were the same trucks that had been used to take the boys away the day before. They were just as dirty; there were only more of them. The hotel staff helped us in, mothers first, their children after. But when the trucks were full, not everyone had found a place—so the soldiers started to push us back to make room, causing wails of panic among the children. The lack of space and the smelly darkness caused by so many people being packed so tightly together was frightening, and the mothers began shouting in protest. This did not help; it only added to the sense of chaos.

Mom, tall and strong, was able to hoist Easabella to her hip, giving Simon space to breathe. I did the same with Emma-M. Then there we stood, packed so tightly that we could not even change position.

The trip was surely worst for poor Simon, who only saw the sky if he lifted his head and who received numerous inadvertent kicks from his little sisters' dangling legs. Mom took the shoes off of the girls, and I tied the strings together and hung the bundle around Simon's neck. He didn't like it, but I was afraid that, left on the floor, they would get lost once we arrived. I began to wonder where we were going and how much longer we would have to stand, packed together, in this sweltering heat.

It was past noon by the time the trucks slowed down to a cumbersome crawl. We had driven to the train station. By the time we were unloaded on the platform, the mothers were bad-tempered and antsy, many of them driven to slap their whiny children into silence.

I looked at the little faces of my baby sisters, wet with tears after Mom had hard-handedly stopped their cries and questions. I felt so horribly for them. They were just scared, being still so very small. I took their hands and dried their faces, but I had nothing to tell them. So I took them aside, and once it was just the three of us, they calmed a bit.

Of course, we then had to be counted again. The same people who had been loaded into the trucks at the Simon Fraay now had to be accounted for on the train platform. As if anyone would try to escape. We'd have had to jump off of the truck somehow—and even off the trucks, the Japanese soldiers were everywhere. Where would we go?

After the endless counting by the screaming soldiers, we were herded into the many empty cars of a train that was used to transport cattle. Some of them had benches, but all of them stank of livestock, and their urine and fecal waste. And it was these filthy cars that were used to transport our luggage and us.

Mom looked disgusted as she stepped in and said she hoped there was no waste left on the floors. Women and children were randomly pushed in, and everyone tried to reach the benches. Inside the cars, families became separated, but getting a seat was more important than traveling together. Mothers called their children and were satisfied when they heard an answer from somewhere in the wagon.

When all the seats were occupied, the rest had to stand. Our family had a bench, and although very tight together, we at least had somewhere to sit. When Mom felt an old lady lean against her legs, she pulled Emma-M to her lap to make room on the bench. The old lady's daughter remained standing and thanked Mom for her kindness. The old lady smiled and introduced herself as Vera Hansen.

It was another two hours before we felt the train move. The temperature in the cars had become unbearable. The smaller kids had thrown off their tops, and the mothers had opened the windows. Although the incoming air was warm, it brought a bit of relief.

Finally, the train moved slowly forward, and away from Langsa and everything familiar. We left behind Sitah and Hassan, without knowing what had become of them. We left the place where perhaps Dad was being kept, but had no way of letting him know. We left behind everything we knew and cherished.

Mom had closed her eyes. Was she having the same kinds of thoughts as I was? Was she suffering from the same fear and insecurity? I noticed how tired and worried she looked, and could almost see her musings about Dad and about what would happen to him, and to us. I knew there were no answers.

I thought about Phaedra's Bible book and wondered if God saw us now. If God was so powerful, why was this happening to us? Was there a meaning to it all?

Struggling with my thoughts, I watched the *sawahs* (rice fields) pass by and envied the few people working them. They paid no attention to the train. They were working, but at least they were free to do what they wanted and go where they liked to go.

We who were sitting all stood at different points to let the standing women and kids rest and stretch their legs. I had given my place to Vera Hansen's daughter awhile ago, and her old mother was now asleep in her arms. Little children fell asleep also, and woke up cranky.

Every so often, we would pass a little train station, but we never stopped. And so we went on for hours, tolerating the sickening heat and the monotonous sound of the wheels, without food or drink. We had brought water and fruit and even some sandwiches that had been prepared by the hotel staff, but that was long gone now.

Further, the toilets had been clogged long ago and were now useless, even though there had been no toilet paper available from the beginning. The odor of the urine and waste became suffocating. The children whined constantly, as their pants were wet and uncomfortable, and the women started to shout for attention, because everyone needed to go to the toilet. The Japanese soldiers on the train were invisible, however, as long as we were moving.

Finally, just outside a larger station, we felt the train slow down. It stopped beside a forested area, and the soldiers let us out to find some foliage to hide behind. We left endless streams of urine, and some left more. The relief was so intense, and we were all so spent from having held it in for that long, that no one complained upon our return to the train. Then, like sedated cattle, we were pushed back into the cars, where the children fell back to sleep and the women, somberly resumed struggling with their endless worry.

Sitting again, I leaned on the window and watched the gradual departure of daylight and approach of early evening. Little lights appeared here and there in the distance. They came closer, passed, and disappeared again behind us, leaving only shadows from trees and a few faraway houses.

When we finally stopped again, we were at a large station. Somehow we understood that the Japanese soldiers' screaming on the platforms meant we had arrived, although we didn't know where.

As I stepped off, I saw a few poorly lighted buildings in the distance but no one on the street. There was no moon, but looking at the dew on the grass along the road, I knew it was very late.

Mom grabbed Simon and Emma-M, and I held Easabella. We huddled together and moved with the mass of people from the train onto the road. Walking that road gave us relief from the endless stillness of sitting or standing on the train, and as long as we knew we were all five together, we felt okay. We just followed the people before us.

Soon, *koelies* (laborers) passed us with little carts full of bags, suitcases, and sleeping mats. They were much faster than we were, hauling the luggage easily and efficiently in the direction of a large light in the distance.

When we finally reached the distant light and passed through a gate, we found our possessions waiting for us. We looked around. Long stretches of buildings stood in unfriendly silence. A single lightbulb on each building illuminated the doorway. We were to learn later, after walking through one such doorway into one of the oblong buildings, that there was also a second doorway at the other end. Each building was the same—two long walls filled with windows and two short ends, each with a door and a light above it.

Simon and the girls hunched in closer to Mom for safety.

"Is this a prison, Mom?" I whispered. She didn't answer, but looked around in disgust.

The *koelies* then led us to a smaller, more inviting building with brighter lights and wooden benches around tables. The lights drove the depressing darkness of the place away and we followed Indonesian women inside where we found clean, cool water and food. Rice, a tasty soup with pieces of chicken, and fresh vegetables. We had to be divided in groups, since there were not enough tables and benches to sit all of us the same time. We got ourselves in the first group and moved to an endless table were all the food was invitingly displaced. Starved we forgot about bathrooms and sleeping arrangements. We just sat and gorged on the rice, veggies, and chicken offered to us as if food had never tasted so good. We were even each offered a banana and bread after that, but we kids could not eat anymore, so Mom took them with her for us to eat the next day.

Mom left to find our possessions and I took Simon and the girls to the washrooms to be cleaned. We then went looking for Mom, who had disappeared into one of the oblong buildings. Entering through one of the doorways on the building, we found ourselves standing in a long hallway that stretched to the door at the other end. Walking through this hallway, we passed many rooms, where families had already settled, though many of the doors to the rooms were broken and hard to open and close.

Finally, we found Mom in a room by herself. Several items cluttered the floor: an old couch, a few washbasins, several bricks, old frazzled *rotan* (cane) mats, two chairs with only three legs each, a broken broom, and a few dented cooking pans. I wondered who had lived here before and why all of this had been left behind. The room was full of cobwebs and dirt, but Mom promised to take care of that tomorrow.

Our family of five filled the small room, so when we saw others passing our doorway looking for space, Mom hurried to spread the sleeping mats on the floor and our few possessions around them. Easabella and Emma-M rolled onto their mats and were asleep before I could cover them. Simon nestled himself against Mom and, despite the noise around us, was out in minutes. Mom asked me something, but I did not want to talk, so I pretended to be asleep as well.

I had so many confusing thoughts that I could not follow. Where were we? Why were we again in a place with a fence, with guards and soldiers, in a place where we were dependant on Japanese men who told us what we could and couldn't do? What right did they have to treat us like animals, and to steal everything we once had and once were? No matter how I tried, I couldn't get rid of the disturbing feelings of protest, anger, and powerlessness.

Behind my closed eyes, the bright, beautiful colors of freedom and happiness changed into drab, dark shades of fear, insecurity, and void. I folded Emma-M's little body against me, perhaps a little too roughly, as she protested even in her sleep. I hid my face in her hair, which still stank of dust and sweat, but also smelled of Emma-M. Then, listening to her breath, I fell asleep.

The next morning, we learned that we had arrived in a *tangsi* (army camp), named Kamp Keudah, and that the gates would remain closed.

KAMP KEUDAH

Kota Radja, June 1942

After the Simon Fraay Hotel, we found things very different at Kamp Keudah, which was an abandoned army camp in Kota Radja, the capital of Atjeh. Each long concrete building housed the main rooms over its entire length, and there were several smaller buildings, all encompassed by a strong iron fence with a gate that was always closed. Guards who looked like Atjeh-Indonesians, paced around the fence. Atjeh-Indonesians lived in the northern part of Sumatra, in the province of Atjeh, and were well-known for their aggressive behavior and their dislike of the *blandas* (white people). We learned later that they indeed were Atjeh-Indonesians and worked for the Japs, but that they were still in training at the time.

The rooms in the concrete buildings had dirty cement floors and were littered with items that had apparently been abandoned by previous inhabitants. We couldn't even guess what kind of people had lived there before and why they had left their belongings behind, let alone in such bad shape. Everything was dirty, old, and in many cases broken. The rooms were small, with damaged doors and windows that could open just a bit. Some windows with missing pieces of glass were taped off with plastic, allowing only filtered light through. And flies had left black spots everywhere—on window frames, on the plastic coverings, on the ceiling and floor. The walls between the rooms were thin too; we could hear people talking from six rooms down. But the hollowness of the empty building disappeared as we all, women and children, found a place and tried settling in.

What *was* like the Simon Fraay was the way we were divided among the rooms according to size. Smaller families had to share a room with each other, but larger families like ours could have a whole room to ourselves. This was nice because we had a space to call our own, and by closing the door as we had done at the hotel, we could shut out the rest of the world. And after cleaning the space, arranging the furniture and belongings that were there, and unpacking our things, the room started to feel a bit more like somewhere in which we could learn to live.

We didn't have a sink though, and had to go to a different building to wash, shower, and use the toilets. There was no toilet paper, so we learned to *tjebok* (rinse our bottoms with water from a bottle next to each toilet and our bare hands). We were supposed to refill the bottle for the next user, but most of the time you would have to fill the empty bottle before doing the job. There was no soap, and to dry our hands, we kids used our clothes or wiped them in the grass.

The morning after we arrived, the Japanese commander came into camp with one of the Atjeh guards and summoned everyone by swinging a heavy, rusty bell. We gathered in front of the kitchen, where the commander stood. This time he was tall enough that he didn't need a box to stand on, but he did need someone to translate. He started to shout out rules in rapid Japanese, which the Atjeh guard didn't seem to have trouble translating into Indonesian. Some rules we'd practiced at the Simon Fraay, but others were new.

- Twice a day, we had to gather in front of the kitchen to be counted. Absence without a serious reason would be punished; no exception for children or sick people.
- No one was allowed to leave the camp, and doing so would be punished.
- Smuggling was forbidden.
- Food would be delivered to the kitchen, but the women must prepare all the meals. We would also receive a meal card, saying how many people were in our family.
- There would be a *toko* (store) in the camp, where needed items would be available to anyone with money.
- Whenever a Japanese soldier passed, we were obliged to bow. If this was forgotten or neglected or even done in a nonchalant way, we would be punished, because it meant disrespect for the *Tenno Heiko* as well as the Japanese guard. In addition, we were not allowed to look into a Japanese guard's face or eyes, as this was considered insulting.
- One of the smaller buildings would be used as a clinic, where a doctor would see patients. There also would be a nurse.
- All women must work; the camp must be kept clean and the buildings properly cared for.

- Certain possessions were not allowed. Books and pictures of the royal family would be confiscated and burned, and the biggest offence would be hiding a radio. If a radio were found, the entire camp would be punished with less or no food.
- Lights in the barracks would go off at nine, and no one was allowed out after that, except to go to the washrooms. No candles were to burn after that time either.
- Each family was to keep its room clean and free of odors, and mothers were to keep their children quiet.

Then, as if in a final blow, the commander announced that we were to choose one woman among us to be a camp leader. He would deal with only the camp leader, which meant that all of his further requests and instructions would go only through her. She would be responsible for anything happening in the camp, and he would be unavailable to anyone else.

After the commander left the camp with his sidekick, the women gathered to choose a camp leader. The women agreed that this would not be simple. No one wanted to be responsible for everything in the camp. The person they chose would have to be a strong person and respected by everyone in camp.

They agreed, however, that once she was chosen, she would assign a leader to each of the buildings we lived in. Each of these leaders would be responsible for enforcing the rules and keeping the peace in her own building.

I left the women and went to look for Peter. When I found him, he was exploring one of the buildings, and we decided to go explore the grounds together. We sauntered from one corner to the other. We both felt discouraged, now driven so far from normal life. Any hope for a return to happier times seemed to recede further. We felt more like prisoners in this camp than we ever did at the Simon Fraay, and neither of us knew how to change that.

We saw papaya and banana trees around Kamp Keudah, but they had no fruit. The trees looked odd without leaves, and were mainly used by bats and sometimes snakes to hide in. The few banana leaves that were left hanging were mutilated, and I noticed later that some were used to protect wounds and others to cover food (to keep flies away).

We found the little *toko* (store) where goodies were available for money or trade. The owners were Chinese, and they sold spices, soaps, pillows, *klamboes* (mosquito nets), cookies, cotton materials, candles, and even shirts and shorts.

There seemed to be plenty of water to bathe with, which I later learned was always deliciously cold. It came out of taps in the *mandi kamer* (shower room), where we would be allowed to shower once a day, as was customary in the tropics.

The policlinic had two nurses, and once a week, a doctor would visit to treat the sick. The doctor also was Chinese and had some medications available, but he was careful handing them out as the Japanese commander allowed him to have only small quantities. But there was quinine, aspirin, cough syrup, allergy tablets, and ointments.

We walked silently around the fences of the entire camp. On each corner stood a guard. The Japanese guards had rifles, but the Atjeh-Indonesians had bamboo sticks, which they wore over their backs, and whips in their hands.

Later, however, we found out that the Japanese officer forbade the Atjeh-Indonesian guards to use the sticks or whips on us, while they were in training. They first had to learn how to guard a camp full of women and children, who had lost their freedom and independence, and who were expected to try trading with or smuggling in things from locals. Only Japanese soldiers could dole out punishment. If an Atjeh-Indonesian guard was caught punishing a prisoner, he would be dismissed from duty. The Japanese army paid the guards, and at that time, no one risked losing his job. Ever since the European men had been taken, and their wives interned in camps, work had been scarce for the Indonesians.

So the guards didn't do much with the bamboo sticks. They sometimes played soldier among themselves, when no Japanese were around, using the stick like a pretend gun. The whips seemed important to them, though, because they practiced using them whenever they could. Of course, they were not allowed to hit us, so they hit everything else: dogs, cats, birds, and even old Indonesian people when they came unsuspectingly close to the fence to beg.

Their favorite whipping sport was to kill chickens. In Indonesia, chickens roamed the roads, looking for worms or other food scraps, and the guards would use whips to slice their heads off, laughing hysterical as the headless chickens walked around drunkenly before dropping dead. By the end of their game, there was not much left of the animal at all, and the Japanese soldiers had never interfered.

That day, and for several days after, Peter and I looked for our other friends around Kamp Keudah, but something had changed between us all. The connection had been lost. We were awkward around one another and, as much as we may have wanted, couldn't find the loose easiness we'd had, in which we could call each other names without causing hurt or offense. Plus, we were missing Max and Erik, who had been the leaders of our *kastie* teams before being taken to the all-male camp. And so our little group of friends fell apart.

Perhaps the transport from the Simon Fraay to the much larger, more intimidating Kamp Keudah had aged all of us. By now, we had gone through what, at one time, would have been the unthinkable. We had been through things that did not belong in any of our young lives, and this had surely altered our thinking and playing. At least I knew this to be true for me. My life in Langsa was long gone. It seemed like years ago that I had lost Dad's bike and even longer back to the time when we'd enjoyed Sunday brunches and carefree swims. Though it had only been a matter of months since then, I had felt much, much younger than I felt now.

So Peter and I stuck together, often playing and roaming the grounds. We shared goodies and watched the guards endlessly. I continued to try to convince him to give me his black-heart hitter, and he continued to tell me no. We never spoke about all the rules we had to follow, even though their oppression never ceased to hover over us, thick in the camp air.

At the end of the day, our camp leader was chosen. Only a few women were interested in fulfilling this task anyway, but Mrs. Elliot was chosen among them. All of the women highly respected Mrs. Elliot for her classy demeanor and her calm way of handling difficult situations, which we had already had the misfortune to experience at the Simon Fraay. Mrs. Elliot started by requesting that each building get together to choose a representative. The next day she would meet with all of those representatives and discuss necessary issues. So that night, our building did get its own representative. Mom mentioned to us kids that Mrs. Winter would be the leader and that when she told us to do something, we were to obey.

In the beginning, we had quite enough to eat at Kamp Keudah. Food was brought in raw by Atjeh laborers in large trucks. They would unload *kangkong* (green vegetables), *ketan* (sweet, sticky rice), beans and peas, sago and sometimes bananas, papayas, and eggs. The women would change it all into cooked meals for the entire camp.

We could also buy *goela djawa* (hard brown sugar) in the store to sweeten the *ketan*. And the rice was, although dusty, filling enough with the green vegetable soup. Sometimes the *katjang idjoe* (green pea) soup or kidney beans replaced the rice, but then we would have boiled eggs or *pisang goreng* (fried bananas) as well. There was never meat, but chicken could be found in the soup on the days the truck came. The chickens came in dead, feathers and all, and the women had to pluck and clean them. When there were many chickens, we'd have a whole piece each, because without a refrigerator, the meat would spoil by the following day.

Sometimes vendors would come close to the camp fence with fruit and pastries, which they would sell or trade for jewelry and other precious items. The Japanese commander frowned on this, however, which meant it usually took place at the end of the day when the lights were not yet burning.

Mom regularly bought stuff in the *toko* (store) like coffee, tea, and soap, using some money she still had, and when the money was gone, she traded pieces of jewelry with the locals at the fence.

Mom was not unhappy. She liked it when things went all right and there was nothing to worry about. She loved sewing, and continued, as she always had, to make matching dresses for the little girls—tight over their little chests, with flowing skirts hemmed in rich lace, which she had bought in the *toko*. There were always sleeveless dresses, too, which had only thin spaghetti straps to be tied. Mom had explained that as each girl grew, she'd only need to tie the spaghetti straps higher up, which would make the dress a bit longer. Our little girls almost looked like twins in their matching dresses. In fact, since Emma-M was tall for her age, the only difference between them was their hair. Mom hadn't even needed patterns before, because she had made the dresses so often.

Now, she had to sew them by hand, because she'd had to leave her sewing machine. But other women in camp were so impressed that she began to get orders to sew for their children.

Simon needed shorts, because he was growing so fast. Mom bought enough of the cheap denim material sold at the *toko* to make Simon several pairs with lots of pockets, just the way he liked them. She then made the same shorts for me, but from khaki material, since I didn't like the blue denim. Besides, Peter's shorts were always khaki, and I wanted the same.

Mom was also a good hairdresser, having learned the trade from her father before she'd married Dad. Her own hair had always been very chic looking, draped around her head. She had never gone to a hairdresser, because she knew how to style her long, wavy hair exactly according to fashion. It wasn't long before the women in the camp found out how skilled she was in this area, as well, and she gladly helped them out when she could. She would be paid for her work, and the extra money and appreciation helped her get through those days when some women got mail from their husbands but she never got anything from Dad.

It was curious. Why did others have the Kamp Keudah address and we didn't? How did those women get mail? Who would know this address, which was so far out in the north of Sumatra?

And what did this all mean about Dad? Could it mean he was not in Langsa anymore? Not even on this island anymore? Where had they gone after they marched past us at the Hotel Simon Fraay, and then around the corner and out of sight?

And without an address, we couldn't even write to him. However, Mom wrote anyway and addressed the letters to a depot in Kota Radja. After all, the Japanese commander had promised to take care of any letter without an address, as long as there was a clear name on it.

Peter's Mom had no mail either.

The good thing was that Mom had made many friends, since she was sewing a lot for others. While sewing or playing cards together, these women would talk endlessly about everything from missing mail and wondering how long this all would go on to longing for the freedom they once had. I listened whenever I was around them and missed Dad being there with us. I wondered whether Mom's letters would ever reach him and whether he missed us too.

Eventually, more people came to the camp from different places, and for many, it was their first time being held prisoner behind a fence; till now, they had been free. After listening to all the rules of the camp, they would look bewildered, staring at the fences, the closed gate, and the walking Atjeh guards.

By now, the Atjeh guards had finished their training and had grown heady with power. They seemed to think they could do whatever they wanted and became mean, always teasing and humiliating the *blandas* (white people). Their training had lasted two months, and although they still were not given rifles, they were allowed to use the whip.

Mrs. Elliot, the camp leader, had warned us not to antagonize them, but she hadn't needed to; their sadistic behavior made us all afraid—not just the newcomers. Further, the Atjeh guards recognized potential traders faster than Japanese soldiers did, and then used their whip on them.

The Atjeh guards were seldom allowed to enter the camp, except to translate, because even the Japanese officers didn't trust them around us; after all, we were a people that they had once worked for and always had resented. So only the Japanese soldiers did the *koempoelans* (gatherings) and the counting. Still, they too were impatient and hit fast when the rows of women and children were not straight enough, or when individuals didn't bow in the direction of Japan as they were supposed to.

We often made mistakes with the bows, after which we'd be forced to stand at the gathering place for hours in the burning sun, till the asphalt under our feet became soft and hot. If we weren't wearing sandals, we'd have to lift one foot at a time to relieve the burning. We weren't allowed to use the toilets during these times either. The children peed in their pants first, but after half a morning of standing, the women also couldn't hold it any longer. Then, the punishment was easy: we'd have to clean up the mess, scrubbing away on our knees with the burning sun on our heads and the flies everywhere.

After more people arrived at Kamp Keudah, the Japanese commander gave each family some money to use in the *toko*, to supplement meals or use for other much-needed things. Mom bought new *klamboes* (mosquito nets) and a pillow. She wanted to use the pillow to hide her jewelry and extra money in at night, so that it wouldn't be stolen, since the people here had begun to steal like magpies. Peter once said the only way to fight thieves was to steal something back from somewhere else, but there wasn't much else at Kamp Keudah worth stealing.

Whenever Mom was out doing her *corvee* (chores), I had to watch Easabella and Emma-M. Simon didn't need watching. He always had his own games, real or imaginary, and besides, Simon was never bad. When Mom returned from her chores, she expected the room to be neat and tidy. That meant it had to be cleaned up and our few possessions put aside in an orderly way, with the sleeping pads rolled up, so we could lean against them.

We needed new *klamboes* (mosquito nets) so badly. In the ceiling of the buildings we had found several large hooks to which we could attach the top of the *klamboes*; the previous occupants must have used them for the same reason. The gauzy sides of each *klamboe* would fall like sheets around us, and they were long enough that we could fold the ends under the sleeping mats. Since the *klamboes* were sized to fit full mattresses, we needed only three of them to span our five sleeping mats. And we would lift the parts that draped between us, so that we could all see one another. In the beginning, this felt like camping, and we had a lot of fun with it.

The *klamboes* that Sitah had brought us at the hotel were starting to tear and had numerous black spots, where the mosquitoes had been smacked dead. I loved to smack mosquitoes. With one hand inside the gauze of the *klamboe*, and the other hand outside, I could clap and crush each blood-filled insect to a sliver. Over time, the blood would turn from red to black, and adorn the gauze with one more hard spot.

Whenever we made a mess, Mom would say, "I know there are pigs, but that doesn't mean we have to live in a pigsty!" Mom had so many of those sayings, and I sometimes couldn't follow what she meant, but in this case I knew she was saying she wanted things to be orderly and everything around the room done properly. In fact, one of her other favorite sayings was, "Sofia, what you do, do that right, or else don't do it at all!" I had tried the "don't do it at all" a few times, but it hadn't worked. First, Mom just got angry, but then Dad's belt came out, which for some reason she hadn't forgotten to take to the Simon Fraay Hotel. Neither had she forgotten to bring it here. After getting hit enough times, though, I realized it wasn't much fun having to sit on my burning bottom or lean away from the back of a chair to avoid hurting the painful streaks on my back. So, I ran whenever I got caught. I was good at it too. Mom never even tried to catch me. But she was always waiting for me when I got back. So after awhile, having no choice, I did what she wanted.

All parents in Indonesia, Indonesian and Dutch alike, punished their children physically. We kids didn't know any different and were used to it. Some parents used their bare hands, others used rulers, and a few Dutch parents even used belts. This was what Mom liked to use when she found it necessary to let me know that I had been disobedient or insolent too many times.

I once had heard her tell Dad that I seemed to need a belt treatment approximately every three months and that, afterward, I seemed much more cooperative and attentive. Dad had not agreed. He had told Mom that no child should be punished with a belt. But Mom had answered that her mother always had the belt hanging on their hat stand, ready to be used at any moment, and that the sight alone kept the children obliging.

When she wasn't using the belt on me, Mom would scoff, "You are a child of the devil, Sofia, and probably will remain that way. I give up on you!" When Dad had been with us in Langsa so long ago, he would frown and become very quiet when he heard Mom say that.

Then once, on one of our wonderful afternoon visits to Dad's barber and the ice cream parlor, Dad had explained to me that Mom's mother used to call Mom a child of the devil whenever she did something that was considered bad or sinful. Dad suggested that when Mom called me that, she didn't mean it literally, but only said it because it was what she had always heard from her mother. At the same time, Mom knew her mother loved her, so she didn't think it was wrong to call her own daughter the same thing.

Then I had asked Dad if Mom loved me, and Dad had assured me she did, but explained that when Mom became nervous or had to face something difficult, she could lose control and say things she didn't mean.

I understood what he was saying. For Mom, it hadn't seemed like such a bad thing to repeat what she had heard her mother call her for so long. I had never known Mom's mother and didn't think I would have liked her, but Mom was just copying her—it didn't mean they were alike. And I still loved Mom. Still, I tried to understand why she wasn't more like Sitah, who had never hit any of us. I didn't say anything to Dad. I just quietly finished my ice cream.

We walked home, and Dad didn't talk the whole way. But when we were almost there, he wrapped his arm around my shoulder, squeezed me against him, and said, "She is trying, Sofie, give her time. She will always be your Mom."

Mom had never called me a child of the devil until after I told her about Jan and his chocolate. I should have talked to Sitah instead.

Jan and his brother Otto were big guys, older than sixteen, and back when things were normal, their parents had belonged to Mom and Dad's bridge club, which played together every Friday night. Although Langsa was a little town and the Dutch people saw each other regularly, I didn't know Jan and Otto very well, because they attended a different school and did not bother with us little kids; they had other things on their minds.

One afternoon, when Mom and Dad were taking their daily siesta, I had found Jan leaning on his bike watching me as I slid down a curving coconut palm.

"You did fine, Sofia," he said, smiling, "getting up that tree like a *katjong* (street child) and coming down like a monkey."

Surprised, I just looked at him, wondering what he wanted and why he was there.

"Doesn't it hurt your legs and your crotch sliding down with only the little panties you have on?" Jan continued to smile, but I moved away from him and collected the coconuts I had dropped from the tree.

He came closer and crouched down, his eyes level with mine. "Come on, Sofia, don't be shy. Look, I'll give you this big chocolate bar if you take off those panties, climb that tree, and come sliding down, just as you did before."

Chocolate was rare in Langsa and I had never seen a bar as big as the one Jan showed me. I stared at him, and he continued to smile, holding out his hand with the tempting chocolate. Big drops of sweat covered his forehead and upper lip. Then a half-loose coconut broke away from the tree and thudded down behind me, breaking the silence.

I turned and picked up the *parang* (knife) I had brought, along with two coconuts, by their stalks. Then I said, "Do it yourself, Jan, and stuff your chocolate!" and ran toward my house, the coconuts bouncing against my legs. When I looked back, Jan was gone.

When I told Mom about it, she became hysterical. Dad took her into their bedroom, where I heard his soothing voice talking between her sobs. The rest of that day, Mom didn't speak to me. She ignored me and didn't answer any of my questions. I started to feel guilty, though I didn't know why I should. I asked Peter if he knew, but he didn't either and just said that parents had weird ways of letting kids know something was wrong without telling them what it was.

After that, Mom had decided that I was a child of the devil. "Good girls don't talk to boys like Jan, Sofia. You shouldn't have been outside in the first place. It was siesta time—you should have been in your room!"

I still didn't get it. Where had I gone wrong? I hadn't taken Jan's chocolate and hadn't climbed back up that tree without panties. So why did I feel hurt when she called me a devil's child? Neither Sitah nor Hassan had ever called me anything but my name. I had heard other mothers call their children nasty names, but ... Mom had called me a child of the devil. What did that mean? I knew the devil was evil, but I couldn't understand why she would call me his child for refusing chocolate. I was not evil.

I decided then to be extra good, to do everything right, and to try not to make her angry. I would watch the little girls more often and not shout back when she ordered me around.

It hadn't worked. No matter how good I tried to be, she still called me a devil's child whenever she ran out of patience. I'd have rather had the belt.

Now that all the prisoners, including us, were getting sick and weak, Mom was calling me a devil's child quite often. She didn't have the energy or strength to use the belt to change me into a good child.

Mosquitoes had become abundant, especially after rainy days, and slowly we had all become weak with malaria. There were days of high fever, followed by days of drowsiness and sleep. The doctor felt so uncomfortable with the large number of us who had come down with it that he started to complain to the commander.

He explained that we'd only become weaker because of the poor meals, with its lack of vitamins and fresh fruit. While in the first months, the food had been passable, lately it had become less so. Breakfast was always the same, either oats or sago, but often unsweetened, as the *goela djawa* (brown sugar) was often not on the trucks. There were never enough vegetables, and eggs were rare. Twice a week, we had chicken in a heavy soup of noodles or peas, and the rice had a dusty taste even when washed thoroughly. To our surprise, we received bread a few times, but it was several days old, perhaps from a large store unable to sell all of it. There were more than enough bananas, but they were overripe and unattractive. In general, the food was the same each day. There was not much variety, and by the time it reached the rooms to be eaten, it was clumpy and cold.

The doctor was also concerned that, with recurring malaria attacks and not enough medication, we'd become vulnerable to more severe illnesses. So after a long discussion with the commander and Mrs. Elliot, the camp leader, it was decided that all of the prisoners of Kamp Keudah would be vaccinated for infectious diseases, and that more fresh food would be supplied. The last thing the commander wanted was a camp full of infectious people, who could die and leave the guards and soldiers infected. He did not enter the camp again till the vaccinations had been completed and the doctor had received more aspirin to treat people with fever.

I asked Mom what the doctor meant by infectious diseases. I thought it sounded ominous. Mom explained that even though everyone already had malaria, vaccinations would protect us from getting sick with something worse, such as typhus, cholera, and dysentery.

When Mom took us to the clinic for our vaccinations, I cried for joy to find Mies Miedema there. I hadn't seen Mies since we'd arrived at Kamp Keudah. She wrapped her arms around me and held me awhile, and I thought I could have stayed with her all day.

Mies was helping the camp nurse, who she called Nadine, care for all the sick people. She called Nadine a nurse, because that's what she was, although there wasn't much nursing Nadine could do; treating people was difficult with only aspirin, quinine, cough syrup, and a few ointments. Even if she could do nothing else, she was always there when you needed her. "If I can't heal you, I can keep you clean and comfortable," she used to say, and that's what she ended up doing.

Everything about Nadine was warm. Her hands were warm and her body was soft and comfortable. Kids loved to be hugged by her. But most of all, her eyes and her smile were welcoming. They seemed to invite you to share whatever might be troubling you. Everyone loved Nadine, with her endless patience and gentle voice.

Nadine could also see things that other people couldn't. Women who didn't know her well called her a fortuneteller, but Mies Miedema called her a lady with visions. Mies was often with Nadine, who had a separate section in the barrack—the room closest to the clinic, along with three adjacent spaces for sick people who needed overnight treatment. Mies not only helped Nadine at the clinic but also took her baby there when she had *corvee* duty.

Returning from the clinic, with two quinine tablets from Nadine and Mies Miedema's hug still around me, I settled outside our barrack in the warm sun, shivering, unable to get rid of the exhausting cold inside me, which I knew by now always preceded the high malaria fever.

Before Kamp Keudah, none of us had suffered from malaria, but after the outbreak, it didn't take long to learn the symptoms well enough to anticipate what would happen to you next. The attacks were exhausting. They would begin with your feeling cold, and then colder, and then eventually so cold that your shivering would shake your whole body. On sunny days, the malaria sufferers could be seen trying to warm themselves on sunny spots. This cold phase would be the draining part, lasting approximately two to three hours. Then the body would relax and the fever would start, quickly becoming quite high. The children often reached a body temperature of a hundred and four degrees Fahrenheit, and the adults just slightly lower. The fever would force you to go to bed, where you would spend hours in a restless sleep, perspiring to slowly rid your body of the heat. The weaker the patient, the more perspiration. Some would perspire so heavily that after waking, a wash and change of clothing was necessary.

For the rest of the day, you would be slightly feverish, lethargic, drowsy, without appetite, but thirsty. That night would be more restful, and the next day, aside from feeling weak, you would feel almost completely okay: the fever would be gone and a slight appetite would have returned. The fourth day, however, would be just like the first, and the process would start all over again.

This time, it took until early evening for the cold to leave me. My eyes had closed long ago, but now I started to relax. The heat felt good. I was too tired to get up to go to bed, however, and decided to stay there. Then drowsily watching the red pumping of my heart behind my eyelids, I drifted off to sleep.

I awoke to Mom gently pulling me up, steadying my body against hers. She felt cool against my hot skin.

Later that evening, waking up on my mat, I remembered something odd: I had seen tears on Mom's face. Could she have been crying for me? Had Dad been right when he'd assured me that Mom loved me and really did not mean the hurtful words she spoke when she called me a child of the devil?

I fell back into my healing slumber, not wanting to forget the tears on Mom's face.

Easabella had started to complain about pain in her tummy. She often fell asleep, rubbing it. I remembered that when Easa was a toddler and had gone from eating baby food to more substantial meals, she often had difficulty digesting the rougher food. Sometimes she would also complain about her tummy feeling funny, and once in awhile, would even vomit, which upset her so much that she didn't want to eat ordinary food. For days, she'd live on porridge and *nassi tim* (a soup of soft boiled rice and chicken).

Mom said that Easa suffered from a delicate stomach and would feel better if her food was soft and easy to digest. But the meals we got from the camp kitchens were not prepared for delicate stomachs. So whenever Mom wanted to cook something soft for Easabella, she'd go to the long line of *anglos* (low wood-burning barbecue units) in the kitchen, which was available for preparing your own dishes.

Emma-M was having problems too. She had learned long ago to go to the washrooms and not pee in her pants, but at night there weren't many lights between our building and the washroom, and she was frightened of the shadows. Mom had put an empty can in the room for her to use, but

Emma-M couldn't ever seem to wake herself soon enough. We would find her wet in the morning, crying and sucking her thumb like a baby.

Simon spoke even less than usual, and his gray-blue eyes somehow became larger in his small face.

Mom's nerves were stretched tight; she snapped more than ever and her hands were quick to strike. There was still no mail from Dad.

So between the bad days, whenever possible, I found Peter, and we had our time together. The days passed slowly but steadily, and began to blend together, as each day was the same. The biggest change in schedule was when the women switched their assigned *corvee* every two weeks.

On days when Peter and I got together, we'd make our rounds on the inside of the fence, following the guards on patrol. Sometimes, we'd play with our marbles and, if we could get enough friends together, would organize a game of *kastie*. At mealtimes, we went to the kitchen and showed our meal cards to get food for our families, which we then took to our respective rooms to eat. We always ate in our rooms, since there were no tables outside inviting meal gatherings, and besides, the flies were too numerous.

More frequently, there were nights we went to bed hungry. Some people who had run out of money could talk the Chinese owners of the *toko* into trading jewelry or other treasures for food; the Chinese *toko* lady even accepted elegant clothes in exchange. The Japanese soldiers had seriously started to punish trading at the fences, but women still did it occasionally, usually surrendering long-kept treasures for more practical goods.

When Christmastime came, the *toko* owners put toys and home décor up for sale, but had to quickly change their merchandise when they realized such wares could not be sold to hungry people. They honestly didn't know anything about Christmas; they only knew that such items had historically sold well to Europeans in December.

New merchandise included bottles of colorful syrups that, diluted with water, would fill a glass with delicious lemonade. A Chinese delicacy, lemonade had little sweet bubbles floating at the top, which, when you tried to catch them with your tongue, would flip between your teeth. The *toko* also began to sell wonderful pastries, cookies, and cakes, which, though brought in fresh every day, were gone by nighttime, since everyone had some money hidden away for holidays. In addition, exotic fruit-filled baskets stood next to the front door. This fruit was grown everywhere in the tropics and had difficult names, and flavors that the Dutch and other *blandas* had needed to get used to when they'd arrived in Indonesia: purple *mangistans*, hairy red *ramboetans*, dark green *sawos*, *blimbings*, papayas, green prickly *soursops*, and here and there a *doerian*.

Seeing these baskets brought up a deep longing within me, and a sense of nostalgia. This was fruit I hadn't seen since I'd visited the *passar* (market) with Sitah before my ninth birthday. Tears welled in my eyes, which I wiped away angrily. Tears never helped, and they certainly would not help right now.

In addition to Christmas, we had to learn to celebrate birthdays at Kamp Keudah. Whenever one of us kids had a birthday, Mom would cook something special, and we always asked for the same thing. Mom would buy flour, *goela djawa* (hard brown sugar sold in large solid discs), a coconut, and a couple of raw eggs if they were available. Then, part of the fun was watching her beat ingredients into a foamy, thick batter and, on the low fire of one of the *anglos,* fry the most delicious pancakes we'd ever tasted.

As soon as a pancake slid out of her frying pan, I would grate the *goela djawa* over it. I had to be fast or else the pancake would cool and not be able to melt the sugar into syrup. The pancakes were so thick and filling that Emma-M and Easabella had to share one, but Mom, Simon, and I could each manage our own. The little girls would have the first one, Simon the second, and I the third. Mom saved the last one for herself, since it took time to scrape out the very last of the batter. This pancake also took longer to fry, and while it did, we would patiently wait for her, inhaling the sweet odor of the syrup. It was difficult to wait until everyone had a pancake to eat, but Mom had always insisted on waiting till everyone had a plate, and the rules hadn't changed.

When money became scarce, she would buy less and create different birthday meals. Although not always available, eggs were cheap so for the five of us, she would buy three eggs, a large tomato and a sweet, juicy onion. With this she would bake a large, high egg omelet, and when our meal arrived from the kitchen at night, we'd each have a slice of it with the rice. With such a birthday meal, we were not hungry going to bed, and Easabella didn't complain about a sore tummy.

As long as Mom cut children's hair and sewed for other people, she could also buy candy on those special days and, if it was there, a coconut cake. The candy in the *toko* was the same as the stuff we could buy in Langsa: rolls of peppermint or licorice, hard sugary suckers, some on little wooden sticks, and little chocolate tablets, which no one bought because they were outrageously expensive. I loved the long strings of dried *assam. Assam* was a sour fruit used in Indonesian recipes, but it was also prepared as candy, with the little, stony seed still inside and rolled in coarse sugar. It was my favorite treat, and Simon liked it too. Emma-M and Easabella spat the *assam* out, however, because it was too sour for them. No matter what special food we were able to get for our birthday celebrations, though, we always all sang for the birthday kid.

The longer we lived in Kamp Keudah, the more difficult it became to celebrate, though I wondered about many mothers who I had heard complain day after day about the bad food, their hungry children, the lack of money to buy shoes, and the shortage of medication, but who still seemed to manage big celebrations. While most of us were hungry and failing, and had nothing, they seemed always able to have something.

After Christmas, the commander decreased the money given to families, making trading at the iron fence a daily occurrence. Mom, too, had to resort to trading what she had long cherished. She sewed things for the Chinese *toko* owners in exchange for needed items, and a few times, she had offered up some of her beautiful dresses, which she didn't dare wear here. None of the women wore beautiful dresses anymore, but were always in easy, loose garments. The beautiful dresses became useless, lying in bottoms of bags, becoming more and more crinkled. So Mom, without seeming upset about it, took her two nicest dresses to the *toko*. She got soap, sugar, and salt for the one, and coffee and fruit for the other.

But when the *toko* didn't want to trade anymore, she had no other choice but to consider something she had never wanted to do.

Off and on, women in the camp had traded with those who lived outside the fence. We always saw these locals walking along the roads, balancing large baskets full of merchandise on their heads. The baskets were flat and woven from thin bamboo strips. They were about twenty-five inches in diameter and folded slightly upward at the edges. Those folded edges would prevent their merchandise from falling out when they lifted the baskets onto their heads. To balance the baskets as they walked, each trader would place his or her basket on a tightly rolled ring of cloth in the middle of his or her head. There, the basket sat snug and safe, able to be carried to wherever the trader wanted to sell.

In the beginning, except for an eager few, the traders had not seemed interested in us. They had watched us from time to time, but then walked off as soon as a guard came into view. Understandably, they were afraid, since anyone caught trading, whether inside or outside the fence, would be severely punished, usually with a beating. But the women knew this and so were very careful, as they began more frequently trading those possessions that were no longer wanted by the *toko* owners. This always happened during dusk, when it was difficult to recognize people.

Some women were particularly crafty at doing this, and had regular contacts. Trudy Sanders, one of the best smugglers, helped many of the other women trade their jewelry for food, clothes, and even medicinal herbs.

Trudy's face was always closed; she never let on how she was feeling, whether angry, happy, or sad. Mies Miedema said she had a poker face and was a great actress, but could also be very dangerous. She didn't explain how.

Trudy Sanders had one son, Herman, who was so beautiful that the

Japanese soldiers thought he was a girl and loved to pull their hands through his silky, fine hair. He was eight years old and didn't like this, however. Though frail and angelic looking, he was acutely aware of his mother's subtle signals. They'd communicate with a wink or a smile, a slight hand gesture or a glance. I envied their closeness. It was just the two of them, and they did not seem to need anything or anyone else.

Trudy traded some of Mom's jewels for her, though parting from them had broken Mom's heart. To begin with, she hadn't had many jewels that were really valuable; most of it was costume jewelry that she had bought to match a new dress she had sewn. Now that all of that was gone, she had only the precious stones that Dad had bought her: the twelve in her arm bracelet and the six smaller ones in the matching earrings.

One night, after the girls and Simon were asleep, she removed two of these stones from their settings and gave them to me. "Ask Trudy Sanders to sell them for me, Sofia. Tell her to get as much money for them as possible. However much she gets, it will never be enough."

Then with tears in her eyes, she rolled the rest of the stones back into a velvet hanky and stuffed them in her bra. Soon after, the lights went out, and I could hear Mom on her sleeping mat, rolling onto her side. I slipped next to Emma-M and stared into the darkness, feeling the jewels in my hand, warm and stony.

"Sofia," Mom whispered.

"Yes, Mom?"

She kept quiet for so long, I thought she had fallen asleep. But then she said, "Don't lose them!"

"I won't!" I said. I closed my eyes, and let myself drift into happier times when I was free to come and go. When life had been simple and Sitah had still been around and Dad had come home each day after teaching school. When Simon's eyes had had no dark shadows and when the little girls had laughed loud and often. I could smell the *saté* (pork shish kebobs) that Sitah prepared over a low fire mixed with Hassan's cigarette smoke. Hassan and Sitah. Where were they now? Would we ever see them again?

I pushed Mom's jewels into Sitah's slipper and tucked it under my face. Then I drifted off and into faraway *gamelan* music (music played on wooden instruments), into warm nights alive with little dancing oil lights, into colors of misty mornings and burning sunsets, and finally into sleep.

The next day, Trudy Sanders brought Mom the money and food that she had gotten for her jewels. Mom was happy and let Trudy take her share for the risk she took.

Trudy then turned and gave Herman half of her portion of the money. "Your share," she said. "You deserved this!" Her eyes were alive with pride and love and camaraderie as they walked away, Herman thin and straight under Trudy's arm. They did not talk, for each knew what the other had to say.

Mies Miedema knew about Mom's belt. Last month, when Mom had been angry because I hadn't bathed Easabella and Emma-M after they had made mud pies, I had yelled at her, and Mies had later seen the welts showing through my shirt but didn't mention them.

It had all started one day after a night of high fever. I had been happy just to be able to sit in the sun and watch the little girls play. The warmth felt good and calmed my upset stomach.

When we arrived at the bathrooms, the bath water was cold, and I had hated to get shivery again, so instead of bathing them, I just washed their hands and feet.

When Mom came back from her *corvee*, she was tired, of course, and then found mud on their knees, and broad rings of sand under Easabella's nails. When she screamed and called me a child of the devil, she suggested it was time for the belt again. My head became heavy, and I felt the hot anger rise inside me.

"You can bathe them yourself, Mom!" I yelled, and then I took off, but not before she swung the belt, slashing my shoulder and instantly causing welts. Mom had then turned and left the building, taking Easabella and Emma-M with her to be washed.

As I ran past the next building, I saw Mies Miedema and was shocked. I hoped she hadn't heard the confrontation. She could have even been watching. I looked up at her furtively and quickly tried to pass. I was afraid she'd think less of me after hearing me yell.

I suddenly felt terrible about what I had done. I had known Mom would be tired and cranky; she always was when she came back from *corvee*. But I shouldn't have yelled. That had made her grab the belt.

But Mies only smiled. "Stay with me for awhile, Sofia. The sun is still warm and the mosquitoes aren't out yet." I looked at her face and saw no evidence that she knew what I had done. Perhaps she had not heard what I'd said or seen Mom furiously leaving the building.

She looked calm and composed, as her baby slept on a blanket in the shade. I walked up to her hesitantly, still unsure what she had seen or heard. We sat together, silent, and I felt uncomfortable.

Then Mies Miedema started to talk. "I heard what Mom called you, Sofia. I couldn't help hearing. You were both close by and the windows were open."

My heart dropped and I felt my face turn red. What would she think of me now!

"When people are upset and tired," Mies continued, "they often react in unusual and offensive ways. Perhaps, something happened when Mom did her *corvee* today or maybe she wasn't feeling well. Mom must have said those things to you without thinking, or meaning it. You know you are not a child of the devil; you know you are always doing the best you can."

I didn't say anything. I was afraid that if I did, I would start to cry, because Mies Miedema's voice had been so soft and sweet, and she hadn't even mentioned my yelling at Mom. We sat silent awhile, and I began to relax. Mies looked at the welts on my shoulder and went for a cold compress. When she returned, she folded the compress over my welts with gentle fingers, and then lifted my chin and said. "Have patience with Mom, Sofia. She didn't mean what she said. She loves you." She sounded almost like Dad had so long ago.

I swallowed the tears in my throat as I stood up. "I wasn't feeling good either, Mies, and Dad always warned Mom that children shouldn't be punished with a belt."

I walked away feeling better, knowing that Mies seemed to understand why I had yelled at Mom.

"Itchi–ni–san–sji–goh–rokko!" Counting and recounting was done over and over again, as the Japanese soldier continually lost track. Becoming angry seemed a way to disguise his embarrassment.

As I stood on the *koempoelan* square, the pain in my back dulled into throbbing. Funny to feel your heart beat in your back in more than one place.

"Itchi–ni–san–sji–goh–rokko!"

My back became hot and sweaty, making my shirt stick to the welts. I made space between my back and the cotton by pulling my shirt taut, away from my body, so that air could get to it. It hurt like hell and I closed my eyes. Mies Miedema had taught me how to deal with pain. "Just move into it, Sofia. Move with it, and it will become part of you. Then it will not feel so bad."

I tried to do that, but it wasn't easy. Finally, the air came through my shirt and, though warm, felt soothing on the hot, sticky, throbbing welts.

This time my crime had come after days of rain and boredom. It had been just yesterday, when Peter had come over with his marbles, and we'd needed to mark lines and holes for our game. I had used Mom's eyebrow pencil to make nice, sharp lines, and then thrown the pencil out, hoping she'd just think she had lost it. I should have known better, of course, but was willing to take the risk for a good game of marbles.

Something unpleasant must have happened during Mom's *corvee*, for when she returned she was not only tired but short-tempered as well. When she saw us playing, she knew right away what I had used to make the marks, and went for the belt without a word.

"Itchi–ni–san–sji–goh–rokko!" Would he ever get it right?

The sun crept higher along with the voice of the stupid soldier. He began pushing women in and out of line, becoming rougher and meaner. In the process, Mrs. Hansen, who was standing next to me, trying to keep her old mother standing, stumbled and smacked into me. I ended up on my knees against Mies Miedema's legs.

Falling, even from fainting, always infuriated the soldiers more, since it never just happened to one person. Since we were so packed together, whenever someone fell, he or she would knock against someone else, and that person, in turn, stumble into a third, sending a whole group of us over like dominos.

This particular Japanese guard was always short-tempered and unable to count correctly, and now that so many of us were down, he totally lost it. He drew his favored weapon, which was not the whip, but a long, slender bamboo stick with multiple fine hairs that instantly opened the skin, causing festering sores that were difficult to treat or heal. The bamboo stick came down over all of us, again and again, hurting necks, heads, backs, legs, and shoulders, as the guard worked out his rage, screaming and raging till his arm became tired and the only sound left was the suppressed cries of women and children.

Finally, Mrs. Hansen got up, still holding her mother, and Mies Miedema bent over Phaedra, pulled Phaedra to her side, and then tried gently to lift me to my feet. The guard stood watching her, and not liking what he saw, used his stick on her. Mies did not move. She continued to help me up with firm, careful hands as she caught the bamboo blows on her back. She then turned and stared the soldier straight in his furious face, unblinking, and towering over him. It stopped his rage. He turned and left, screaming something to another guard.

All morning, we stood in the burning sun, on the hot asphalt, thirsty and weak. Mies kept her hands on my shirt, gently pulling it off my back. Though by this time, I didn't mind that my back hurt, since hers must have hurt more.

I went to see Mies often after that. In my mind, she had grown into someone brave and untouchable. I wanted to stay close to her, to learn what made her so strong, so defiant, and so beautiful. Mies was not a beautiful woman, but after that day, she had become the most beautiful person I had ever met. I wanted to be like her so much that I was sorry that my eyes were also not gray. I tried to walk straight like her, taking large, long steps with my bare feet, which reminded Mom to tell me to start behaving like a lady.

I made my voice soft like Mies's when talking to Emma-M and Easabella. And I talked a lot to Mies Miedema, who looked at me and talked to me, and smiled with her eyes.

Now more than a year behind barbed wire without access to the outside, a horrible boredom set in at Kamp Keudah. The women had told everyone their life stories and became crankier by the day. They had daily quarrels, were short-tempered, and often worked their chagrin and unhappiness out on their children, who wisely stayed as far from them as possible.

We children continued to play with each other, but we also fought quite a lot. At one time, the mothers had tried to organize something of a school, but there were not enough teachers for all the different grades who were willing to put up with insolent, often-hungry children. Regular attendance was difficult, too, for children and teachers alike, because of the recurring, frequent malaria attacks.

Also, paper and writing materials, such as pens and pencils, were forbidden. The Japanese commander didn't want to risk prisoners' stories being smuggled out into the public eye. Whenever diaries were found, they were immediately burned, and their owners usually punished by having their hair shaved off.

By this time, the food rations had again become smaller; we hadn't had *ketan* (sticky rice) and *pisang goreng* (fried bananas) with our meals for weeks.

The guards became more vicious, less patient, always ready to use their whips or bamboo sticks. The lights began going out earlier at night for no reason at all.

More rumors came and went. Rumors about the return of the men, pockets of escaped prisoners, transports, and war victories and losses. And there were promises, too, of more food, and of forthcoming mail. Every time, word spread quickly and changed as it went, but none of it became reality. And every time we heard planes pass overhead, our hopes went up but came down faster.

Nadine had visions, but no one wanted to hear them. They were not happy visions and we needed to believe this would end sometime.

Easabella and Emma-M had become visibly taller and lost their baby fat. Simon grew little, however, and his gums bled a lot. When Mom took him to Nadine, she said that he needed better food, with more fresh fruits and vegetables. Simon didn't complain much, but as soon as Mom got back from *corvee* duty, he'd show her his painful gums.

As for Mom, she left each morning without speaking, and more often than not, had that faraway look in her eyes that meant she was depressed.

That made me angry. She had no right to turn inward and leave us hanging every time things got tough—we needed her! Of course, I had Peter and Mies Miedema, but Simon suffered, and the little girls needed her more than ever, with the malaria fevers every few days, and the constant hunger. All we kids ever felt like doing anymore was crying. I started to resent Mom and hated myself for feeling this way.

For once, I wanted just to sing, to really sing, because I was happy. I wanted to know that tomorrow would be a good day and that we would have enough to eat. I wanted Simon's eyes to lose the lost look, and the little girls to laugh—to really laugh. I wanted all those things that I hadn't known I'd had before. What I really wanted was just to be ten years old. Instead, with Mom slipping into her faraway world, to that place where she would not be disturbed, it would be entirely up to me to take care of the younger kids.

Looking at Mom these days and listening to her silence, I longed for her angry eyes, her impatient replies when she didn't have an answer, or even her whips with the belt if she thought I needed it. Looking at Mom, I was scared.

Thank goodness for Tuesday afternoons. They made Kamp Keudah almost bearable. They were the highlight of every week, brightening the monotonous days like a silver coin between coppers. The guards would come in and rope off a six-by-six meter square, and everybody would crowd around it. Sharp at two o'clock, a couple of *betjaks* (two-wheeled carriages pulled by a man) would arrive at the gate, loaded with delicious food: pastries in multiple colors, many covered with shredded coconut; fried plantains, fresh fruit, *pisang goring*, candied pineapple, and rolls of cookies; little fish, meat pies, and *loempias* (egg rolls). When the *betjaks* stopped, a sweet Atjeh woman and a teenage boy came out, both weighted under a shoulder pole bent by trays and trays of goodies. The guards had to make a path for them from the gate into the square, where they then spread out their wares and started selling. Everybody bought something from the *passar* (market) woman, which they would carry back to their rooms to savor, taking little bites for as long as possible.

Every week, Mom gave us kids money to buy things. We each got just a bit, but we felt as rich as kings. Peter and I wriggled ourselves forward between other wriggling kids till we reached the ropes, and then we would lean over them. All the while, hands were waving and women were shouting orders, and the wonderful little *passar* woman was staying calm. With not a hair out of place, she carried a white melatie flower in her *kondé* (hair knot) and wore a spotless white *kabaja* (shirt blouse), which set off the earth tones of her sarong. Her feet were hidden in little beaded sandals just like Sitah's. She turned and twirled to serve everyone, her tiny brown hands, light and fast, counting cookies, egg rolls, and money. Her whole face smiled, making her look friendly and compassionate.

Her food was not expensive. She also gave out credit and readily believed anyone who claimed they had it. And when she was not able to give back correct change, she would promise to make up for it the next week by bringing either the correct change or new wares that would be available free of charge. Peter and I abused her trust ruthlessly. We took turns convincing her that she had short-changed us the week before and always got a few cents out of it, which we'd then use for *pisang goring* or *loempias*. Since we did this every week, she probably recognized us after awhile, but she continued to believe us (or pretended to), and gave us the few pennies we asked for.

Every week, she never failed to come. And every week, when I saw her leave with the empty trays, it never failed to fill me with an even deeper longing for freedom. I would imagine her going to a place without guards and barbed wire that, for me, existed only in memory. There were only a couple of times that she didn't come, for some reason or another, and then she was sorely missed.

One Sunday, I promised God that I would not cheat the *passar* lady out of pennies anymore if he would just save Mies Miedema's baby. That morning, I had won ten of Peter's most beautiful marbles and offered to give them back in exchange for his black-heart hitter, but he had refused. I got mad and wandered off to Mies's room.

When I got to her building, Phaedra was sitting outside, under a little shade made from a piece of banana leaf. She looked solemn.

"What's up, Phaedra?" I asked, rolling her name extra long-like. I had never understood where she'd gotten her strange name until I'd asked her once, and she'd explained that it was because her mom and dad were poor. Mies had told her, "Since I can't give you wealth, I'll give you something you'll enjoy all your life. You'll have a name richer than wealth. I'll call you Phaedra. No one will ever forget a girl named Phaedra."

"Baby is going home today," Phaedra said.

I looked at her in stunned silence. What did she mean by that? Was something wrong? I knew Baby had not been healthy and that Mies was always extra careful with her, but Mies had never explained what was wrong.

"She can't stay any longer," Phaedra continued. "They are waiting for her in heaven."

I hurried to Mies's room and found her leaning against the concrete wall, Baby cradled in her lap. The little girl looked like a doll and was as white as Sitah's melatie flowers. I didn't say anything but just looked at her. I never noticed before how long and dark her eyelashes were. Against her now-stark white face, they were the only color, forming perfect little bows, floating in shadow. She lay quiet and still, her little chest barely moving. I looked for movement, going from her closed eyes to her tiny chest and back again, fearing the moment I wouldn't see any. I waved at the flies coming for her face.

I had seen people die at Kamp Keudah, but never a kid, and never a baby so small. Yet kneeling next to Mies, I knew that's what was happening.

"I never named her, my baby," Mies said finally, lifting Baby up close to her face. "I knew she wouldn't stay with us very long and that God has always known her name." Her large hands formed a cradle around her baby's head.

I had nothing to say, but my throat wouldn't let me speak anyway. Why wouldn't God let Baby stay with Mies and Phaedra? How could Mies be so calm? Why wouldn't she cry? Mies Miedema always spoke about God as if she knew him, or as if she had seen him and talked to him. Maybe she had; maybe she knew where to find him. I didn't. I knew for sure that I had never seen him anywhere. But taking the chance that he might be somewhere, I made deals with him in my mind. I promised to give Karel and Peter all my marbles, except my gold hitter, if he wouldn't take Baby home. I promised not to cheat the *passar* lady. And I promised to love Simon just as hard as I loved Easa and Emma-M and Peter, and to always be good for Mom, if he would just take someone else home instead of Baby.

More flies. Swiping at them angrily, I wanted Mies to keep on talking and Baby to continue breathing, so I wouldn't have to face the truth that kids could die before they grew up. Baby opened her eyes and looked at her mother. The two were still, speaking only with their eyes.

Then Mies whispered, "Do you want to leave us so bad, my love? Are you so very tired?" She lifted Baby a little higher and put her lips against her daughter's cheek. "Then go, my darling. I'll tell Daddy what a sweet little girl you have been."

Baby's eyes closed then, and life gently slipped away from her as she lay in Mies's arms, her little face cradled against her mother's throat. I scrambled away before her chest stopped moving and ran. I ran to the end of the camp and back and to the end again. I ran till pain shot through my side, making breathing difficult. I enjoyed the pain and wished for more, so that I'd have a reason for my screaming and crying. I wondered if my screaming had reached God, and then I wondered if he really was God.

Nadine had a little, empty tea box, which Mies lined with the best she had—a crocheted tablecloth hemmed with lace. Nadine laid Baby inside, and Phaedra closed the lid and tied ribbons at the corners. Mies carried the little coffin to the gate, where a guard pushed it into a *grobak* (open cart) pulled by a tired, white ox. The sound of the wooden wheels over rough ground hammered in my mind long after the *grobak* was gone. Mies Miedema never knew where her baby was buried.

After that, I gave all my marbles, except for my gold hitter, to Peter and Karel and Herman Sanders. Karel and Herman thought I would ask for them back the next day, but Peter didn't. Peter didn't say anything, but gave his to Phaedra.

The days passed, one after another. Malaria kept our activities low-key, but despite hunger, fevers, soreness, and diarrhea, we continued to play. Rain was the very best for playing; fever and stiffness were quickly forgotten. And when it came down in torrents, it would create nice, muddy streams along the slightly sloping ground around the buildings. We'd make mud men and other "sculptures" from the clumpy clay, and then mud balls to attack each other's creations.

We fought in two teams: the Dutch against the Japanese, only the Japanese weren't aware of the game. When the soldiers were hiding indoors from the rain, we dared make fun of them, stomping around on bowed legs, screaming at each other, stretching the corners of our eyes outward, and waving imaginary whips.

Karel would shout, "Itchi–ni–san–shi–goh–rocco!" He would also make "bullets" by packing mud around a stone and aiming it at a guard. When a mud bullet landed perfectly on a soldier's boots, as it often did, all hell would break loose. The Japanese soldiers were proud of their shiny, black boots; they spent hours polishing them with a soft cloth, sometimes using spit, until they could see their own ugly faces reflected in the black leather. The victim of the mud bullet just about lost his voice screaming at us. He would storm through the gate, swinging his whip, which swiped many of us over our backs and shoulders, but the mud helped as it built up on the whip and soon made it too heavy.

We'd be so covered in mud that even if you soiled your pants, no one would notice it running down your legs. We'd squeeze the mud between our toes, forming fat worms. Karel, with his big feet and wide-spaced toes, could make the fattest!

Karel wasn't the only mud hero though. Once, Kees managed to fly down the hill riding a large piece of bark from a banana tree. The trunks of banana trees are soft and shrivel when old; they are then easy to cut down to make place for the next tree, which is already sprouting. Kees found a large piece from one of the dead trees and rode it down a hill, banging hard into the back of a soldier's knees, sending him crashing to the ground. He looked like a giant upside-down turtle, choking on mud and fury. And by the time he got up, we were gone.

The *passar* lady was forbidden to come that week, but seeing Kees's trick made up for it. We all called him hero.

I often wondered why Mom said she was collecting quarters for rainy days, since we never used them when it rained. So I started stealing them. Easabella and Emma-M had started crying a lot, complaining about being hungry, quarreling, and fretting to the point that people in the rooms around us started to shout, "Keep the little buggers quiet, goddamit!" This usually happened when Mom was at *corvee,* and I was watching the kids. Simon was no help, but he was no problem either. Simon was just Simon—there, but not there.

So with the first quarter I stole, I bought a big roll of *katjang idjoe* cookies (cookies made with ground green peas) from the *passa*r woman. Later, I gave each of my little sisters one as soon as they started to whine. It worked. They were surprised at first, but then smiled. Their happy, thin faces soothed my guilt. I was not proud of what I had done, but the girls were so small and often so sick, and they had so little food to be content with. I felt tears coming when I looked at them and saw them carefully licking their treats, so they would last longer.

I brought my face close to theirs and whispered, "We have a little secret, you guys and me, okay? We are not telling Mom any of this. When it hurts too much in your tummy and it keeps on rumbling, you'll get a cookie just like now, okay?" The girls nodded, still sucking on the last crumbs.

"But only when it really hurts, okay?" I said. "I don't have too many!"

More nodding. I then took them by their sticky, little hands to go play with Phaedra.

I felt guilty about Simon too. He hadn't been around when I'd given the little girls their cookies, and I hadn't wanted him to be. But why had I shut him out? And why had I not included him in our little cookie secret?

Simon was too close to Mom. I didn't trust him. Stealing was wrong, and this was Mom I was taking from. If he knew, he surely would tell her. Not to mention that I envied Simon for the love and attention he got from Mom. Simon always got the best of the special little treats. I couldn't remember him ever being slapped by Mom, and I never heard her say rotten things to him. I resented Simon for bringing out the light in Mom's eyes, the smile on her lips, and the tenderness on her face whenever she watched him absorbed in one of his games.

I also made the excuse that Simon couldn't be as hungry as Easabella and Emma-M, since Mom often gave him a little more than she gave the rest of us. And when there were choices in food items, she always allowed him to pick first. Easabella and Emma-M didn't notice, but I did. I would watch Mom silently, and when she saw me catching her, she'd explain, "The girls are still small, Sofia, and he is a boy. He needs more to grow strong."

What about me? I'm not still small. What am I? I griped in my mind. Shouting it out like I'd wanted to, and straight into her apologetic eyes, would have brought her hand out like a flash. *So what if the girls are still small? They are hungry too, and so am I!* I told myself these things to quiet the voice that warned me that stealing quarters for cookies was not the right way. It wasn't. But then what was?

When I took the third quarter, Simon saw me do it. It was Tuesday, the day the *passar* lady would come, and I had only three cookies left.

"What are you doing?" he asked quietly.

"None of your business!" I snapped, putting the coin in my pocket and Mom's sock of quarters back in its hiding place. She kept it between two planks under her sleeping mat.

He looked at me with his pale gray eyes. Why didn't he say something? Why was he just staring at me like that? Was he trying to make me feel guilty? So what? I already felt guilty!

Then Simon walked away. I watched his straight, narrow back move away and out of the building. Stealing the second quarter had been much easier than the first, and with the third one today, I had hardly felt anything—till Simon fixed his eyes on me, open and clear.

"Simon!" I called.

He turned.

"I want to tell you something!"

He came back, hands in his pockets, eyes on my face. Not angry or nervous or accusing, he was just cool, calm Simon.

"Let me tell you something, Simon, and then you keep your mouth shut. You are not talking to Mom, you hear!"

No answer; not even a nod.

I continued. "This is the third quarter I've taken. I buy *katjang idjoe* cookies with them, and when the little ones become really cranky and hungry, they get one and feel better. Mom will never know."

We looked at each other, Simon and I.

"I am hungry too, Sofia," he said, "only I don't talk about it."

More guilt for Sofia. So I divided the three cookies among the four of us and felt much better. Better enough to keep up the stealing, until four weeks later, when one day, Simon met me and the girls coming home from our visit to Mies and Phaedra. I knew Mom was about to return from *corvee* and would be tired.

"You'd better be warned," Simon said. "Mom found out about the quarters."

Staring at Simon, my heart began to pound. "Is she mad?"

He nodded.

I told him to take the girls to Mom and took off. I knew there would be hell to pay. Well, so be it. It wouldn't be the first time, and I would get over it. Still, I wanted to delay facing her for as long as possible. I looked for Peter and we wandered around, along the fence, between the barracks, around the bathhouses, looking for anything to keep us occupied, but finding nothing. Then eventually, it became dark and Peter headed off to his building.

It was time to face Mom, just like that time I'd lost Dad's bike. Only this was worse. *Oh, Dad, where are you?*

When I walked in the room and saw her face, my heart sank. It was worse than I could have ever expected. Strangely calm, Mom didn't look at me and then spoke in a flat tone.

"Sit down, Sofia, and listen carefully. I am only going to say this once. When I am done talking, you get out of my sight. I don't want to see you for one week. You can come in to eat and to sleep, but I will not talk to you and will not see you. You do not exist for me because you are not my child. As I said and knew before, you are a child of the devil. What you did clearly shows how very bad you are."

Her words fell on me, one by one, like stones. I felt like mist, without form, just floating. I looked at Mom but she had already turned away. Hurt set in. I walked outside and sat on the steps of the building, listening to the familiar sounds of my family on the inside. I felt dead and wished I were. Mom hadn't even asked if I had taken the quarters; she had immediately assumed there couldn't be anyone else.

I sat in the shadow of the roof, which was darker than the rest of the night. Mosquitoes were zooming around me, biting. Here and there, a sleepy bird chirped. A guard passed, and I remained unnoticed. I hadn't eaten since morning, but I wasn't hungry. When the guard was out of sight, I slipped away, running silently from building to building. Mies made a space for me on her sleeping mat when she saw my face at her door. She didn't ask.

That night, the monkey on my chest moved in, and it didn't leave me for a long time. It settled in when I recognized what I was and accepted my place—in the family, in Kamp Keudah, in my mother's heart. I accepted that Mom couldn't give me what she didn't have—or, if she did have it, that she would never share it with me for fear it would leave her empty. I wondered if she knew me at all, and why she found it so difficult to find out.

I spent the night listening to Phaedra's breathing, and was gone at first light. I hadn't slept, but didn't feel tired. I still wished I were dead. I made a plan, however. I couldn't live with Mom's cold eyes and her totally ignoring me. So I would work to change her mind, to make her admit that I had a place in her heart after all.

I didn't know much about God, but I knew enough about the devil to realize the comparison. It was like the difference between light and dark, warm and cold, good and bad. So I would prove to Mom that, in me, there was light and warm and good.

I would give her back her quarters, since they seemed so important to her. But first I had to earn them. I made a deal with Trudy Sanders' son, Herman, to borrow his axe. After I had explained what I needed it for, he said he wanted 20 percent of each quarter I made, and I thought that was fair. So armed with Herman's axe, I went to work.

I started collecting the bigger pieces of wood around camp and cutting them into smaller pieces. Wood was popular, since the women still used it to cook on the *anglos* (open barbecue units) whenever the kitchen food wasn't sufficient and they had food from the *toko*. As I chopped, I imagined Mom's stunned, happy expression when I gave her back the quarters. I felt better knowing I had a plan in place.

That afternoon, I took a break from collecting and chopping, and went around to each woman to ask if she would buy a basket of firewood from me for a quarter. Mies Miedema, Nadine, old Mrs. Hansen, and all of their friends signed up. So, with more names than I needed, I went home to see Mom. There is where my good day ended. I had hoped that she would have been at least a little worried that I hadn't shown up to sleep last night. She wasn't.

Emma-M was fidgety, and Simon told me she had missed me sleeping next to her, but Mom said nothing. She spoke to Simon and the girls, as she moved around the room, preparing for dinner. When she filled the soup bowls, there were only four. Simon looked at me, took the fifth bowl and filled it with what was left in the soup pan. He brought it to me and neatly put the last spoon next to it.

"Here, Sofie, your soup," he said and sat down to eat his.

Mom didn't look and didn't say anything. She just ate and helped Emma-M keep her spoon straight, which I usually did.

Good old Simon seemed just fine in the middle of all the mess. But then, he always had Mom's love. I admired him anyway. He was almost seven, but often acted much older. I finished my bowl and, on my way out, rubbed his head a moment. He didn't look up. Maybe I would cut one more basket of wood to give Simon a quarter.

Once outside, I ran. I had work to do. I was not planning to go back before I had earned all of Mom's quarters. The chopping had turned out to be a lot harder than I had expected with Herman's clumsy axe. The blade often flew off, and I had no nail or screw to fasten it back onto the handle.

After awhile, Peter came to help me chop and tried to repair the axe with a narrow wire he'd found. He wasn't very successful, though. The blade still flew off if we weren't watching, and then the wire broke. It didn't help that the logs were hard and cumbersome to lift, and that millions of insects lived under them. We especially had to be careful of scorpions, which we tried to split through the middle with the axe.

Peter kept asking me why I was doing all this chopping, and at the end of the day I told him. He didn't say much, but just sat and listened with his face closed. After that, he helped me on the days when he had no fever. I still worked when I had fevers. Like clockwork, the cold spells came every few days followed by high temperatures. The more frequent the malaria attacks, the stiffer I was, until my joints became quite sore, and I had to rest quite often. But even then the work left me tired, weak, and listless. Sick-smelling sweat drenched my clothes.

Simon came to see me every day too. He sat watching, while Peter and I handled the wood. On days Peter didn't come, Simon picked up the cut pieces and arranged them in the basket without saying much.

I decided to spend the nights with Mies, if she would let me, until I had cut and delivered all the baskets. I didn't feel like seeing Mom before I could give her back her quarters. Mies said it would be okay, and Mom never came looking for me. Mies told me that Mom knew where I was, though, because she had told her.

Every night before I went to sleep, I took out the quarters, one after another, in the dark, and just looked at them. I didn't need light to count them; I knew exactly how many there were.

"Why don't you cry for once, Sofia?" Mies asked me one night. "It doesn't hurt to cry, you know. Tears can flush out some of the pain."

I rested on her mattress, too tired to sit. Her building was close to the spot I had chosen to cut the wood, and she had seen me leave every day. My head pounded relentlessly and fever burned my face. Holding my hot hands in a wet towel helped, but I could hardly hear what Mies was saying.

"I don't want to talk about it, Mies," I told her.

But she went on, her soft voice wrapping around me and making its way through the fog in my head. "Remember, Sofia, people often say things they don't mean and do things they don't intend to do. They themselves are in so much pain that they can't carry on anymore. To not drown in it, they say and do things that hurt. If you don't understand why they do this, you will hurt too."

Mies stroked my hair as she continued. "Pain is not bad, Sofia. It cleans you so that you can feel free. If you let it wash over you, you can understand better after that. But if you are afraid of the pain inside of you and avoid it, it will stay locked inside you and change you into someone else. It will make you hate, and hate only hurts you. The more hate there is, the less room you'll have for love. Then you will be starving." She paused. "Leave space for love, Sofia. You can't be without it."

I didn't want to hear it. Tears were falling, and I turned my back toward her. This didn't silence Mies.

"It is necessary in life to feel pain and to bend under it, so you will not break when love is hiding and you feel so alone. Perhaps you do not understand all of this now, Sofie, but you will. You have been in the rain; you will feel the sun and wind again."

I turned back and looked at her. Her light-filled eyes and her soft voice, along with my realization that she loved me enough to share her wise and strange thoughts with me, brought out more tears.

She cooled the wet towel once more and folded it around my pounding head, then wiped away my tears. I would have to think about all of this more after the fog lifted.

I knew it would take weeks to fill the eleven baskets I needed to earn back Mom's quarters, but exactly one week after that black day when she disowned me, I went home to see Easabella and Emma-M. I had so missed sleeping next to them in the dark nights, when they were the most sweet and quiet. I had seen Simon almost daily, but we never mentioned Mom.

Mom acknowledged my existence, but didn't say much, and when she did it was in short sentences and even shorter answers. Apparently, she was having difficulty forgetting what I had done and forgiving me. She never asked me why I found it necessary to steal the quarters, never gave me a chance to explain why I did what I did. I could've brought up the subject, but I had a feeling she wouldn't have accepted my explanation anyway.

As I looked at her, I thought about what Mies had said and suddenly started to feel sorry for Mom. Was she in pain, as well? Was hate growing in her?

But if it was, she had no reason! Dad loved her. She had always had tons of clothes. Before our being taken prisoner, she had laughed a lot, and when she hadn't gotten what she wanted, she had pouted and gotten it anyway. Dad had joked often that she was spoiled, but he had also been proud of her, the way she had looked and moved and danced and entertained. She had always been a good seamstress and hairdresser, even before she married. Dark and wavy, her hair, swept up in a rich roll around her face during the day, had been the envy of every Dutch woman in Langsa. She also had tubes and jars of makeup, of which she used just enough to make her look beautiful. She had been a proud woman then.

But I suddenly saw how little of that was left. We'd been without shampoo for some time now, and her hair was stringy and without shine. She had it tied with a ribbon, but it just hung listlessly down her back. She had only three dresses left, which were beginning to show wear because she had to wash them over and over again. Her nails were bitten down to the quick, her lipstick was long gone, and I had finished her eyebrow pencil. Her bra had become much too large for her, and her usually full breasts were hanging like Dad's old socks, filled with marbles. Dad had been gone for such a long time, too, and she missed him. She missed him terribly.

Poor Mom. Looking at her now, I had the strangest feeling that I was the older person and that Mom was the girl. I smiled. She would be so happy to get her quarters back. She would smile at me again, like she still did at Easabella and Emma-M. She would start loving me again, maybe even as much as she loved Simon. She would fill my bowl with food, and I would again be her oldest daughter and belong to our family.

She would be proud of me. I was sure of that.

For some reason, and at some unidentifiable moment, trading had gone from being discouraged to being forbidden. It was now considered smuggling, and if caught, punishment would be harsh and painful. Being kicked or beaten no longer seemed so bad in comparison to the new threat of having your clothes ripped off or your head shaved in public, which would be humiliating and degrading and surely never forgotten.

Still, out of necessity, the trading continued. We were always hungry these days. The food supplied by the kitchen was never enough, and everyone was running low on money for food from the *toko* and the *passar* woman.

Plus, the Atjeh-Indonesians liked trading with us. They knew the value of our jewelry, and they wouldn't hesitate to make a fair exchange. Much of it was solid gold bought mainly in Holland and seldom available in Indonesian jewelry stores.

There may have been another reason they liked bartering with us. The other day, I'd heard a woman tell Mrs. Elliot, the camp leader, that she sensed a hint of malicious glee in the Atjeh-Indonesians, an eagerness to buy that came from their pride in seeing the roles reversed—they enjoying freedom and we being kept as servants to listen obediently to orders.

Trudy Sanders and her son Herman were still the most trusted couple to do the trades. However, on one particular day, the Japanese soldier on guard, after he had disappeared around the bend, decided to circle back around immediately, to catch any offenders unaware. Herman, on the lookout as usual and still hidden behind the bend, didn't see him return. So when the soldier rounded the corner and saw the action, he roared, and as he ran toward the gate, slipped the gun off his shoulder and used it to charge the slight Atjeh man. Without stopping, he drove his bayonet through the vendor, who had been standing completely still in utter terror, seemingly unable to move or run. He had remained fixed on the spot like an animal caught in the headlights at night. Thrown back by the force of the furious soldier, he died where he came down. Trudy had slipped away, but not before the soldier had seen her.

An instant later, he rang the *koempoelan* bell, and the ring seemed loud and insistent. Women stopped their *corvee* duties and children their playing, and all went running to the square, where two Japanese soldiers were waiting—one of them was the guard who had seen Trudy Sanders.

We formed our rows in frightened haste, as the soldiers worked their way through the throng, hitting, pushing, and screaming orders that none of us understood. The guard who had seen Trudy seemed to grow angrier by the minute and began to kick women's legs with his heavy boots. Children started to cry. Mom tightly clasped Easabella and Emma-M against her. Simon and I were in the row behind them, silent and afraid.

Suddenly, the lights went on around us, and the guards began jerking up the women's heads and looking at their faces. Mom's head snapped up as a soldier hit his fist against her face. Her lips began to bleed. What did they want? Why did we have to look up at them now, when that had always been a sign of disrespect before?

Then a high-pitched scream drew everyone's attention toward the middle of the square. It was Trudy Sanders. The guard who had caught her at the fence had found what he was looking for right in our midst. He had twisted her hair around his hand and was dragging her to the front. Trudy, holding her head and running next to him to try to relieve the pulling, stumbled and fell, causing the guard to lose his grip on her. So using his gun, he repeatedly hit her on the back until she stood and walked the rest of the way to the front. Once there, she looked the soldier straight in the face, which made him wild. He yelled something, and the second soldier disappeared into the guardhouse and returned with scissors. Herman, who had come running after his mother, was now hopping and screaming in the first row, his eyes filled with terror.

Using his bayonet, the first soldier ripped Trudy's clothes off of her body, and then turned to get the scissors from the second soldier, which he then moved roughly over her head, butchering her long hair into jagged, uneven spikes. She cried in pain, and when he had finished, he pointed at her and stood laughing.

I glared at him, looking smug and powerful with his gun, hurling one insulting jeer after another. His laugh was mean and ugly, and he formed a picture of everything I hated. I looked around and saw the drying blood on

Mom's mouth. I saw Mies half-hiding Phaedra in her skirt. And I saw the faces of many other women and children reflecting various degrees of fear, terror, and disgust. Mom started to tremble, and suppressed sobs began to sound all around me. I felt humiliated and scared, angry and powerless. I hated what I saw. If eyes could kill, that Japanese man would have been stone dead.

So we waited, with Trudy in front, dressed only in rain and trails of blood. The soldier had pierced her body while removing her clothes with the bayonet, and her head while cutting her hair with the scissors. Still, her blazing blue eyes never lost sight of the sadistic soldier slowly moving around her, ridiculing her. Her eyes scared me. They were so unblinking, and the guard so furious, that I was afraid he would poke them out in an effort to kill the accusation and pride that shown through so clearly. And then he might kill her, as he had done the Atjeh trader.

In a Japanese man's mind, a woman was not much. She was to serve, to slave, and to bear and raise his children. And she was not to be seen or heard, unless prompted. Trudy Sanders was none of that. Trudy Sanders' silent voice set free a scream that no one heard but everyone felt. Trudy Sanders was a hero.

When the first soldier tired, the second replaced him. As we continued standing on the *koempoelan* square, the day disappeared and the slight rain picked up. Old Mrs. Hansen fell down, but was quickly picked up by her daughter. As I watched them in the eerie dusk, when people became unrecognizable and shadows melted together into a solid black mass, the two of them looked like one. A few minutes later, when Mrs. Hansen fell again, she was cold and unconscious. Her daughter picked her up again, and held her until after dark, when we were released back to our rooms—all except for Trudy, who had to stay standing in her spot, alone and naked in the rain.

Mrs. Hansen's daughter carried her mother to Nadine's clinic, where the old woman slipped away during the night. Her daughter was grateful for her passing. She told Nadine her mother was better off this way.

Back in our building, no one spoke except for a whisper here and there. Somewhere, a candle burned, and then a soft voice started to pray. Others followed. We had not been allowed an evening meal from the kitchen.

Mom put Easa and Emma-M to bed, but Simon stayed up, just sitting and leaning into Mom. I left and went to Nadine's to look for Herman, but he wasn't there. So I went to the *koempoelan* square and found him; he had stayed to watch his mother from a distance, as he was not allowed to go near her. She seemed to stand very still at the end of the *koempoelan* square. All I could see was a formless shape in the dark of the rainy evening, and Herman's eyes remained fixed on her.

When the lights in the buildings died, Nadine and Mrs. Elliot walked past us and went through the gate to the guardhouse. They disappeared behind the door, followed closely by the guard. The guardhouse stood outside the fence, but close to the gate.

There was not a sound. No shouting, no talking, no moving. The crickets shrieked.

Herman's tear-streaked face, a white blot in the darkness, faced the shadow that was his mother. I put my arm around his shoulders, and we waited. Nadine came out of the guardhouse and walked straight to Trudy, then half-carrying her, guided her carefully toward the only lighted place left in camp—the clinic. Herman joined them, moving silently to his mother's side and slipping his arm around her. I lost sight of them when they turned the corner of a building. Mrs. Elliot then came out of the guardhouse, and not seeing Trudy on the square, also walked in the direction of the clinic. I admired her courage. I wondered what had been discussed in the guardhouse after Nadine had left. I wondered if Trudy would be safe now.

Then staring in the dark, I wondered where God was and why he hadn't been here today. I wondered where Dad was, too, and whether any Japanese soldiers would beat him like they had Trudy.

The following day, Herman became ill, so he stayed at the clinic. He was vomiting and had a high fever. He screamed in his sleep, reliving the agony of his mother's punishment.

After four days, the fever left and I went to see him. I wanted to return his axe now that I had filled all of the wood baskets. I found him sitting next to his mother's bed. He looked pale and weak, but didn't mind seeing me.

Putting the axe next to his feet, I took his hand and opened it, and placed two shiny quarters in his palm. "These are yours, Herman, for the axe. I won't need it anymore."

He looked at me and picked up the axe, his small hand tensing around the wooden handle, knuckles standing out, his thin, pale skin stretching in between. Herman's hands were clean, not like mine, which were blackened and had cuts around the nails; I couldn't always scrub the dirt out after cutting wood.

Herman looked at his mother. Her face had lost most of the swelling, but still had blotches of yellow, green, and black, and colors in between. Her eyes were closed. She didn't look like Trudy Sanders at all.

"Do you think she will be all right, Sofia?" Herman whispered, afraid to disturb his Mom, yet anxious to know. I didn't know and didn't answer; we were both quiet.

Nadine looked at us and then pulled Herman close. "It's too early to tell, love. Give her time. She had a rough spell."

Herman opened his mother's hand and kissed her palm. Then he put the quarters inside and slowly closed her fingers, one by one, around them. Her fingers were still swollen and bruised.

When I left, Herman was still watching over his mother, holding her closed hand against his face, waving the ever-present flies away from her bed.

I gave Mom the eight quarters when Simon and the girls were playing outside. For reasons I couldn't explain, I had wanted her to be alone. I talked matter-of-factly, hiding the tremendous effort and stubbornness with which I worked for three long weeks.

"Here is the money I took from you, Mom." I laid the quarters neatly in two rows of four. "I took eight quarters. Here are eight quarters back." I looked at her and saw her eyes widen, shifting from the money to my face.

"How did you get those, Sofia, did you steal them from somewhere else?"

Something deep inside me moved, and for an instant, I saw Hassan's face lighted by the flames of the fire, the shadows moving from his cheeks to his eyes. "We all have a monkey on our chest, Sofia … keep it caged … do not let it loose." His soft voice sounded as clear in my head as it had that night.

Then, whatever had moved became quiet, and I started to tremble. I crept slowly back toward the door, stood up straight, and looked at Mom through a mist. If only this once she would fold her arms around me. I needed so much for her to be proud of me for what I had done.

"Don't worry, Mom, I didn't steal them. I cut wood and sold that to people. If you don't believe me, ask Mies Miedema." I walked out of the building and into the sun. The light irritated my already burning eyes.

Simon saw me and stopped playing. I didn't want to speak to Simon; I didn't want to speak to anyone. So I ran. I tried to outrun the hurt, but Mom's words followed me, resounding in my head. "Did you steal them somewhere else, Sofia? Did you steal them?"

So long ago, whenever one of us kids would take a cookie from the jar without asking, Mom would say, "Don't steal, kids. Just ask. All I can say is no." She loved little phrases like that, that made a point and left you to draw your own conclusions. Now I hated her for them.

Feeling hungry and betrayed, I looked for Peter and spent the rest of the day with him, not so much playing as picking fights. I cheated Kees Vermeer in marbles, and when his brother William challenged me, I was happy to punch him, sending him home with a bloody nose.

I didn't get home till after dark. Mom had food ready, but, though my stomach groaned with hunger, I turned my back on her and refused to eat. Simon ate most of my meal, too, and then washed the few dishes alone, while Mom washed the girls and put them to bed. I gave him my last shiny quarter, and, of course, he did not understand why. Perhaps he, too, would think I stole it.

When the lights went out, Mom started softly, "Good-night, Simon."

"Good-night, Mom."

"Good-night, Easabella."

"Good-night, Mom."

"Good-night, Emma-M."

"Good-night, Mom."

"Good-night, Sofia."

Silence. Still, I didn't feel any better.

Rumors were flying: the war would end soon, the emperor was negotiating surrender, and liberating armies could be expected any day now, and many others.

Nadine had had no visions; she didn't believe the rumors. But she did seem to know something as she told Mies Miedema. "This is only the beginning. There is more to come."

Rumors had come and gone so often that no one took them seriously any more. This rumor, though, was persistent. It had started as a whisper, which someone else repeated, and so on and so on. But finally it seemed to hold some truth when it was partially confirmed by a smuggled-in newspaper, at which point the news spread like wildfire: we would be leaving Kamp Keudah and going somewhere else.

This was alarming. We were not happy in Kamp Keudah—awful things had happened here—but we had settled into a routine, and the unknown change could turn out worse than known imprisonment.

Not even "the fortuneteller" was prepared. Nadine had had no time or energy for visions; she'd had her hands full with increasing numbers of sick people.

Mrs. Elliot brought it up to the commander, in hope of getting solid information, but he wasn't ready to give her details.

"Later, later," he said and pushed her out the door. But a week later, he confirmed it: we would be transported out of Kamp Keudah.

So, on a hot day in September, we found ourselves walking to the train station we had forgotten was there, struggling under the weight of luggage, food, and other possessions. When we had arrived at Kamp Keudah, we'd had *koelies* (laborers) carry our things in little lorries; now we did the carrying ourselves. Walking on a cobblestone-and-dirt road didn't help, as many of us had only sandals. Every so often, we'd pass older and weaker women who had sunk down to rest awhile, before being chased forward again by the guards with their ever-ready sticks and whips. Everywhere along the road, the Atjeh guards and Japanese soldiers stood, prodding us all to walk faster.

Children cried, and mothers, exhausted of their patience, pushed and yelled at them. Simon pulled Emma-M, while Mom carried our valuables, and I lugged the sleeping pads. Whenever I dropped one, Easabella was there to pick it up and shove it back over my shoulder. We were all weaker now and quickly tired, but above all, we were afraid for what was to come. At the train station, we found chaos. Shouting guards, mothers looking for their kids. No one seemed to know where to go or what to do until the familiar counting began, followed by our being loaded into the train wagons. We five were fortunate enough to find a place to sit together—a small miracle since everyone was being pushed in, regardless of who belonged where. The bench was not wide enough for all five of us, but we made it sufficient.

I took Emma-M onto my lap and pressed as close as possible into the side of the wagon, and then we all leaned into one another. But we could sit, while many others were pressed standing into the open spaces till there was no room for even one more.

When the train finally moved, the monotonous rhythm of the wheels soon put Easabella and Emma-M to sleep. Simon just stared, hugging the heavy water jar. *Sawahs* (rice fields) and mountains with misty tops moved past the windows. I watched the people working in the fields—they were free. They had no guards to punish or beat them, or to count them twice a day. They did not live behind barriers. They had enough to eat and were not always sick. And they were not afraid of what the future might hold.

Mom closed her eyes, and I thought about Dad, about the last day we'd seen him in Langsa, his smiling face and his reddish stubble. Tears came to my eyes. Thank God Mom's eyes were closed.

The train stopped at many small stations but we were not allowed off until just before noon, when we hid behind the shrubs and bushes for much-needed relief. After that, we went on again for hours, and the second time, stopped for a meal.

That meal was better than we'd had in a long time. The rice didn't taste dusty, and the soup had vegetables and chicken. *Pisang goreng* and fresh fruit were put out for us on long, low tables. Mom, and most of the other mothers too, took our bananas with her so we could snack on them later. After eating, we stood in long lines behind a single tap, where we could fill our empty water bottles and drink as much as we wanted. Mom warned us not to drink too much because the toilets on the train were already dirty and full. It had nothing to do with the odor, which had filled the wagons for so long that we had gotten used to it—but we couldn't add more waste to toilets that were already overflowing.

As we reboarded the train, I watched the Indonesians clearing off the tables, and felt pangs of yearning. They would go home tonight, while we would disappear on a smelly cattle train, headed to somewhere we didn't know.

We rode the train into the early evening and then deep into the night, without room to stretch, let alone sleep comfortably. Mom sat up straight, and Simon had been able to put his head in her lap, though his back looked unnaturally bent. Easabella leaned into him, heavy and formless. Emma-M sat at the window this time, slumped in a little heap. I leaned my head over her against the wooden frame. I could expect bruises tomorrow, as the train rumbled furiously over the primitive rails.

When we woke up early the next morning, we were more tired than before. We stopped for another pee break, this time along *sawahs* where locals were working close-by. They stared as we did our business, but none of us cared—or, at least, none of us had the energy to protest. Or even complain.

The second time the train stopped that day, we walked out to find a large *passar*, where we were offered a breakfast of porridge and bread, but weren't allowed to buy anything. Then we reboarded and went on into the hot hours of the afternoon.

About midday, we changed trains, having to suffer yet again the endless counting routine. By now, any food and water we had brought was long gone, and the stinking toilets were worse than the heat. With the slow speed of the train and the endless stops where nothing happened, I had the feeling we would never get to where we were going. And after a final pee break that evening, we prepared ourselves for a second night.

Mothers had long since stopped telling their children stories to pass the time. Children had stopped singing all the songs they'd learned in happier times. We were all too tired to complain to each other or to the Japanese soldiers who traveled with us but remained invisible. The only sound was the harsh rumbling of the wheels.

And then the train stopped. Silence. No engine sound. All of a sudden, soldiers were there screaming and waving us out of the train. We stumbled out of the wagons, and then stretched and hopped around in the open spaces. The day had cooled, and life returned into women and children. Here and there, someone even laughed. Then looking around, we discovered that we had arrived in Medan, the capital and the largest city of Sumatra.

Langsa was not far from Medan. Mom and Dad had taken us there a few times. We had spent a few nights in a hotel. We had visited the cinema. And after swimming in the hotel pool, we had gone out for a Chinese meal. These were supposed to have been good memories, but now they were painful, and I shoved them away as soon as they entered my mind.

Busses were waiting and, without delay, took us outside the city to a large building that we later recognized was an empty school. But we had light, washrooms, fresh air, and water. And there was another tasty meal: rice and meat and soupy vegetables. The meals on this trip were so much better than we had gotten used to at Kamp Keudah, and it made me wonder whether it was a better place we were traveling to, with bigger, tastier meals. We went to bed on the floor on our sleeping pads, happy and tired, full of food and water, and without a thought for the next day.

The next day came early, and bread and porridge for breakfast was more than enough, since we were not yet fully hungry after last night's meal. So we ate the porridge and kept the bread for later. Then on we went into the same waiting busses, and past the endless *sawahs,* hour after hour. We stopped twice for a pee break and walkabout, but there were no other meals.

The busses were small and crowded, but had many windows through which we could see the beautiful *sawahs* promising a rich harvest. The road had many curves that, without exception, threw us against one another when we went around them. We went past deep ravines, where I detected narrow creeks and rivers that, way down at the bottom, glistened in the sun. At times, we drove so close to the road's edge and next to ravines so deep that I made sure Easabella and Emma-M stayed away from the windows; they would panic if they saw how dangerously steep they were, especially Easabella. She would totally stiffen up. I just hoped the driver had come this way before. In fact, I hoped he'd come this way many times before.

As we traveled lower, the landscape changed. Farmland still stretched widely along the road, but had fewer workers. In the distance, I saw *alang-alang* grass instead of *sawahs.* The land had an isolated, abandoned feel. I missed the cattle, the traffic, and the power lines, and the turkey hawks in the sky. Mom had, long ago, sold her watch to Atjeh traders, but when we thought it was the right time to have lunch, we ate the bread saved from this morning.

When finally the busses stood still, we were looking at something very different than Kamp Keudah. In place of cement buildings stood wooden barracks, with *atap* roofs (layers of dried palm leaves).

Surrounding all the barracks were two fences, each with a gate, and there was a walking path in between. The gates were locked with heavy chains, and, of course, a large guardhouse stood outside the outer gate.

The prisoners who were already there showed us inside a barrack, where we found a wide-open space. Wooden platforms spanned the length of the building on two sides, and there was a path between. The current occupants, more women and children, watched us come in, and one woman led us to an open, unoccupied space. Soon we had our belongings lifted off the ground and on the planks, and the lady who had showed us our space brought us a jug of water. She told Mom we were too late for food; the meals from the kitchen had already gone out.

Mom didn't answer. We'd had to go without meals before, and after sitting for almost two days in trains and busses, we didn't really feel hungry. We cherished the water, but were not interested in more.

I went outside with Simon and the girls to find the washrooms, while Mom spread out the sleeping pads. When we got back, I saw that we had not much space, but didn't need more. The sleeping pads took up little room. We had no *klamboes* (mosquito nets) tonight—they would have to wait till tomorrow—but the sleeping pad felt good as soon I lay down on it.

I closed my eyes, trying to block out the sounds around me. There had to be hundreds of us in this barrack, and I missed the separation and privacy of the walls and doors at Kamp Keudah. As the hammering of train wheels resounded in my head, I wondered if we would spend the rest of our lives like this, going from camp to camp. Would we ever be free again?

LAWE SIGALAGALA

September 1943

Though bearing a name like a melody, Lawe Sigalagala was a camp where many died. It was named for the nearby lake, known for its cold, clear, fast-running water that flowed down from the mountains. Thanks to the river, many of the surrounding villages and cities had sophisticated waterworks. The mountains could be seen at a distance all around the camp, partly hidden in mist.

The camp lay in the Alas Valley in the southernmost part of the Atjeh province, where the hot air of the day would settle low and linger into the evening, only to become cold at night and rise hot and humid again the following day.

Lawe Sigalagala had more barracks than Kamp Keudah had had buildings. The barracks were built of wood and bamboo, with roofs of *atap*. The kitchen stood a fair distance from the barracks because of these *atap* roofs. The Japanese guards were petrified of fire and *atap* would burn fast and fiery. The kitchen had a zinc roof.

There was no electricity in this camp either. For light, kerosene lamps hung everywhere and had to be extinguished by eight o'clock. No candles were allowed after that either.

Inside, each person was given ninety centimeters of space to live, sleep, and eat, so for the five of us, we got four-and-a-half meters, which Mom closed off with *sarongs* she had bought at the Kamp Keudah *toko*. She couldn't live without privacy, she said. With the curtains, I felt crowded. It would take time to get used to our new, enclosed space.

I was surprised at Mom. She had been so particular and used to good things in Langsa that I couldn't follow her apathetic acceptance of a life not only in captivity but also one enforced by brutal, merciless guards. Yet, on the outside, she didn't seem upset. She didn't fret or complain. She didn't even seem disgusted with the fact that our circumstances seemed to deteriorate with each relocation. Each passing month, we lost more of ourselves by way of losing our possessions and our values. Though Mom scoffed at this, her apathy seemed only on the surface, while her real emotions, I imagined, lay deeply hidden and denied. I missed seeing what was inside of her, as I had in peacetime, when Dad had been with us. Without Dad, she was a very private person, a person who was almost a stranger to me. She buried her feelings and thoughts by escaping into depression and mental absence. It seemed she needed his presence, as if it gave her confidence. Well, what about privacy now!

Life in the camps had blunted any feeling of decency or modesty. Like Mom, every woman in our barrack had found a way to separate her family's space. Some used sheets, others old newspapers; the family beside us had used sarongs just like we had. Above the dividers, though, everything remained open, so sounds were audible throughout. We had all grown used to it, though, so as long as the children didn't make too much noise, no one complained.

The prisoners, however, were different than we were used to. Many were the wives and children of native Indonesian KNIL soldiers. At the Simon Fraay and Kamp Keudah, we had lived with only European and Indo (mixed) women and children. Fortunately, due to our previously intertwined lifestyles, we could all understand each other.

With so little space and privacy, I now doubted that we would have better food, as I had hoped during our meal in the empty school building. I started to feel more a prisoner with each camp, and it made me angry. We hadn't done anything wrong, so why were we being locked away with so many people? Why did Japanese soldiers have the power to treat us worse than we had ever treated our pets, even our cattle?

I turned out to be right about the food. There was even less here than there had been the last few months at Kamp Keudah. I should have known better. And indeed nothing else improved. In fact, not much changed at all. Japanese guards circling with suspicious eyes, long *koempoelans* on the hot tarmac under the burning sun, harsh rules and even harsher punishments all continued unabated. Worse, *corvee* duties were given to us kids, as well.

On the other hand, here our guards were called *heihos*. These were not the nasty Atjeh-Indonesians trying to get back at the *blandas,* but were Indo-European prisoners of war (POWs)—KNIL soldiers who had surrendered and were now forced by the Japanese army to guard the prison camps where women and children were interned. Later, we heard that they also had to watch over male camps and that, while doing so, a guard would sometimes find his own son and refuse to do the duty, which would result in either execution or starvation.

The *toko* here was smaller than in Kamp Keudah, and only open a few days out of the week, but food and fruit could be bought there in exchange for money, jewelry, and even clothes. For some reason, clothes were still valuable here, not only in the *toko,* but also among locals outside the camp. They actually preferred to trade for clothing than for jewelry.

It was a good thing, since the kitchen meals were so skimpy and, more or less, the same every day: a watery soup made of rice or *oebi* (sweet potato), and sometimes a bit of chicken or beef in vegetable broth. The prisoners who had been at Lawe Sigalagala when we arrived told us that the little bits of floating meat was from dogs or cats. I told Easabella and Emma-M that it was goat meat; neither of them would have eaten it otherwise. I said nothing to Simon, but he remained suspicious.

Of course, to buy anything in the *toko,* we needed more money. Mom did her best, and soon had people coming for haircuts again. And since there were more women at Lawe Sigalagala than there had been at Keudah, she had added clients.

All around Lawe Sigalagala hung a musty odor. The rains and hot, damp air bred thousands of mosquitoes, and malaria attacks remained a daily occurrence. We lived our lives around fever, headaches, and diarrhea. We remained a tight family group, always looking out for one another. When one was ill, the others felt the pain as well. Easabella and Emma-M were always together and when one was sick, the other stayed close, which I found endearing. Simon could still bring out the smiles in Mom's eyes and occasionally even make her laugh. I was content with a day without fevers and with normal behavior from all of us. How happy we were with so little, and how far from what we had known just a few years before.

Women's *corvee* duties included keeping the campgrounds clean or planting vegetables outside the fence, which would be cooked in the kitchen for everyone. Mom's new *corvee* duty was with the women in the kitchen, sorting rice. Inside the large jute sacks, they would find rice riddled with *padi* (inferior rice grains, still in their husks). Rice bugs had woven nets between the grains, and the raw rice was clumpy. The women had to sort the rice from the *padi*, before they washed and cooked it. Some bags had more *padi* than rice, however, and after cooking, still tasted like jute sacks and the inferior grains. We kids were too hungry to complain, though, and when she could, Mom added salted fish from the *toko* to cover the musty taste of the rice. But the inferior rice was difficult to digest and I was afraid for Easa and Emma-M.

Over the months, Emma-M's tummy became rounder and Easabella's complaints about tummy ache became more frequent. Simon sometimes did not want to eat, saying he felt nauseous and was "sick of always having the same stupid, dirty food." Then he'd give his share to Emma-M, who, in turn, gave Simon her banana.

We were happy when Nadine got herself back into the clinic, where they, too, were very happy with her. Wherever she was, she brought with her a sense of competence and peace, and people trusted her immediately, steadfastly taking her advice, which was often all she could give; her treatment option had been whittled down to cold compresses and sometimes aspirin.

There were two other nurses at Lawe Sigalagala, who had been there before we arrived, but Nadine seemed to be the chosen one to deal with the doctors, whenever they came. Once in awhile, we saw a Japanese doctor walk through the camp with Nadine, listening carefully as she told him about the many sick people and the near nonexistence of medication and equipment to treat malaria and tropical ulcers. The Japanese seemed paranoid when it came to infectious diseases, but not much else; therefore, as it turned out, all this doctor was doing was listening for reports of dysentery, typhus, and cholera. Since there were none, he'd leave in a hurry, and all Nadine would get for the visit was a few bottles of malaria tablets, aspirin, and bandages with tubes of soothing cream. Another physician came in once a month. This doctor was British-Indian, very large, and to us children, an imposing figure to say the least. Of the two, the Japanese doctor was in charge, but the other physician was more humane.

Nadine used the malaria pills on the children first, and the women agreed that the children needed them most. Later, she discovered that some medication had disappeared without record. She went to the camp leader, who she didn't know, since Lawe Sigalagala had already had a camp leader when we arrived. Her name was Mrs. Frost. Nadine explained her worry and asked for a padlock for the little medicine drawer. From then on, she always carried the key in her pocket. When she had asked the other two nurses if they knew of the medicine's whereabouts, they acted offended, and later resented her for keeping the key to herself rather than somewhere they could also have access to. Nadine was firm and kept the key, however. If the other nurses needed it, they would have to ask her for it.

Once, Nadine had to ask Mrs. Frost to contact the commander and ask for one of the doctors to come and take care of Karel. An ugly sore had been festering on his leg for a long time, but then it formed a red line aiming at his knee. The doctor took a sharp little knife, which he sterilized in a wood fire, and then opened the sore with a nifty little jab. Karel yelled at him but by then the sore was open and the puss running out. Nadine took care of the rest, and

Karel left later with candy. He proudly showed everyone his clean snow-white dressing and bragged about the deep incision and the "enormous knife."

Mies also went back to the clinic to help Nadine. She endlessly boiled water in large black pots, which, when cooled, they gave to small children to drink. This was to prevent the kids from becoming sick after playing in the stream that ran along the fence, which they often did, splashing water at one another and sometimes swallowing it. Nadine also used the boiled, cooled water to wash out festering sores and insect bites.

When Christmas came around, Emma-M and Easabella couldn't remember what it was. Simon tried to revive the story of Jesus's birth, but needed help from Mom at times when he mixed it up with one of the other Bible stories. Mom bought some extra nice stuff in the *toko*, although she had less money now. She had felt weaker lately after her malaria attacks and had had to cancel some appointments.

Christmas was good enough though, since Mom did not have *corvee* duty and only Easabella was feverish. Easabella had been feverish for a week, and was very listless, wanting to lie on her sleeping pad all day. She napped a lot and, when awake, constantly massaged her tummy with careful, gentle strokes. Nadine had promised to come get Easabella and to take her to see the doctor as soon as he visited. But that had been ten days ago, and Easa still hadn't seen one.

For Christmas, Mom gave her the best she had—soft pudding with plenty of sugar and decorated with banana and papaya. Easabella loved it, but could only eat half. The rest of us had bread and fruit and peanut candies, and each a large piece of *goela djawa* (brown sugar) to suck on. We let it melt slowly in our mouths, savoring the sweet gooey taste as long as we could.

The only thing we missed that Christmas was Dad, and Mom didn't want to talk about Dad, so we sang carols instead—mostly Mom and I, as Simon had forgotten the words and the little girls had never known them.

The day after Christmas was not as good. Easabella's fever became high and she constantly rubbed her tummy. All day, she lay moaning and scaring me with her small white face and closed eyelids, which looked bluish. Mom couldn't get her fever down. She constantly changed the cold compresses, but the water in our bucket quickly became lukewarm, after which I'd have to go to refill it.

Passing the clinic on one such run, I saw Nadine and Mies. Nadine waved and motioned for me to come nearer. She listened silently as I told her about Easabella, and escorted me back to the barrack, where Mom was telling Simon and Emma-M to keep quiet so as not to wake their sister. Nadine looked at Easa and went to work. She carefully turned the blanket back and removed

Easa's clothes. Even with all the jostling, Easa seemed too weak to wake up. I looked at my little sister lying there, without clothes and so thin I could count her ribs. I turned to dip the towel into the water can to make another cold compress—I had to do something to help Easabella wake up! Nadine took the towel from me and draped it carefully around Easabella's little body, and suddenly Easa started to shake and jerk. Her legs and arms swayed high and bounced back on the planks, her head bent upward, and her eyes opened slightly. She looked frightful.

Simon and Emma-M started to cry, and, mesmerized, I watched Nadine hold back Mom, who had reached out to help Easabella. Nadine told Mom softly not to touch Easa, assuring her that this would pass quickly, and that she was not in pain and would get through it. I held Emma-M and Simon close, and the three of us watched as Easabella fought through her first convulsion. Mom's tears rolled down on her outstretched hands.

Slowly, Easabella quieted until, at last, she lay still, her eyes again closed and her breathing returning to normal. Nadine applied a new cold compress and told Mom to continue this until Easa woke up. She expected the fever to go down later in the day, and once it did, Mom was to try to get soft baby food into her.

Walking with me to the kitchen to get the baby food, Nadine explained that convulsions could happen in little kids when they were undernourished and had high fevers. It could also happen again, she warned, and when it did, we were not to touch Easabella during the jerking and bouncing; that would only make it worse. Then, after we left the kitchen, she led me back to the clinic, where she handed me a small rubber toy made for kids to play with in the bathtub.

"Try to get this between her teeth, Sofia, when it starts, so she will not bite her tongue when her teeth clamp down. Otherwise, she will bite her tongue and it will be very sore afterward. Tell Mom to watch her closely."

Easabella was sleeping when I got back. I told Mom what Nadine had said and gave her the rubber toy. Simon and Emma-M had stopped crying and sat quietly watching Easabella. We were all exhausted and, as always, hungry.

Hunger was a part of life now. Peter and I would roam the camp, looking for food, fruit, anything to eat. We played marbles for food, and, sometimes, if we found one, shared a discarded banana, which we ate without peeling. If we could get away with, we would steal.

Stealing a chicken from the Jap's guardhouse outside the fence was a real art. Chickens often came through the outside fence to look for insects or worms on the walking path between the two fences. As soon as a soldier caught it, he'd send it cackling and flying over the fence with his boot. Sometimes though, instead of walking around to patrol the area, the guard would just sit in the guardhouse, watching from a chair. Then we had a chance to catch a bird.

The chickens were noisy and the job needed to be done in silence, so we would cover ourselves in mud and, ever so slowly, move forward over the clay earth toward the fence. Peter was much better at it than I was. His thin body would slide silently forward, slowly and steadily, closer and closer to the chicken. At times, alarmed by what must have looked like strange, moving clumps of mud, the chicken would cluck excitedly and trot a few steps away, its head bobbing back and forth. Peter would keep still for a few minutes until the stupid bird headed back his direction, and then continue sliding forward. Once close enough, he'd stretch his disguised hand under the fence, and his fingers would shoot up as inconspicuous as a shadow, simultaneously grabbing its neck and twisting. There was no pity and no mercy—just joy over knowing we'd have a great meal.

The next time we saw a chicken slip in between the fences, the guard was dozing. Now, it was my turn. I grabbed it, but couldn't kill it instantly, like Peter did, so it fluttered, screamed, and threw up dust, awaking the guard. I pulled it under the fence, but we had nowhere to hide it from the slowly approaching guard.

If I'd have been wearing a skirt, I could've hid it underneath, but I had on shorts. Peter, however, was wearing long pants that were too wide around his thin frame; he'd had to hold them up with a piece of rope.

I shoved the bird at him. "Sit on it, Pete. Hide it under your pants. They are big enough!"

Grabbing the bird, he sat on it, the wings spread under his thighs and the body between his knees, just as the guard reached us and poked his rifle through the fence.

I quickly took Peter's marbles, formed his feet into *V*-shape, and pretended total concentration in aiming the marbles between them. Moving around on my knees, I made dust, hoping to give the guard the impression that I'd been the one to kick up the dust before.

Peter sat waiting for marbles to hit his heel, and then, knowing the guard would not understand him anyway, said softly, "The f—ing bird is still moving, Sofia. Do the job better next time!"

I started to giggle, and then laugh. I rolled over against his legs, laughing so hard that tears rolled over my cheeks. Finally, I wiped my face against Peter's pants and looked at the guard, who seemed convinced that nothing suspicious was going on. He was still close, though, so we played ourselves away from the fence. Peter moved slowly, heaving his butt slightly with his hands. The chicken squeezed between his knees, its wings scraping the ground. Finally out of sight, we picked up the now surely dead bird and ran, hooting with triumph and feeling like hunters with their prey. We had a good day, that day. A day to remember.

Soon after that, though, the chickens by the guardhouse disappeared, so we looked elsewhere. Early one morning on our hunt, I found a big snail stuck against the barrack wall. He had crawled up really high and didn't seem to know how to get down again, as his long feelers were frantically moving. His house sat on top of him like a large, circular wart, and he had left a slimy path behind him. I grabbed his shell and pulled him off. He let go with a soft sucking sound and smoothly curled away inside his house.

I liked him. He was alive and curious. I held him and watched for awhile. Now and then, his feelers would come out, and when I touched them, they'd immediately pull back in. *How could such a big, gummy animal fit in such a small house?* I wondered. Showing him to Peter was a mistake. Peter wanted him out and started to poke inside the snail house with a twig. But the harder he poked, the deeper it burrowed.

Mom absolutely refused to have it on our space, so Peter took it to his. Letting him do that was my second mistake. When I showed up the next day, Peter had thrown it into his mom's pan of hot water and smashed the little brown house. The snail had changed into a pale gray, crinkled up, juicy chunk of meat, which Peter neatly cut into two equal parts. I stared at it for awhile, feeling sorry for the snail. In my mind, I saw his hesitancy and his frantically waving feelers. I would've liked to have kept him, to have something of my own. And for a moment I hated Peter. Because of him, something beautiful was gone. That animal hadn't done anything, and it was so small and only had his house to hide in. But then the chickens hadn't done anything either, and I hadn't felt so strange killing them!

I looked at Peter chomping away on his piece of snail, juice running down his chin.

He smacked and swallowed, and then started digging in his mouth for any pieces stuck between his teeth. "It's good, Sofia, you should try it. Really good!"

I picked up my half and bit off a little piece, feeling like a traitor. It did taste good, however, and hunger took over. I ate the rest of my share, savoring the flavor and pushing aside all of those feelings I didn't need.

After that, we went snail hunting every morning. There was a field behind our barrack, filled with long grasses, low undergrowth, and mosses. Each at his own slow pace, the snails moved between the grasses as they had done all the days of their lives, somehow knowing where to go. I loved the hour just before daylight, when the sun wasn't quite up and fog clung to the ground, keeping the dampness and coolness of night a little longer. Carefully moving one foot after the other, so as not to step on a snail, I bent low, moving my hands to separate the grass while looking for the lumbering, shiny snail houses. Sometimes when I found one, I just watched it for awhile as it went up and down over the mosses, sailing like a ship on the waves. Little pieces of moss would stick to the flat part of its body when I picked it up.

These mornings were the best part of the day, when no one was up yet and I could touch the dew and smell the wet moss and hear the few birds already stirring. By the time the sun had soaked up all the mist and the barracks had come alive with people, I had collected six or seven snails.

I would take them back to Mom, who boiled water till it rolled and then dumped them into it all at once. She would then quickly lower the lid so we wouldn't see the snails die. They boiled for fifteen minutes, were taken out, and cooled. Then Mom slowly pulled them out of their shells with a large, straightened safety pin. A string of slimy stuff and dirt followed, which I had to rinse away, since Mom did not want to touch it. She would cut them up into small chunks and mix that with vegetables and boiling rice.

We kids watched her prepare the meal, patiently waiting until it was finished. Then Mom would skim off the top layer of soft, soupy rice, and offer us each just a little.

"Just to tide you over!" she'd always say.

It wasn't much—not more than three spoons for each of us—but it was worth waiting for.

After that, the rest of the dish sank into the hot house, which was a box that Mom had lined with half of an old blanket from Emma-M and kept warm with a hot stone. The freshly cooked food would go on top of the hot stone and be covered with the other half of the blanket. There it sat, staying warm until dinnertime, when we would eat it together with the little bit of food we got from the camp kitchen. We looked forward to it all day.

Karel de Boer died within minutes on a day as murky and yellow as the snake that got him. The sun was out enough to make it hot and sticky, but couldn't burn its way through the heavy, low clouds. There was no wind and no birds. Just hot silence.

Kees and William, Peter and I, and Karel and a boy named Jaap Martelaar, our usual group of friends, cleared an area to play shanghai-stick. It had become one of our favorite games because it could last all morning, but took little effort. It didn't require running, either, which just made us tired; the nighttime fevers had sapped any energy we'd had left.

One played while the others sat around and watched. The player worked with two sticks, one long and one short, and we all took turns. A small, narrow ditch was made in the clay, and the short stick bridged over it. The player had to place the long stick in the ditch under the short stick, whip up the short stick into the air and then whack it away with the long stick as far as he could.

The distance between the ditch and the spot where the short stick came down would be measured with the long stick. But if you were skilled enough to hit the little stick one more time upward before whacking it away, you could count the distance with the short stick, starting from the place where it came down back to the ditch. This would make your score three times higher, since the long stick was three times the length of the short one.

When it was Karel's turn, we all watched him closely because he would never miss a chance to cheat. He balanced the short stick over the ditch, whipped it up two times, and sent it flying far beyond the cleared area, close to an old, sagging banana tree.

"All right!" He ran toward his stick, ready to measure.

William went after him Since we couldn't see the stick from where we sat, he wanted to make sure Karel didn't try to cheat and overcount.

When he reached the area where the stick had landed, Karel swept away the old leaves to find it, and after that, things happened very fast. He snatched his hand back, yelling something. William, behind him, pushed him aside and saw movement behind the banana tree. We all ran over to see what had happened. Karel was sitting among the leaves, cradling his hand against his chest. Then William pulled him away and we saw the brownish-yellow viper flash under the sagging banana trunk.

Karel cried soundlessly, and his breathing soon became noisy and ragged. Lying next to his knee, there was something gross about his hand. It looked as though it belonged to someone else—someone much bigger and fatter.

Then he cried out loud, full of terror, and slowly fell to his side. "Help me, Mommy," he whispered. "Please, help me."

No one moved. None of us knew what to do or say. Time stood still, as we watched his eyes close. Then Karel stopped breathing. A bit of saliva dribbled out of his mouth, and blue smudges moved over his closed eyes. His hand still looked grossly swollen, and a spot below his thumb showed where the snake had bitten.

Kees broke away on his knees, leaving a trail in the clay till he got himself up and ran. Jaap Martelaar followed. William, Peter, and I stayed with Karel, unaware of the time passing. As I watched flies arrive and settle on Karel's hand and eyes, I scoffed, wondering where they came from so fast, as if always waiting to move in on something sick or dead. I swept them away till Karel's mother came running with Nadine and Mies.

The three of them carried him to the clinic. A doctor did not see him. Neither did Mrs. Frost, the camp leader, inform the doctor about a death in the camp, since when death was not caused by something infectious, they did not investigate further.

In the afternoon, we all went with Karel's mom to the gate in front of the guardhouse. She had wrapped her best towel over his head before he was to be put into the rough box to be buried.

"His face will not feel the rough wood now," she said, but she had no tears. Her hair, which had been shaved off a few months ago, had started to grow again, but in a different color. Karel had been her only child.

I missed Karel. He always cheated, was always mean, and was always on my back. Perhaps, that's what I missed, but I wasn't sure. Mostly, I just felt uneasy. Karel was a kid like me. We went to the Simon Fraay Hotel together, fought and played at Kamp Keudah together. I won his marbles, and he won mine. And he was gone now, killed by a snake. Proof that kids died too. If Karel died, so could I, or Simon, or one of the little girls. Especially now that both Easabella and Emma-M had convulsions with high fevers.

In addition, Emma-M, after seeing Easabella have her first convulsion, had had repeated nightmares. She was deadly afraid of going through the same thing. At night she wanted to be kept very close before she went to sleep, and I promised to wake her if I thought she might have a convulsion, so she could fight it.

What would I do if one of us died? I wasn't willing to think it through. Just the idea of it made me restless enough that for days, I avoided Peter, who only wanted to talk about Karel and the viper. He told me that he and William later hunted for it, but that it was gone.

Nadine didn't help much either. "Karel is better off this way," I heard her tell his mother. "He had a difficult life ahead of him."

Karel's mom still couldn't cry, and when I asked Mies why, she said, "Her heart is frozen, Sofia, and the cold also froze her tears. Pain is the key that keeps her heart locked. Time will have to melt the pain and unfreeze the key. When that happens, she will cry."

I had questions for Nadine too. "How did you know Karel would have a difficult life ahead of him?" Nadine could see things other people couldn't. Perhaps, she had seen Karel grow up. But then, if life always happened as it did in her visions, how could Karel be dead now?

Watching Nadine, I was suddenly reminded of Sitah. Nadine looked nothing like Sitah; Sitah was pure Indonesian, while Nadine's father was French, and she never spoke of her mother. Yet they both belonged here on this island, and Nadine had the same wisdom and gentleness as Sitah. Nadine, too, preferred being alone over being in a crowd, and seemed to trust only children.

Easabella adored Nadine. She had taken care of Easa several times, when the diarrhea wouldn't stop and when Easa endlessly complained of a bellyache.

"Karel traded peace for conflict a long time ago," Nadine finally answered. "Breaking was more fun for him than mending. He took what was not given to him, and it didn't make him happy. He liked the shadows, which gave him comfort and shelter, because light asked from him more than he was willing to give. Perhaps, now he will find what was already his to take."

I didn't understand everything Nadine said—just some of it. But if Nadine knew what kind of person Karel would have been when he grew up, then what might she know about me? Afraid that she could see inside me—my angry thoughts about Mom and my dark moods—I moved away from her and her direct stare, and lay down on one of the clinic's sleeping mats.

What kind of a person would I be when I grew up, with all these horrible memories in my head? I wondered. *I don't want to remember any of them!* Then I promised myself never to be hungry again, for sure. I would have soap and clean clothes every day. I would have a washroom and a toilet, just for me, and without flies. I would find Sitah and Hassan and join them again in front of a wood-burning fire, cooking and eating with my hands and savoring the odor of spices mixed with smoke. I would hear the peels of peanuts, and their crackling as they burned in the fire.

Thinking about Sitah's delicious cooking brought water to my mouth, which pulled me back to the present. I bolted up and was surprised to see Nadine. I had forgotten about her. She must have been watching me for awhile.

"Did you find peace, Sofia, for a moment? In a place no one knows about?" She smiled, her eyes filled with something I couldn't name. Had she seen what I was thinking? Could she really read people's minds?

I lowered my eyes and scrambled off the mat. "I've to go, Nadine, I'll see you next time." Then I ran away.

Nadine laughed. "Run, Sofia, and run some more. The only way to outrun your demons is by finding out who they are!"

There were no snails left to hunt. They had all been found and eaten, or had escaped the area after the women had cut the tall grasses to plant potatoes. There were rats, however, but once caught, we had no way of cooking them— till Peter found a way.

We had discovered that the rats roamed the warehouse, which was a room without windows and a single lightbulb on the ceiling. The door to the warehouse was only unlocked when the women were cooking in the kitchen, and because bags of rice and *oebi* (potato) were kept there, it offered the rats plenty to eat. By suddenly flipping the light on, we could see them scurrying away between the bags. The rice bags were too heavy to move, but the potato bags rolled when we pushed them, so Peter and I made a plan.

Peter, armed with a big stick, hid in the warehouse on top of the bags. He went as high as he could climb and waited. A half hour later, I slipped through the door, flipped on the light switch, and Peter would go after the rats who were running for shelter. Sometimes he missed, but when he was lucky, we had a dead rat. In those instances, we'd sneak out of the warehouse with it, and Peter would hang the beast somewhere off of a tree branch, blood leaking from its nose and mouth, making me nauseous. Peter promised it would be better once we had it roasted, and when evening came, he'd take it home in his pants' pocket.

After dark, we'd sneak out, hiding in the pockets of shade along the barracks, and meet in the kitchens. Between the cooking stones were always smoldering ashes and glowing coals left over from the daily cooking, so we gathered them, heaped them into a bed of fire, and buried the rat in it.

Once the small body was covered in the hot ash, the waiting began. We didn't talk, as there was nothing to talk about, and we were comfortable with each other. We just lay back on the kitchen stones. Sometimes the wide, black *wadjangs* (shallow pans for holding large amounts of food) were still warm from the evening porridge, and we could crawl into them, completely hidden in the bottoms. To pass the time, Peter would exercise his arm-farting skills. He'd cup his right hand over the hollow of his left armpit, and then pump his arm up and down with short, jerky movements, making little puffing sounds. He could make them really loud, but never did on these nights.

When at last the rat changed into something we could eat, Peter pulled it out and blew the ash off the charcoaled skin. The head was hopeless, as it always fell apart, but we shared whatever was left. We each pulled out one leg, then another. It wasn't much, but it had the taste of meat and stilled the ever-present gnawing in our stomachs. With each bite, we'd spit out the black stuff and swallow the rest. We never caught two rats, since there wouldn't have been enough coal and ashes to roast it. And anyway, eating just the one often left us nauseous.

After our ratty meal, we'd bury any leftovers under the ash and sneak back to the barracks. Slipping in between the little girls was easy. If Mom ever noticed my absence, she never let on. I never saw her wake up, and the next day, she never asked where I had been. Besides, one of her other famous sayings was, "What you don't know can't hurt you." So, good-night, Mom!

Easabella started to scare me. She still had not seen the doctor, and she had become very pale and thin. She and Emma-M were both very thin; well, we all were. But they cried a lot and often wet themselves during the night. Even though Mom still had the mutilated tin can on our *tampat* (living space) for them to pee in, they often were too sick to make it in time. And I couldn't wash the urine odor away anymore, for we had very little soap.

Easabella's tummy was always tender and swollen, but now it felt hard on the days she didn't want to eat. Some days, she had terrible diarrhea; other days, she couldn't go at all. Mom had asked Nadine for help many times, but Nadine couldn't do much. She told Mom to give Easa only boiled water and as much warm rice water as she would take. But often, Easa brought the rice water up as soon as she had swallowed it, and then turned her head away after that, only taking water.

Easabella had been on her sleeping pad for an entire week when, one morning, she suddenly seemed worse.

I sat next to her all morning, watching her little hand rub her tummy, around and around and around, moaning at times. Her hair was stuck wet around her face, and I wished it were less red, so it wouldn't make her face so frightfully pale.

Mom, exhausted and having stared at Easabella day after day for over a week, didn't seem to notice the gradual, slow decline in Easa's condition. That morning, after returning from *corvee,* she had stretched out on her pad and fallen asleep before I could talk to her about Easa.

Her eyes were dull and worried, and I sensed her going inside her self more and more. She seldom laughed, even at Simon.

So I continued closely watching my little sister, hoping to see a change for the better. I was afraid for stillness and hated the flies that swarmed, trying to sit on her. I changed the soiled sheet under her bottom, afraid to turn her over because every time I did, she moaned and whimpered in pain. I longed for her to sleep, so she would be more comfortable, and I longed for her to wake, so I would know she wasn't dead; this was how Baby Miedema had looked when life had slipped away from her.

I tried to work some rice water between her dry lips, but it ran down her chin and neck, and woke her, her light brown eyes widening and searching and finally settling on me.

"Am I going to die, Sofia?" she whispered clearly and shocked me. Easabella knew how ill she was.

"I won't let you, Easa. Don't think about that. You are not going to die. I won't let you!"

"I feel so bad, Sofia, there is so much pain in here." Her hand kept moving over her tummy as she closed her eyes, sinking away from me.

Pulling her to me, I kissed her feverish face.

"Don't let me die, Sofia, I am so afraid to go to sleep."

I started to cry, which didn't help Easabella. "I'll watch over you, Easa, I promise. Go to sleep. I won't let you die!"

Easabella slept then. I could feel her tired heart beating against my arm. I held her awhile, until I had to clean her again, gagging from the smell. Although she hardly ate anything, Easa had diarrhea almost every hour. After being cleaned, she laid still. Her eyes were closed. Her hand was not moving over her tummy anymore. Her forehead was dry and burning hot.

A wave of fear swept over me. I got the gut feeling that Easabella was slipping away from us. Shaking Mom, I cried and screamed, and then finally pulled her up out of her sleep. Mom woke and suddenly, now with different eyes, saw her little Easa. She wrapped a towel around her, picked her up, and walked out of the barrack. I followed her through the camp and into the clinic. Nadine saw us coming and, without speaking, went to Mom's side and walked with her to the gate, where a guard was standing outside the gatehouse.

Nadine took Easabella from Mom and, without hesitation, passed through the gates, went up the steps of the guardhouse, and through the door. The guard trailed behind her. Mom and I waited, holding onto the gate's bars. Behind us, life went on as usual, as we stood in our little world of panic and foreboding, afraid.

After awhile, the door opened and Nadine came walking down the stairs alone, her arms empty. Mom started to cry.

Nadine held Mom awhile and then told us that Easabella would go to a hospital, that transportation was on the way, and that she would not be back soon. She didn't know much more—not the name of the hospital, or whether doctors would be treating her. Not if Easa would be strong enough to survive. When the guard came back to watch us, Nadine gently took Mom with her, away from the gate.

I stayed, staring at the guardhouse, wondering how Easa was now. Would she be awake and looking for me? Would she remember my promise? Where would she go? Would she ever come back? She was still so very small and now all alone. Very ill children had been taken out of the camp before, and every so often, one would come back, looking healthier and better fed. But the rest disappeared; no one knew where they were or what had been done with them.

Awhile later, a little horse-drawn carriage rattled up the road, stopped at the gatehouse, and carried Easabella away.

We were left guessing and scared. Mom couldn't help Simon and Emma-M feel better, as they had many questions for which she had no answers. I, too, found it difficult to get used to the empty space left by Easa. But, of course, Emma-M missed her most. She cried herself to sleep every night and started to suck her thumb again. So I started taking her to Mies Miedema's place more often; she liked it there, and she and Phaedra got along very well.

Then, a few weeks later, we had a fabulous surprise. A little truck stopped in front of the gatehouse, and the guard took from it a large bag filled with postcards. It seemed that almost every family was receiving a postcard from a husband, father, or son, and the excitement was incredible. All of us were so ready for a bit of sun, a bit of happiness, and a reason to laugh and sing. And then we received one from Dad!

It didn't tell us much. None of the postcards received that day told much. In fact, all of them were very much the same, varying only slightly here and there. It must have been awhile ago that they were written, though, because some were wrinkled and others smeared from having been wet. They had no address and no date.

Our postcard was written in blue ink, in a slanted handwriting that Mom immediately recognized as Dad's. Elated, she caressed the bold letters. Dad wrote that all was well. He lived in a plain bamboo building with lots of other men. The food was okay. They had clothes and medicine, and they did building jobs for the Japanese army. He wrote nothing personal, nothing indicating what had happened to him or where he had been since we'd seen him when we'd still been at the Hotel Simon Fraay.

Mom kissed the postcard, folded it in two, and stuck it in her bra. It stayed there, day and night, till the ink smudged and came out, leaving marks on her skin. Then the words on the postcard ran together, till eventually we couldn't read them anymore. But Mom knew the text by heart and showed Simon which smudges had been which word.

But what did all these letters mean? At least for us, it meant that Dad was still alive and still thought about us. Could it also mean the end of the war was near? Perhaps the Japanese soldiers were getting scared knowing that we'd soon be free, and they were trying to make us forget their cruelty. Or, was this just another of their merciless jokes? Of course, there were always as many camp pessimists drowning our joy with talk of gloom and doom, as there were optimists lifting spirits, sending our imaginations soaring with talk of what they would do once they were free—what to plan, sing, buy, eat, and wear.

All I knew was that after that letter, for the first time since Easabella had left us, Mom washed and brushed her hair again. She wasn't able to bring back the shine, but certainly some of the curls.

A few days after, another bag was delivered, this time with blank postcards. Each family received one postcard on which to write back to their fathers, sons, or husbands. When we were commanded to write only what was dictated to us, however, I realized that most likely Dad had been told, as well, what he could and couldn't write.

The letter would have no heading, as a date was forbidden and we didn't know our address. The message we were to send was similar to the one we'd gotten from Dad: We were okay. The food was sufficient. It rained a lot, but the house we lived in was dry. Messages without a message. Words without meaning. But, perhaps Dad would receive it one day and be just as happy with it as we were with his. The commander made it clear that if we did not write what we were supposed to, the postcard would be torn and not sent.

Simon wished there were a way to let Easabella know about Dad's postcard. Mom and I didn't allow ourselves to think too long about her. Easa had been so ill when she had left, I couldn't help but wonder if she was still having the pain and convulsions, though my biggest fear was that she had died like Baby Miedema.

"When will she be back?" Emma-M asked at least once a day. So I promised her to go to the gate each morning to wait for the *grobak* (an open cart, pulled mostly by one or two oxen) to arrive with our supplies and food, and see if Easa might be delivered along with them.

The *grobak* was loaded high on some days, but carried only a few boxes on others. Sometimes the *grobak* even carried boxes or baskets for people who had died in the camp to be buried in somewhere outside. We didn't know where the graveyard was, if there even was one. There were always two oxen pulling it, because one wouldn't have been enough to haul all that weight over the sloped sand roads.

Perhaps one day, I would see Easabella arrive on that *grobak,* smiling and waving, and then Emma-M would be happy again and not so terribly lonely, asking for her sister all the time. I often thought fondly of how they'd been like twins, playing and acting just alike, although they'd looked very different. But, over time, they had begun to look more alike. In fact, it seemed that all of us began to look more alike, and maybe it was because we all had one thing in common: we were thin and starving. At *koempoelan,* when Mom had wrapped her arms around us, keeping us together until we were counted, we'd needed less than one meter of space—and that had been when Easabella was still with us.

The food in the kitchen was always the same and made diarrhea regular. Although some still bought from the *toko,* there were far fewer supplies than ever, because they had far fewer clients. Most of us had no money left to spend. Our jewelry had all been traded and the money we were given by the Japanese commander through Mrs. Frost was scanty. Mom had sold all her garnets and even traded her wedding ring for milk powder to give Easabella.

Peter and I still roamed the camp, looking for live things to catch and cook. There was no more rat hunting for us, since the warehouse door now had to stay locked because of theft. Once, we tried *tjitjaks* (small lizards) but the ashes burned them away to nothing. We sucked at the trunks of the banana trees, hoping to find any last trace of their juices, but usually found them dry and cut our lips on the bark. I really didn't like to do that, though, as I had become terrified of snakes after Karel had died—although snakes usually were not seen around banana trees, which had smooth trunks and provided little cover. I couldn't explain this unreasonable phobia.

We didn't talk about food, yet it seemed to be the only thing on our minds. Even the mothers didn't let their kids play rough or running games, worried it would make them hungrier. Except Mom, who, after the excitement of Dad's postcard wore off, really wasn't Mom any more. She went into herself, where she liked to be whenever she was unhappy. She slept in the daytime, and even when she was awake, her eyes were dull when she looked at us. I often had to wake her when it was time to eat, after I had collected the food from the kitchen, though sometimes she would push her food away, roll over, and go back to sleep. And on other days, she would eat half a portion and put the rest back into the pan, which, without a word, we kids divided among us. She didn't care. She was no longer interested in anything we did, even in where Emma-M was during the day. She let us be, and often didn't hear our questions or didn't want to answer. Still, Simon stayed always with her, playing quietly with old toys. It was difficult without Mom, and I resented her for abandoning us.

The loneliness and hardship we experienced at Lawe Sigalagala was depressing enough, without also having an emotionally absent mother. Day after day, we saw the same people and the same camp. We ate the same food and did the same boring things. The Japanese soldiers and native *heihos* walked the paths around the camp day and night. There was no outside traffic. No noise. Apart from the daily *grobak* arriving and leaving, and the occasional appearance of a truck, there was only silence.

There was, however, always activity around the clinic, where increasing numbers of patients came for aspirin or, when available, quinine for the exhausting malaria attacks. The area around the kitchen and washrooms was also consistently busy.

The biggest commotion, though, came from the barracks, where the women constantly quarreled, frustrated and irritable after years in captivity with still no end in sight. Children often stayed away from their mothers to avoid being slapped or beaten. And after *koempoelan,* whenever the whole camp was punished for the misgivings of one—forced to stand for hours in the hot sun until the soldier let us leave the soiled, stinking square—the woman at fault would be scolded by her fellow prisoners in no uncertain terms and then ignored once back in her barrack. The atmosphere in the camp had become one of misery, in which everyone seemed to have lost hope. No one was content anymore, and the littlest, stupidest thing would cause full-blown reactions.

Mom stayed away from all of it. She had little interest in what was going on around her. Every day, she just did her *corvee*, came back to the barrack, and went to sleep. She left it up to Simon and me to go for the meals and to watch Emma-M. Of course, Simon didn't move away from Mom. He always found something to do around her and often did things for her. He waved away the flies when they sat on her and brought her water when she awoke thirsty. And when she didn't need him, he went to his mat and rested. Suffering with regular malaria attacks, Simon, too, felt poorly, and didn't play much anymore. His face had become very thin, and although he had gotten older, he still looked like a five-year-old.

Out of all of us, Emma-M seemed to manage best. She always ate her entire meal, played with Phaedra (whenever Phaedra had no fever), and sometimes even skipped a few days of regular malaria attacks. She still asked for Easabella, though, and her eyes filled with tears each day when Nadine told her there was no news. She would walk away, bravely hiding her tears, but with dejection in her little figure. It was painful to see her so disappointed time after time, but neither Nadine nor I could help.

Still, Mom worried me most. When we'd still lived free in Langsa, I had often seen her lose control. Her nerves always seemed to be stretched the tightest right before her slow descent into depression. Before Dad had been taken, he had always been there to guide her through those periods of melancholy, and, after awhile, I would just watch her come back to her normal self.

Now that Dad was not around, it all fell onto me. I was the one expected to keep our little family together and to help her come back. But as I watched her sink further into her self-chosen isolation, I had no idea how. I was not Dad, and my back, neck, shoulders, and knees had become chronically stiff and painful from malaria attacks. It was all I could do not to go to bed for a rest during the day; there was Emma-M to watch, and I didn't trust Mom even in the rare times she awoke. She was liable to do something stupid—upset other people or start a confusing conversation that would end in a fight.

We had been close to two years behind fences, we had had hopes and disappointments, we had seen cruelty and each of us had at one time or another been hit or beaten or kicked. Lots of women had had their hair shorn or still felt the sweep of the whip or bamboo stick over their bodies whenever they caught glimpses of their scars. We had bowed for screaming Japanese soldiers, bent humbly down when they despised us for no reason. We had descended into a way of life, which was appalling, degrading, and inhuman. We were sick and remained sick with no outlook on a change and without hope of change or better. We had very little hope left; where would we end up without hope? We felt a forgotten people.

It was almost three months later when I went on my daily trek to the gate one afternoon, and, leaning lethargically against the fence as usual, I watched the familiar *grobak* come around the bend in the road. The two chunky oxen were pulling hard, which meant the cart was full. I wondered why and left my post to get a closer look. Anything coming to Camp Lawe Sigalagala from the free, beautiful world behind the high, dense forest had my attention. The *grobak* wheels groaned and squealed. It was difficult to see, for the sun had just risen above the mountains. The air was still chilly.

Shading my eyes from the sun, I could see bags of rice, *oebi* (cassava), and wood, as always, but there was something more today. I started to walk faster, then run, and strained to see better. For a moment, I couldn't believe my eyes, for there appeared to be nicely wrapped boxes on the *grobak,* as well—they almost looked like presents. Each box was square with a large red cross on each side, and they were piled very high. No wonder the beasts were having trouble pulling the load!

Then, as the cart neared the fence, my heart skipped a beat. I swallowed. For there, surrounded by the Red Cross boxes, sat Easabella like a little queen in her carriage. I reached the gate, still doubting my eyes, and watched until the *grobak* came so close that I could see the large, tired eyes of the oxen.

The little girl among the boxes started to shout, "Sofia, Sofia! Look at me! I am back, Sofia, look at me!" She waved a cotton doll with ridiculously long legs and arms. It really was Easabella! And she looked clean and healthy, with color back in her cheeks.

The guard swooped her off the *grobak* and she came running, laughing and crying at the same time. What a sight she was! She came through the gate, jumped up on me, and locked her little arms tightly around my neck. I stumbled backward under the new, healthy weight of my little sister and smelled her sweetness. She smelled like a child—no more urine odor, no more sweat and fever, no more illness or worries about death.

As we walked in triumph through the camp toward our barrack, kids surrounded us, hopping and laughing and shouting.

"Easabella is back!"

"Hello, Easa!"

"Easabella is back—look at Easa!"

I felt like a queen in a parade, like a hero—like I had cured Easabella myself and saved her from dying.

In a minute, Mom came running toward us with Simon and Emma-M. Someone had run ahead and told them. We met them halfway, Easabella running the last few meters into Mom's arms. And as the five of us stood there between the barracks, holding one another in a tangle of arms and heads and bodies, Mom started to cry. Not just a little. Not just softly so that only our family could hear. But with big heaving sobs. And she didn't stop. She let go of everything that had bothered her for so long and that she'd had to carry alone, without Dad. All of us cried then.

After a few minutes, we walked together, still crying, to the barrack, where we found the *tampat* (living space) we called home. There, we calmed down, and Easabella shared rice cookies with us from a small package the hospital nurse had left in her pocket.

Mom's tears didn't stop flowing the rest of the day, though now they gently left her eyes without the heaving sobs. She kept looking at Easa and sometimes even expressed admiration for the way she looked and spoke.

That evening, when I came back from the kitchen with our food, I found her asleep, propped against our rolled up sleeping mats, with one arm around Easabella and the other around Emma-M. Simon watched over the three of them, waving away the flies.

Easabella was back. We were five again.

The Red Cross parcels were little wonders. The camp leader and lots of other women carried them from the gatehouse to the kitchen, where everything was taken out of the boxes and shown to us. Half of it went into the warehouse, and the other half was divided among families according to size. Though the goods had to be shared and rationed over time, there was a lot to go around. Plus, Mies gave Easabella a whole extra pack of cookies, since she had brought us all of the goodies to begin with.

We kids waited on our *tampat* for Mom to return, and when she did, her arms were full of delicious things we had forgotten. Butter and cheese, crackers, milk powder, dried fruits, beef and salmon in cans, and even vitamins and cigarettes. She had traded her share of cigarettes for soap and shampoo. She also had packets of coffee, tea, and soup stuffed into her roomy bra. And best of all, she brought large bars of chocolate—milk chocolate with big, hard almonds. Mom spread our goodies over the *tampat,* and Simon gaped while the little girls shrieked, dancing with Easabella's long-legged doll between them till they dropped, totally spent. I felt so rich and happy, and especially now that Easabella was there to enjoy it with us.

Mom started with the chocolate, breaking off a big piece for each of us. Simon kept his so long that it started to show white spots. He just licked them off and kept the smaller dark brown chunk for the next day.

The Red Cross parcels brought more questions and rumors to the camp, as well, but these were the same as always, centering on whether the end of the war was near and whether, perhaps, the Japanese soldiers were becoming afraid. Together, we thought out loud how it would be wonderful to receive these parcels more often, like every month. And Nadine wondered, if that happened, whether they might also include much-needed medications.

Maybe, some said, the Red Cross boxes had been sent to us to let us know that we weren't forgotten and should continue to hope—and this idea had some truth to it, as they had brought with them at least a small amount of long-lost hope. We felt that somewhere, someone must have known about us after all.

More hope came soon after, when the nurses were informed that another doctor would arrive to replace the Japanese one. We hadn't seen much of either doctor for awhile, and many were seriously ill.

The new doctor arrived a few days later and, to our delight, turned out to be Dutch—someone who spoke our language and someone who we could trust. Particularly the older women, who seemed to suffer from pain and illness more than the rest of us, were happy about this. A doctor was someone to be trusted—someone with whom you could discuss problems and be sure they would not be shared. Confidentiality among the women no longer existed—everything discussed became common knowledge—so the opportunity to talk to him about their pain and illness itself worked healing. They had not been able to open up this way with a foreign doctor because of the language barrier.

His clinic was a separate little building close to the gates, where Nadine and the two other nurses assisted him in treating and sharing information about the patients. The Japanese guards had provided benches from the gates to the little clinic, where patients patiently waited for their turn to see the doctor. Some women were so bad off that they had to be carried in.

One day, Mom wanted this new doctor to check out Easabella's tummy and Simon's gums, which constantly bled and hurt. Easabella had not wanted to go, so I had carried her to the waiting bench. As we quietly waited, Nadine came out to the gate asking for help to get a very ill woman into the clinic. Mom had not heard Nadine, as she was half asleep, and the other women were all too sick to help. So I sat Easabella on the bench and helped Nadine. When the doctor saw the condition the woman was in, he didn't speak. He just listened to Nadine as she filled him in on the patient's needs. Then, just as

I was leaving to get back to Easabella, I saw the shocked glance he exchanged with Nadine and heard his soft whisper: "Good God, how is this possible?"

He must have been upset and shocked about all that he had seen that day, because the next time he came, he brought presents. He also brought news from the outside. But the latter he had to dispense secretly. He'd had strict orders from the Japanese commander not to speak or ask about anything beyond a patient's condition or treatment, and was told that if he did, he would be punished by execution. In addition, a Japanese soldier was always present in the clinic. But knowing the soldier couldn't follow the Dutch language, the doctor would carefully, while discussing the condition and treatment of patients, sneak in reports of things that had nothing medical about them.

I learned about all this one day while at Mies's *tampat.* I had gone to pick up my little sisters, who'd been there playing with Phaedra, and found Nadine discussing the doctor's news with Mies. As I helped the little girls clean up their mess, I caught enough of the women's conversation to understand the gist.

He had told Nadine that he was prisoner in an all-male camp not far from Lawe Sigalagala, and that their conditions were much better than ours. For one, they had several doctors, all of them European. He said he had told the men in his camp about our horrible conditions, that he had seen patients with horrific edema where the fluid had entered the abdomen and even the chest cavity. He had described the undernourished children, some so thin he was afraid of hurting them when he lifted them to his examination table. He had talked about the dysentery and the unending diarrhea, and the many women in hysterics or psychologically disturbed. The men, he said, had listened silently, anger and hate in their eyes, and then had gone through their camp and collected items for us. He promised to bring us more each time he came.

This time, he had brought soap, medicine, toothpaste, and even bottles of an iron solution that had been prepared by doctors in their camp. The Japanese soldier hadn't seemed to mind, as he'd let the doctor give the items to the nurses.

About three weeks later, we also learned that this doctor knew how to put pressure on the Japanese commander, because chicken livers and goat meat was delivered for the most ill patients. He seemed like an angel sent from heaven.

As always, when the Dutch doctor wasn't there, Mies and Nadine and the other nurses kept up the clinic, and as I had begun to spend more time with them, I learned that Mies and Nadine shared a strong faith in something, though maybe not in the same thing. Or perhaps it was the same thing, but each gave it a different name. All I knew is that through our years of abuse, hunger, and death, they both believed in something good and strong that made them a source of help to all who came looking for it.

They helped wherever and however they could, even if it was just by listening. Nadine spent many a night at the bedsides of terminally ill women and children, filling a writing pad with names and notes, messages for husbands and sons in case the patients died. She would promise these women that she would personally write or visit their men, if necessary, and take them their wives' last words. Usually they did die, too, and then Nadine added a date next to their names and messages in her tiny scripted handwriting before taping the notebook back under her mattress pad. She knew no guard would check there, since the Japanese were so afraid of illness.

Mies did *corvee* just like everyone else, but when she was done, she went to the clinic where she had left Phaedra, to give Nadine a hand. Nadine let her help but also made her lie down a few hours to rest.

"Mies has a heart condition," she explained to me one day. "Phaedra has no one else, so Mies should be careful with her health."

Mies smiled when Nadine said this, but rested anyway, since she was tired. She often worked for two by taking over the tasks of weaker women, yet she got the same beatings and she was just as hungry; in fact, with her tall, large body, she probably needed even more.

"Life is given and will be taken," she'd always say. "What will you do with it before you give it back?"

Mies made everybody think. Even the meanest, most selfish bitch showed respect for her. On days she called Sundays, people came to her barrack and sang sweet melodies together; some hymns sounded full of longing for a better time. Then Mies would speak about something and end up listening to many others, as one by one, each woman spoke about what frightened her or what she couldn't handle alone. When Mies spoke, she talked in a singsong way about what was in all of us: grief after losing a child, anger for things that could not be changed, hate and bitterness, and so much more. She then sang again, though often alone, since many women didn't remember the words; but they all hummed the melody. Mies had also read from a Bible before it was taken and burnt by a guard. He'd been looking for radios and, not finding one there, destroyed her Bible instead. But Mies didn't need it; she knew the text by heart. Mies hummed the psalms and hymns for the rest of the day.

I liked to be in the group who went to Mies Miedema's place on Sundays. Not because I wanted to sing her hymns, which I didn't know, but just because I liked to be with her. I admired her low voice when she taught the other women the hymns. I loved the light in her gray eyes and her quiet way of listening when another woman spoke. A Sunday afternoon with Mies was so healing that I could put aside my worry about Mom and forget our troubles for awhile. Nadine thought that what Mies did was better than church.

After one of those Sunday gatherings, I followed Mies to the clinic. Then catching up to her, I felt her arm over my shoulders.

"Talk to me, Sofia," she said as we walked on. "There is so much bothering you. It is time to talk about it."

"I don't need to talk about what is bothering me, Mies," I began. "I cannot ever get rid of it. I don't ever want to forget what the Japanese conquerors did to us."

Her arm around my shoulder choked my voice. "I can't stop thinking about what they made of us," I continued. "I feel like an animal. Always dirty, always hungry. We had a dog when I was small, and it lived better than we do. We never kicked it or beat it.

"I can't let go of the hate inside of me, and I don't even know if I want to. It'll keep me from changing my mind if years later I see a Japanese person who had nothing to do with all this, and I don't want to change my mind. I want to spit and puke and stomp on everything they hold high. When this war ends, I hope to never see one of those flat faces again—with those dark mean eyes!"

I started trembling and found it difficult to continue talking. "I promise myself never to be so afraid again, never to bow for anyone or let someone touch me with a stick or a whip!"

My voice broke and tears started. "And when I die, Mies, I don't want to be buried and still be part of this earth. I want to burn and flame and become ash. Someone will throw me up and I will move into the wind and no one, *no one,* will ever see me again!" My hands were shaking, my legs seemed cabled together, and I felt as though someone had ripped me from the inside out.

Having finally reached the clinic, I sat on a bench, not wanting Mies to see how upset I was. I wished she weren't there. I couldn't think clearly anymore. I wished I hadn't talked to her. I felt dizzy and wanted to disappear, to be gone. Just gone. I longed to be somewhere and nowhere all at once. And I longed never to have been, to have thought—or to have hurt.

Mies sat next to me and held me close. I leaned into her, rigid, unable to get too close or even to sigh, fighting her sympathy, yet needing her empathy.

"You'll be carrying this around in you for a long time, Sofia," she whispered through my hair. "Your young years are shattered now and maybe your future. But you'll have other years and other dreams, and you'll have a future that you make. You have much to give, and there is little you will take."

She paused, and then said, "A gift born in pain will always be a gift. It will stay in you and heal your pain."

I didn't understand. I couldn't think. Yet, her soft voice had calmed the trembling and released the stiffness in my body, making room for exhaustion. Getting up, I looked at Mies and saw tears in her eyes. I didn't need that—I had enough tears of my own! So without saying more, I left.

After that, I didn't go to see Mies for a whole week. I didn't dare look into her eyes and see more pity or compassion. Mies and I never spoke about the conversation again.

Not long after, the busses came again to move us out of Lawe Sigalagala. At least on the busses, most of us could sit, and I was looking forward to seeing the beauty of the land closer to the mountains, watching the soaring turkey hawks in their splendid flights hunting for small animals far below. As long as we had lived here, I had not seen the turkey hawks that had been so numerous on our trip to Lawe Sigalagala, and I had been longing for a time when I could see them again. They must have avoided our place of tears, knowing there would be nothing but empty valley left among the starving prisoners. Though, as it turned out, we left behind more: graves in unknown places, most of them shallow and without names, likely never to be found.

Walking from the barracks, the children fell behind, thin and unhappy, unable to be carried by their weak mothers, who also had very little patience and often pushed or slapped their children to stop their whining. The guards, who were constantly screaming at the mothers to keep their children quiet, were also pushing the poor scared children.

There were screams and yells and hysterical cries as the guards tried to keep the order, screaming at the *heihos* to load us onto the busses and perform the ritual counting. They seemed to scream because that's what they wanted to do, to get rid of their own fury, their own bitterness for having to do what they considered totally demeaning.

I felt sorry for Emma-M and Easa, who had to fend for themselves under muted protest, tears running down their little faces, as they remained perfectly silent. Their luggage was heavy for them, and they were already tired. They kept asking for water, but after they had finished half our water bottle, Mom silenced them each with a slap, afraid we wouldn't have enough to last the rest of the day. Simon didn't cry, but his gray eyes looked huge and miserable in his too-pale face. He didn't seem interested in what was going on. I hugged him, but he didn't seem to notice.

Walking behind my two little sisters, I tried to make them laugh, but wasn't very successful.

"Stop that nonsense, Sofia," Mom snapped. "Nothing is funny now!"

But Emma-M and Easabella had stopped crying, so I continued, this time softly telling them the story about Snow White and the seven little dwarves. I told the girls that they were as little as the dwarves had been, and called them Dwarf Em and Dwarf Bella, which made them smile and giggle.

At the bus stop, two busses were already filled with luggage and sleeping pads. We let go of our loads, too, though Mom was worried we would never see them again. Getting into the busses was not simple. The steps were high and difficult to climb especially for the children and the old, sick people. The only help offered was pushing and pulling by the guards, and there was much crying and protesting, as many would stumble up the steps, falling, and scraping their legs.

Mom's long legs helped her in, after which I handed up Easabella and Emma-M to her. Simon didn't need help, going in on hands and feet. I followed, unintentionally mounting the steps with a woman who had been pushed roughly by one of the soldiers. As she stumbled up beside me, I fell against the iron partition behind the driver's seat, knowing there would be bruises tomorrow.

Mom had been able to save a place for me, but the little girls had started to cry again, and this time Simon also sobbed. I looked at Mom's closed eyes and saw that her face looked wet. I touched her cheek, wiping away the wetness, and then wished I hadn't, as her closed eyes then released tears.

Hours later, we left for an unknown destination. We lumbered on over the rough roads in the humid heat, along the fields and little houses. Simon and the girls fell asleep, and Mom kept her eyes closed as I watched the endless panorama of *sawahs*, so close, yet so far. I missed the turkey hawks since the sky was cloudy.

The busses stopped once to let us hide between the shrubs and bushes. I was grateful for the opportunity to relieve my full bladder, but then this feeling made me furious. I despised myself for wanting to thank someone for something as primitive as a pee break. I felt humiliated and degraded.

Finally, in late afternoon, the sun came through, her sharp light nearly blinding, and we stopped. I looked up to see a sign: BELAWAN ESTATE II.

BELAWAN ESTATE II

October 1944

Soldiers mounted the bus and shoved people out with their gun butts; stiff and sore from the long trip, our climb down was not fast enough for them.

In our group, Mom went down first, an arm over each little girl. Simon held my arm like a vice, so we went down together easily and helped the little ones get out of the way. Mom could barely move, so Simon and I searched for our belongings among those spread along the road. By the time we found all of it, scattered in various places, Mom had recovered.

We followed the line of people already moving through a gate, into a silent, lonely place that was, as always, enclosed in a barbed-wire fence and filled with long barracks. The last light of the falling evening threw a threatening shadow over it, intensifying its aura of emptiness. Little animals made tiny noises among the grass and low shrubs. We had arrived in another camp with another name, and yet it was the same. We later learned that it was an abandoned tobacco farm.

A few kerosene lamps at the entrance of each barrack illuminated the doorway. Further down the camp stood an open building without walls, where more kerosene lamps shed light over clay and cement floors. We learned later that this was the kitchen, where we would also get our drinking water. Here, the water had to be collected in large drums from a tap outside the camp, since there was no plumbing. We also had no electricity.

We stood in the dark, no one speaking, but everyone knowing that, here, nothing would be better. We followed some others into a barrack to see the familiar wooden planks on both sides, a clay path in between. Not expecting to be allotted a larger space, we spread our mats over the estimated four-and-a-half meters and arranged our few possessions around them. People we didn't know became our immediate neighbors, although scattered around the barrack were familiar faces.

Somebody came to tell us that there was food in the kitchen. I was not hungry but went to collect our share, and Simon came with me. As he walked next to me, I noticed his worried expression. Simon was eight by now, and though he never said much, I knew he was keenly aware of everything around him.

As soon as we joined the long line of people at the kitchen, Simon began to talk. He said that things only seemed to be getting worse. Mom showed hardly any interest in him or the little girls.

I tried to convince him that Mom was stronger than he thought, that when the war ended, we would see Dad again, and then Mom would come out of her isolation. I encouraged him to keep entertaining Mom with stories of what he did from day to day.

He listened, and though he didn't seem completely convinced, by the time we were walking back with the food, he seemed more himself. In the barrack, he scooped the porridge into bowls and took one to Mom. She smiled at him and the sun returned to his worried eyes. He looked at me and winked.

We didn't wash the dishes that night; we had no water. Simon had filled a bottle in the kitchen just for drinking.

Then everywhere in the barrack, people began to retire on their sleeping mats, so we did the same.

The camp leader from Camp Lawe Sigalagala agreed to continue at Belawan Estate II.

I had seen her in Lawe Sigalagala but had only known her name. We had little contact with the camp leader and I wasn't interested enough to get to know her better. She was already the camp leader when we had arrived at Camp Lawe Sigalagala. I wondered why she wanted to continue to be responsible. But no one else seemed interested in taking over the responsibility. On the first day, she again explained the rules, which were the same as before except that we would no longer receive money. Some women still had money left over, but there was nothing to spend it on, as there would be no *toko*. In addition, smuggling or trading would be impossible, since this camp was far removed from local *kampongs* (villages). No individual cooking was allowed either, and we couldn't burn candles—no one had any of those left anyway.

Mrs. Frost spoke with a monotonous, uninterested voice to the large group of women, who, in turn, listened apathetically and, in the end, had no questions. Mom, too, was uninterested; in fact, I didn't think she had even listened. She just quietly waited till the info session was over, and then returned to our *tampat,* where she resumed arranging our few possessions. I helped her span the dividing *kains* (large dye-printed sheets) around our space, and then watched as she went to the women next to us and politely excused herself for hanging the sheets. She explained that she needed her retreat and that she wouldn't feel safe otherwise. The neighbors looked at Mom and just nodded.

I asked her why she had found it necessary to explain why she had done something that everyone else here did and had done before at Camp Lawe Sigalagala.

Mom looked at me for a moment and then went on rearranging our possessions as she said, "Hanging the sheets makes it more difficult for thieves if they have plans to steal them, Sofia. They'd have to bring them down first and everyone would notice. There is so much theft around us, and the sheets are all we have. I wouldn't know where to hide if we lost them."

I watched Mom's hands tremble. Her face was devoid of expression. She had become paranoid and I didn't know how to help her. Like Simon, I had been worried and uncomfortable with Mom's periods of unreality. I had even tried to talk her back into the moment we were living in, back into reality. Sometimes she responded, but not today; she would not listen to what I had to say. She wouldn't look at me but just continued moving our sleeping pads around; twice, without noticing, she moved them back to where she had just taken them from. Her mind had gone away.

During our final weeks at Lawe Sigalagala, Simon had had to urge her to eat at every meal, and at every meal, she had patiently explained that the food didn't taste right and that she did not want to eat it. Then once, following her explanation, she had told him with disgust, "Look at the cockroaches. They are all over! And the stinking flies. And where is my silver—how can we eat this? Do they want us to eat with our fingers? We are not barbarians!"

Of course, this had terrified all of us. Most times before, when Mom had gone away into her self-centered world, she had at least made sense when Easabella or Emma-M had needed her, or when she'd had to do *corvee* duty with other women. But seeing cockroaches that weren't there and talking about silver we hadn't had since leaving home years ago—that was different. We had all looked at her, and then Easa and Emma-M had started to cry. Simon had brought Mom an old cardigan and had carefully draped it around her shoulders, but she hadn't noticed. She had not even looked at him. Simon had been terrified. He was not used to being ignored by Mom; he had always been able to elicit a special expression from her.

I had hoped that the commotion of moving to Belawan Estate II would bring her back to us, but it hadn't. She had become so slow and dreamlike, and her mind seemed always to wander through abnormal visions. Simon continued talking to her a lot, as I'd suggested to him that first night in the kitchen line, but she still seldom answered. When she did look at him, it was with empty eyes. Often, this brought him to tears, and ultimately caused him to stop talking altogether, unless it was to her.

What was worse, I couldn't talk to Mies or Nadine about this. Mom would never forgive me later, when her head cleared again and she found out they knew. It was better to try to handle this on my own.

After about two weeks at Belawan Estate II we surrendered most of the other "luxuries" that we had still believed in. There was no water and no electricity, which meant all the cooking was done on wood-burning fires. *Koelies* (laborers) from outside the camp brought in logs but left them uncovered, resulting in wet wood that, when burned, caused a lot of smoke. This was good for keeping mosquitoes away, but made our food taste like smoke.

We had no sinks to wash in, but there were bathhouses where we could shower. Water had become too valuable for everyone to shower daily, so Mrs. Frost organized a bathing schedule, together with all the barrack leaders. Each of us was allowed a bath twice a week with a strictly measured amount of water.

Each day, a group of women collected the water in large drums from a tap outside the camp and brought it in to be used. All day long, water was carried in, to the kitchens, the latrines, the bathhouses, and the clinic. This was heavy work, and all the women were a lot weaker now. So they took turns with those in their *corvee* groups, allowing some to rest while others carried water.

The latrines were in a different place than the showers, and basically amounted to a building with a wooden floor that had holes sawed into it. When you crouched over a hole to go, you could hear the stuff fall on top of what was already there, and smell the stench of what had been left before you. Each toilet hole had a wooden lid that you could close when you were finished, but as people became sicker from dysentery and diarrhea, the holes often remained open, making the whole surrounding area stink.

For *corvee*, Peter and I were added to the garden group. We left early in the morning when the dew made our feet wet and the fresh coolness made us shiver. But within an hour, the humid air would lean heavy on our backs.

Walking through the gate this morning, I'd had difficulty staying in line, and now that the hot sun was out, it was making my head pound. Breakfast had been the old, slimy porridge, tasteless and nauseating. Normally, I ate it just to stop the hungry gnawing, but this morning I hadn't been hungry. All I'd wanted was water.

Worse, malaria had kept me up most of the night. I had suffered through the hours with high fever and images wandering through my mind, and Mom hadn't helped. She had been dreaming out loud, as she did a lot lately, calling out in a low, demanding voice, as if seeing something scary, and then waking up exhausted.

I would have to be careful today. We did the weeding on our knees, and straightening myself up invited black spots to dance in my eyes and dizzy spells that made me stumble for balance—and this, sure as clockwork, would give the Japanese guard reason to whip or kick.

Peter and I only whispered to each other when the guard was out of earshot. We became silent when he neared, and once I saw the shiny, black boots pass, I dared to relax and lean back for a moment to rest. Fever and sun was a bad match. It caused imagination to run, and made it easy to sink into an unreliable world without my noticing.

Now, squatting on my heels, I lost awareness of time and place. For the sole reason of survival, I allowed myself to sink into the unreal world, where everything seemed possible. From a distance and in slow motion, I heard the whip coming and knew it would land somewhere over my body. I saw the cutting string fly through the air, and nicely curl on the way up until it straightened over my back, which soon would begin burning and stinging, and give me the power to master the whip. I would break it and use it on the faceless guard, shoving it all the way into his soft, fat body. Descending into such visions helped control the bitter feeling of utter helplessness and total powerlessness; even reality would not take that away.

It had rained during the night, clearing the sky of clouds, and now the sun burned on my almost hairless head. Mom had shaved my hair short so that she could hunt for lice easier. Most of the girls at camp had very little hair and all the boys were bald; we all had eczema, and there was no other way to get rid of the itchiness. And as with the more important medications, there was no supply of anything for the lice problems. Simon, too, was bald, and Emma-M and Easabella had both had to let go of their hair. Emma-M was still upset about it and refused to let Mom check her for lice. I had checked Mom's hair and had enjoyed the loud snap each time I squeezed one of the fat little creatures between my thumbs. Too bad we couldn't eat them!

The reality of hard clay on my knees, stubborn weeds, painful fingers, and dripping sweat off my face brought back the existence of the softly passing guard and the palpating tension between us. With nothing else to do, we children had spent hours watching the Japanese guards and had become very skilled in measuring their temperaments. It seemed anything would do to relieve the boredom that they had to fight daily; if there was no incident, they would create one just for fun.

I could tell by looking at this guard that I seemed to amuse him, as he stopped and watched me for awhile. I knew I had fallen behind in my weeding, as Peter was almost a yard ahead of me. I tried frantically to speed up under his watchful eye, but my knees were stiff and sore, and I became dizzy again. My mouth was dry and my lips cracked, and we were not allowed to leave the gardens to get water. I sat back in a daze, no longer caring about the guard. I just wanted to move through the red heat, into a cool gray. *If I could only get into that cool gray, I would be all right*, I thought.

Then something soft hit my face. Something gooey and stinky. The cool gray moved away and so did the hot burning. Opening my eyes, I saw the hated black boots shining next to me. I saw pants emerging from the tops of the boots and, higher up, buttons gleaming on a tunic, a fat broad face, and a cap. Everything looked distorted. The soldier blocked the sun as his shape moved in front of my eyes, coming close and then moving away. I tried hard to focus and finally made out the bamboo stick in his hand. Then at the end of the stick, I saw a big blob of chicken shit. It was the gooey, smelly stuff on my face.

His mouth opened, showing gold teeth here and there like fence gates. His loud laugh pounded my ears. It swelled and waved over me, till I drowned in it. For a moment, everything went black, and I found a nice, peaceful place where I wanted to stay. Then something jerked me back to the stink and pounding anger in my head: I felt warm urine coming from somewhere. This puzzled me. Where had it come from? Then I watched the stain in my shorts grow bigger and thought it must be coming from me. I didn't mind. The sun was hot enough that I would dry again.

I turned my head to see Herman Sanders weeding next to me. *Why Herman?* I wondered. Shouldn't Peter be next to me? But Peter had gotten ahead of me. Looking at Herman now, I wondered why his shorts were dry. Shouldn't his shorts be wet also? Herman was always away, somewhere distant, after Trudy's face had healed and she had had trouble recognizing him. His mind had gone away, looking for her, searching and silent. He never spoke, never answered, never smiled, laughed, or played anymore.

Forcing my mind back to the Japanese soldier with his stinking bamboo stick, I stood and looked into his smirking face, the drying chicken shit still reeking on my face. My actions would be a clear sign to him that I hated him.

His grin disappeared. *"Keirei!* (Bow!)" he shouted.

Not moving, let alone bowing, I kept looking into his angry face. Down came the bamboo stick with sweeping force. It hit the back of my leg and hooked over my ankle. I felt the skin on my ankle split and then saw bubbles of red pushing up through it and coming down in a steady, fast flow, settling on the dry soil. The pain was excruciating. Bending down, I closed my hand over the slashed skin. The blood was frighteningly red, and I couldn't stop it from coming.

Mies Miedema, suddenly crouching next to me, forced me down into a squatting position, her arm around my shoulders. She whispered something I didn't understand, trying to coach me back to pulling weeds, but not before the soldier had whipped her arm with another of his bamboo blows. Seeing her arm remain around my shoulders, the guard then swished his stick through the air, and, shouting angrily, sauntered on, down the rows of bent heads.

Once he was out of reach, Mies took a rag from her pocket and wrapped it around my bleeding ankle, which was already covered in flies. I looked up and saw her gray eyes looking into mine and felt safe. I was so exhausted, I could fall asleep. But I knew she would take care of me. Someone would take care of me.

Christmas Day brought another postcard from Dad. Like the first one, it didn't tell us anything, and though not completely his handwriting, the scribbles came close enough for us to believe that he had written it. Anyway, we wanted to believe it came from Dad. We needed to trust that he was still alive. And it made for a wonderful Christmas present!

Christmas Day also brought extra food. Five bananas, three eggs, and sago porridge with brown sugar and coconut milk. In the soup, we even found a few chunks of chicken. Having all this together with Dad's postcard, we felt richer and happier than we had for a long time.

Even Mom was happy, yet something was still missing in her. After we'd eaten, she took Dad's postcard, read it for us a few times, and then laughed and kissed it.

"He must be still okay," she said. "He is still in the same place. Not much change in his conditions." Then she put the card on the tea box that we used as a table, and planted her soup bowl on top like a paperweight.

There it stayed the rest of Christmas day, seen by all of us, and close enough to be touched, but driving the end of the war, the end of all this, farther away than ever. Would we ever see Dad again, be together again, all of us as a normal family? If only we could, I was certain that Mom would become Mom again.

That night, staring into the dark, I saw Dad the way he had looked one day when we had walked home together from the school where he was a principal. I had told him that I would be a doctor when I grew up and would specialize in finding out why some people lost their minds when there was trouble, while others always found a way out.

He had laughed and swung his arm over my shoulder. "You are a strong girl, Sofia. You'll always find a way out!"

Now, I didn't want to be strong. I wanted to be the way I had been when I was nine years old and happy, without a care in the world. I wanted clean clothes, a bed, and school every day. I wanted a full stomach and buckets of cool water to drink from. I wanted to sing and run and play games with my friends. I wanted to be just the way I was before this mess had started.

The wind roared outside, rustling the dry, old *atap* roof. I was afraid, since sometimes fine dust came down when the wind blew with so much force, and sometimes even would blow a hole through the roof, letting the rain through in a filmy spray that dampened the *klamboes*.

"Do your very best, Sofia," he had said, "and then go the extra mile."

More wind, more rattling, and sudden roof jerks.

My very best isn't good enough, Dad, I thought, *and the extra mile is just too long!*

Mom started to sing in her sleep, softly. It was a nursery song. But she couldn't remember all the words, so she would hum till the words came to her again. Her spirit was spending more time where she felt safe. In a place where she wouldn't have to see her starving, dirty kids, full of lice and crusty eczema. Her once beautifully dressed, clean children who now had knobby knees, spindly legs, and large tight bellies. Bellies filled with nagging hunger, worms, dysentery, and other disease.

Our bellies always hurt these days, and when Easabella and Emma-M tried to squat, they were so weak, they would topple over. Simon and I had rotting teeth, and I often heard Simon moan during his sleep while rubbing his sore gums.

"The extra mile is much too long, Dad," I whispered. "We are all alone now!"

Listening to the wind outside, blowing to somewhere far away, I gave it a message for Dad. "I am not strong, Dad. Please come back. Please don't let me go it alone. I am all empty now and I can't remember where it all went. We can't hang in there much longer!"

Then as Mom hummed her lullaby, I fell asleep.

The next morning, I took Dad's postcard. We'd had it for two weeks now and Mom kept putting her soup bowl on top of it after she ate. It had soup stains from the bowl.

Folding it in two, I spread it against her skin between her breasts, where she had kept the first one until the words had faded. Her bra had kept it in place.

"Dad's most recent postcard, Mom," I told her. "Remember, you kept the first card close to your heart?" I closed her dress over the card. "Keep this one in the same place, Mom, so the words will float into your heart and you'll remember him."

She looked at me, not really seeing me. I was so used to it by now that I didn't really mind anymore. She started to rock, wrapping her arms around herself.

"Not too long anymore, Sofia, not too long," she whispered.

I nodded, not understanding, and actually not wanting to understand, but saying anyway, "No, Mom, not too long anymore. It all will soon end."

As in the last camp, many died at Belawan Estate, and to haul away the bodies we often only had baskets. These baskets, which were large enough to hold the average-sized woman's body, were woven on a regular basis by a group of older women. From working constantly with the rough twigs, these women had fingers that were as raw as their conversation. Often, they would quietly speculate whom the current basket might hold, while cynically joking that it might be one of them. We used to have pre-made baskets brought to us on the supply truck, but as soon those were used, the long pliable twigs came instead, with clear orders to use them to weave more.

Still, sometimes there were more dead people than baskets; the supply of handmade baskets ran out before the weavers had another one ready. In those cases, baskets in which we had already sent our dead off would be sent back to us, and we would have to reuse them till more were made.

I had seen the nurses prepare many bodies and didn't think too much of it anymore. First, the body would be wrapped in a sheet. Then the nurses would open the lids that had been woven over each end of the basket, put in the wrapped body, and pull it to the top end. The lids would then be closed and each lid would be tied to the basket with a separate stringy twig. It would not open again, unless someone would undo the stringy twigs. A few times when tall women died, the baskets were not long enough and their feet would stick out so far that only the top lid over their head would close. Then Nadine would leave the bottom lid open and wrap towels over the body's feet.

Once prepared, the baskets were lugged along the "drag path" to the gate. The drag path was created by the large bags of rice and *oebi* (potato) flour that were carried daily from their delivery spot at the gate to the kitchen warehouse. Often, the bags were too heavy for the women, and had to be dragged over the ground, creating a path.

At the gates, the makeshift casket would be met by a *grobak,* which would then carry the body away to be buried. No one ever knew where.

It was heartbreaking to witness the grief of mothers not knowing where their children went. Regularly, it seemed, there was a mother standing at the gates, crying and staring endlessly in the direction in which her child had disappeared, as if hoping her baby might come back.

"What happens to the dead people, Mies?" I asked one day. "I mean when the baskets come back?"

"You don't need to know, Sofia." Not able to avoid my eyes, Mies then explained, "Our dead people are rolled in an extra sheet and then in a tarp before they are laid to rest in a grave. They don't feel it anymore, Sofia. Their spirit has left their body, which they do not need anymore."

I had nothing to say. It made no difference to me. By now I had seen so many baskets.

When Jaap Martelaar's grandmother had died in the middle of the night, Jaap went to Nadine for help, and then lived with her after that, since he had nobody else. Nadine had washed his grandma and, with the help of another nurse, tried to fit her into the largest basket they had. Jaap's grandmother was tall, however, so the lid had to be tied up with her feet sticking out. Nadine wrapped them in a towel, as usual, but then, because it was so late at night, did not take her to the gate. Instead, they left her in a supply room next to the clinic. The supply room had a clay floor, which kept the room a bit cooler, and Nadine figured this might help preserve the body until they could move it in the morning.

Early the next day, Jaap followed some women from the clinic over to the supply room, and when they lifted the basket, they revealed thousands of crawling maggots underneath. The women had expected this; they had seen it many times before. But Jaap had not.

Peter had been walking with Jaap and had seen what happened, and when he told me the part about the maggots, I remembered Sitah and Hassan. I had seen maggots before when I had gone with Hassan to the market to buy firewood for Sitah. Before we had entered the market square, I had seen a dead little dog lying next to the road. Traffic had covered it with dust.

I had told Hassan that dead animals should be buried; they had spent their lives guarding and loving their owners and therefore deserved this last honor. Hassan looked at me and turned back. He pulled a fresh banana leaf from a tree and cut it away from the core. He threw half of the leaf on the ground, and then using the other half to cover his hands, he carefully lifted the dog onto it. Then he carried it deeper into the gutter, in a place no one could see it. The dog had left white, wormy maggots swarming over each other; there were thousands of them.

Appalled at the sight, I looked at Hassan, who explained that maggots were necessary and useful—they were the garbage cleaners of everything dead. When maggots were done with a body, he said, all that was left were bones, which the earth would eventually swallow.

Hassan had had admiration in his voice when he'd said, "Maggots are great, but they also look scary. Never be afraid of them, Sofia, they are harmless."

Peter told me that after seeing the maggots, Jaap, walking next to his grandmother's basket, had started to shake and then wrapped his arms around himself. Then he had started to walk so slow that he fell behind everyone else.

Halfway down the path, the towel around his grandma's feet loosened and then fell off. Not noticing, the women continued to pull the basket toward the gate, and Jaap started to scream as he watched his grandmother's feet dragging on the path the rest of the way. The clinic women took him back to Nadine, who tried unsuccessfully to calm him down.

For the rest of the day, Jaap wouldn't eat, and when evening came, he continued screaming, disturbing the patients in the clinic. So Nadine left him with Mies for the night. Despite neighbors in Mies's barrack yelling at him to shut up, he screamed the whole night, even after his voice had become a hoarse whisper.

The next day, when I went to Nadine to have the sore on my ankle looked after, Jaap was there. I could tell by his bloodshot eyes and his pale skin that he hadn't slept, and he came up to me as soon as he saw me.

Grabbing my arm, his face came close. His staring eyes scared me and his hands were strong, as if he didn't want to let me go. "Did you see her feet, Sofia?" his voice finally squeaked out. "You must have seen her feet! The nails are gone, gone, gone!"

And a few days later, when Jaap's voice came back all the way, this was all he said, over and over again, to anyone who would listen.

I couldn't help Jaap, but he filled my head during the day, and Peter didn't want to talk about him. Then the nights were worse. I saw his grandmother's feet sticking out of the basket, her body falling apart neatly—toes first and the feet next, followed swiftly by the knees, the body, and the head. I ran away from it, but the basket followed me.

Upon waking, I couldn't stop the jittering. My knees knocked the *tampat*, right through the thin mattress pad, banging out a haunted rhythm: "*Ratta-tat, ratta-tat!*"

I sat up the rest of the night, my arms tight around my shaking knees, to make sure I wouldn't fall asleep again.

The sore on my ankle that had been opened by the Japanese guard with his bamboo stick was starting to fester and hurt. Nadine explained that tiny bamboo hair had been left behind in my skin and that bacteria had started an ulcer. To make it better, the bacteria should be killed, but there wasn't anything in the clinic to do that, so Nadine did the best she could. Each day, she pushed out a thick blob of puss, cleansed the wound with boiled water, and put a new dressing on. Still, the sore slowly became deeper and bigger. It hurt a lot, and for awhile I tried to put as little weight as possible on my left leg.

Peter also had become weaker. While working in the gardens, he tired quickly, so whenever the soldier wasn't looking, I tried to do some of his work. Then one morning, Peter didn't come to the *koempoelan* square. We were excused from *koempoelan* only when we were extremely sick or unconscious. When you didn't show up because of illness, the Japanese soldiers didn't touch you, but always checked on you, and you usually had to show up anyway. If you were a sick child, you may not even be checked on; your mother was just sent to bring you out. This is what happened to Peter. Weak and feverish from malaria, he stood leaning into his mother with his head under her arm. Still, the soldier, after counting us several times, always looking closely at Peter, decided that my small, sick friend was fit enough to work that day.

So after *koempoelan*, Peter walked next to me in the long row of tired children, out the gate and into the wide-open fields. He said he was short of breath and dizzy, and as he worked, he just looked straight ahead. When I could, I worked parts of his stretch. One of these times, we didn't see the guard approach.

Peter was leaning on his hands, trying to gather his strength. His arms were trembling and he was breathing deeply. His face was flushed from fever and heat. Then suddenly, there were the hated black boots accompanied by soft but dangerous laughter above our heads. We froze, fearing there was worse to come. A few seconds of nothing. Heat waved around us, and the buzzing of mosquitoes became more shrill, all backed by the soldier's soft laughing, which rose to a growl. Then he moved.

He put his boot on one of Peter's hands and pressed down hard. Pete screamed, but didn't try to move his hand away from the boot. Instead, he bent down lower, elbow on the ground, as if to give his hand more space. There wasn't any space.

The soldier laughed louder and pivoted his foot to one side and then back, before stepping away and moving farther down the row of bent backs, laughing the entire way. Peter left his hand there, partly pushed into the clay. It looked bruised and pitiful.

"Bastard, goddamned bastard," he whispered. "I'm going to kill you as soon as I'm free. I am, you bastard, you'll see!"

He said this over and over until finally he gathered enough courage to pick up his crushed hand with his good one. Cradling it carefully, he shoved it between his skin and shirt, which was now held together with just one button.

"God, that hurts, Jesus, that hurts, ahhh, man, this hurts like hell!" He bent over his sore hand, almost touching the weeds with his face and stayed there, suffering, softly cursing and whimpering.

I searched down the field for the soldier, and when I saw that he was close, I nudged Peter. "He's coming, Pete, get up!"

Peter straightened, but kept his hand hidden in his shirt, working feverishly with his other hand to pull up the weeds.

The soldier came by and laughed uproarishly when he saw Peter working with one hand. The rest of the day, whenever he passed us, he sneered and snickered, leaving Peter cursing and hating.

I did most of Peter's stretch that day and helped him to Nadine's at the end of it. By that point, I couldn't think straight anymore, and the absolute worst part was that I had wet my shorts again. If Pete had noticed, he'd never mentioned it.

The next day, Peter gave me his black-heart marble. "You take it, Sofia," he said, putting it in my palm with his good hand. "I have no use for it anymore."

I looked at him, puzzled. His hand was swollen and blue, and he winced when anything touched it, even his shirtsleeve.

"The flame inside used to move and show signs of life whenever I looked at it," he said. "It used to tell me the most gorgeous things. It took me to foreign lands and showed me colors without names."

He took it out of my hand again and looked at it, rolling it between his fingertips. "I have not seen it move for a long time. I can't remember the colors or the foreign lands. I must have imagined it all."

He gave it back to me. "You have it. You are my friend, Sofie. You have wanted it for a long time. It is the best thing I have."

The whole rest of the day, I thought about his words. I knew they should have meant something, but I didn't care about the black-heart marble any longer. I hadn't played for so long that I couldn't even understand or remember why I had wanted it so badly. Why had it been so important to me? Marbles were for kids, and I didn't feel like a kid. So what did that make me—a grown-up? But grown-ups were twenty years or older.

I was almost twelve now, but often felt older than Mom. My body felt awkward and clumsy, thin, and swollen at the same time. My legs were the same width from above the knee to below the ankle. They looked awkward and felt heavy. When I pushed my thumbs into the skin of my knees or ankles, they made hollows, and it took awhile for the indents to come out again. My legs didn't fit my body anymore. Was this feeling like a grown-up?

At the same time, I always felt scared. I could think only about food and how to get it. I reflexively bent down for punishment and bowed in subservience. And I longed for simple things that I could not have, silly things like ripe mangos, *saté* (pork shish kebabs) at the end of the day, riding my bike, and Sitah's arms around me. Plus, I had peed my shorts several times just recently. Grown-ups didn't do that!

I felt around in my pocket for Peter's marble and touched it. Warmth filled me all the way up, starting in my tummy, reaching my chest, and saturating my heart.

"You have it, Sofie," Pete's voice rang through my mind. "You are my friend!"

I did Peter's stretches of weeding for the next two weeks, which is how long it took before he could use his hand again, although it stayed blue for a long time after that.

Hope had left, and despair and indifference had taken its place. There was nothing left to look forward to.

The Red Cross boxes were forgotten, as no others followed.

The mothers were fighting with each other and screaming at their children daily.

The camp began to stink and become littered. Water that had spilled during various transports mixed together with miscellaneous debris, and formed trashy puddles throughout the camp, randomly mixed with spots of diarrhea and urine left by the increasing numbers of sick people who couldn't reach the latrines in time. The flies celebrated. They came down on everything—mud, sores, shit, dead bodies—and then moved on to eyes, lips, hands, and food.

Disease and hunger was all around us. The Japanese soldiers didn't even walk through the camp anymore for fear of the sickness, the dysentery, the fevers, and the numerous festering sores. But they circled the fences constantly, and when bored or ill-tempered, continued to amuse themselves by making blows to prisoners and loud conversation among themselves.

Mies often got hit because she did things the guards didn't like. She helped others carry too heavy loads. She shared *corvee* duties with the sick. She talked too loud or didn't bow deep enough. Yet, she remained the same. She did what she wanted to do, calm and determined.

But for the rest of us, the grim days and weeks and months had taken too much of a toll. People forever complained. They could no longer find anything to rejoice in or laugh about. Whenever women were together, all they could talk about was food and medication.

Mies always said that hope worked better than food and medication, but she laughed once when I said, "I would prefer food and medication at this time, thank you very much."

The rations became smaller and the quality poorer, if that was possible. We went weeks without fresh fruit or vegetables. Meat and eggs were only a memory. Salt and sugar became rare and were often taken away as punishment. The daily soup consisted of a few noodles floating between some beans or peas. And the bread failed to rise, since it had to be baked from *oebi* flour without yeast, which had run out long ago. The raw rice from the sacks was filthy, covered with insects that had gotten in and had a feast. Strings of webs, spun by rice bugs, glued the grains together. Some grains were half-eaten.

Simon couldn't eat the bread without soaking it in the soup, because it made his gums bleed instantly, and when there was no soup, water did the trick. Easabella refused to eat the rice when it smelled bad and traded it with Emma-M for soup. And when eating the soup, Emma-M's tummy grew tight and hard, after which she said she was full and then had to puke. While squatting in the latrines, she had to wait so long for anything to come out that her little rectum had come down. When I saw this, I was more alarmed than Emma-M, and asked if it didn't hurt. Emma-M seemed used to it, for she said it never hurt but only felt bulky down there. Emma-M never complained much, and she was very independent, wanting always to do her own thing and refusing help even when she actually needed it, so I thought she was lying to me. But a few months later, I learned that she was right: it didn't hurt, and it only felt bulky.

Still, no matter how bleak the days, and no matter how many baskets were dragged off to the gates, Mies and Nadine never seemed to lose hope. They always talked in a "once this is over" way, and Mies kept promising that there would come an end to it all. Sometimes people believed her, especially when Nadine pointed out that the Japanese soldiers had been acting extra cruel lately, screaming until they were hoarse. They also had been patrolling in pairs, she noted, possibly afraid that they might soon lose the war.

When asked for visions, though, Nadine only shook her head and smiled, saying only one thing: "It will soon end! The end will be soon!"

Then one early morning, though we did not see them, we heard the drone of airplanes in the distance. It was as if a wave of electricity had gone through the camp. The guards seemed jittery, possibly fearing the throngs of desperate, dirty, and diseased women. Hope soared, and a feeling of expectation buzzed over us like a swarm of bees. More whispered rumors came from women claiming to still have hidden radios: "The Japanese army has suffered enormous losses," "The Allies are closing in each day," "They have bombed a Japanese island and are starting to win back what the Godly Emperor conquered!"

The response was nothing short of *"Banzai!* (Hooray!) Banzai, Allied soldiers and flyers, Banzai!

Our glory ended, however, when the radio was discovered and destroyed, and the guards, once more, worked out their anger on us. Nothing ever came of the rumors.

After not seeing Peter for several days, I checked in with Nadine. Nadine had looked him over and then had addressed the Japanese commander, arguing that Peter needed to stay in the clinic, as he was not fit to go to *corvee* or *koempoelan*. She had gotten her way. Peter stayed in the clinic during the day, except when he had to leave to go to the latrines. He was weak and miserable and spent all his time lying in bed or crouched over a latrine hole. His belly was constantly cramped with pain and there was blood in his stool every day. Sonja, his little sister, cleaned him before Nadine took him to her clinic, whenever he let her.

Nadine told his mother that Peter had dysentery and shouldn't have anything but boiled rice water. So every day before she went for *corvee* duty, she got a bowl of rice water from the kitchen, which Sonja took to the clinic and patiently gave to Peter each time he opened his eyes. And each time, Peter spit it out, saying it didn't taste right.

When I wasn't at *corvee* or taking care of the little girls, I sat with him at the clinic. Sonja would then leave to help her mom wash Peter's clothes. On one particular day, he had slipped into a half-sleep, his fists pressed into his belly as if to hold back the painful, draining cramps. His pants were soiled again, but I didn't want to disturb him. I looked at Peter. It seemed the bones in his body had given up holding him. Always small for his age, he now looked only slightly older than Simon.

His eyes shifted under the glassy eyelids, and I swooped my hand over his face to chase off the flies. The mosquito net around his bed was pulled back. Peter had torn it this morning, when he'd rushed off to the latrine and gotten his foot caught in it. The net hadn't given much protection anyway; it had been riddled with holes. His Mom had tried to tie the worst holes, but Peter just hooked his toes in them and opened them back up.

He moaned and rolled on his side, pulling up his knees to his chest. I reached for the rice water, but before I could give it to him, he rolled off the bed and ran off toward the latrines. I jumped up and followed him. He never made it. Before he reached the building, the stinky stuff came out of him, darkening his pants and running down his legs in a thin brown liquid, streaked with blood.

"Goddamned shit," Peter yelled, squatting over the closest hole he could reach, panting, without even the strength to remove his pants. He started to cry.

I ran over to him. "Let me help you, Pete, please. You are shitting your pants."

Eyes closed, Peter leaned forward, not wanting any part of my help, but too weak to say so. Then he slumped over onto his side next to the filthy hole. I dragged him away from it and through the door toward the washroom. There were instant flies on his pants, on his skin, on my hands. He didn't seem to notice; his eyes remained closed.

There was no warm water, but cold water would wash him just as well while also cooling his fever. In the washroom were towels and clothes that had been washed by the women and then hung to dry. They were not completely dry yet, but they were clean. I grabbed a towel and used it to carefully wash him. The cold water brought him to. He looked at me, but didn't say anything, for which I was very grateful.

Peter was my friend. We had gone through this mess together. He felt more like a brother to me than Simon. I turned him over, looking with horror at his raw rectum. The turning had hurt him and brought soft moaning. I felt my own tears falling on my hands. I didn't need tears; I needed clean clothes. I grabbed some that I thought would fit him, but it took a long time to change him, as he wasn't much help and I hesitated to move him too quickly. I started by sliding the pants gently under his legs, and by the time I had the shirt on, his pants were dirty again. I had no strength left to start the process over and just sank next to him. Tears again—unwanted and useless. I angrily wiped them away. My hands stank, even though they were clean. What would I do now?

Peter opened his eyes and looked at me. "It's no use, Sofia, I'll be dirty like this all day. Don't even bother. Just keep the flies away from my face."

I didn't answer; I couldn't trust my voice. I felt the flat desperation in Peter's voice deep in myself and knew that if I started talking, I would cry, which wouldn't help Peter. I felt helpless and depleted. I wished I would stop feeling, just for awhile.

"Do you think all this will ever end, Sofie? Will we ever hear music again or listen to the birds singing in the morning?"

I pulled him up against my shoulders and so we sat for awhile, Peter and I, until he fell asleep. Leaning against the washroom wall, I let my mind go empty. Too tired to think, I felt content, sitting on the hard floor next to the stinking washroom with Peter against me.

I was not lonely there with Peter.

When he woke up, we stumbled back to the clinic together, where Mies took over, changing him again and helping him to bed.

As I watched, fear washed over me like a storm. I could tell that the short walk between the washroom and the clinic had exhausted him. What if he died? He looked dead already. The only sign that he wasn't was his open mouth, breathing hard.

"Will he be all right, Mies?" I was afraid of her answer, but I was aching for hope.

"I don't know, Sofia. Peter is still young. He has a lot to live for." Mies looked at me. "And he has a good friend!"

I stayed with Peter until I had to leave for *corvee*. I had a feeling that if I hung around doing little things for him, I could keep death away. I didn't want him to be put into a twig basket, to disappear forever in some faraway hole.

Peter didn't die, but he remained so weak that he couldn't join me to roam the camp or check out the kitchen scraps. He got better food in the clinic, anyway: soft soupy rice boiled in a broth prepared from cubes, with mashed peas and a bit of ground meat.

After *corvee,* I wandered alone along the fences, touching the spikes between the spaces of barbed wire and spitting on the ground whenever a guard passed. It had just rained. The sun was still hidden and the damp air hung heavy around the buildings. Everything was wet and gray, giving me a feeling that I could not identify. It was somber and nervous all at once.

If the rain came back and went all night like it had been doing regularly, the ground would be flooded by morning. Then Easabella and Emma-M would not be allowed to play outside until the overflow had sunk into the mud, leaving soggy kitchen waste and little dead animals behind—scorpions, flies, and beetles.

Wandering on, I looked for my enemies, the flies, and whenever I stepped on one, I squeezed it dead with my bare foot. I was proud of my calloused feet. I could kick apart hot ashes without getting burned, fish a thorn or splinter out of my heel that I hadn't even known had gone in, pass the afternoon hours standing on the hot asphalt of the *koempoelan* square. I was only barefoot, though, because I no longer had sandals to wear, and I wasn't the only one. Almost all of the children went around on bare feet. Thousands of foot and toe prints were visible on the square from our standing barefoot on the asphalt, which softened in the heat of the day and hardened again at night. My soles were forever brown and dirty-looking from the clay, and the flies that I'd smashed into bloody, flat masses had left their prints in the criss-crossed lines and grooves of my calloused feet. Although they were not orange from betel juice, Hassan would be proud of them. I wondered if Hassan had felt the way I did now before becoming *mata-glap* (crazy). Maybe this feeling was the monkey in my chest, waiting to be freed.

That thought really got me going, and I moved faster, almost running. The day was gone now; the wind grew stronger and hard rain would soon follow. The dark shape of our barrack loomed, the door illuminated in a faint rectangle. Lifting my face to the sky, I felt the cool wind and saw the highest trees fading spindly and black into the eerie gray distance. Somewhere far away, the rain began to fall, and as it neared, I knew its soft whisper would grow gradually into a loud roar.

Sitah, Hassan, Dad. Where was Dad? What if, perhaps, he didn't think about us anymore? Pain and longing and homesickness churned inside me, making me uncomfortable. Searching the sky again between the spooky treetops, I found it now colored a deep red, and melting into purple. What caused the sky to have such wonderful clouds? It was too beautiful for prisoners dying prematurely and alone. I longed to touch it and bring it down to share with everyone. A bit of beauty to help us all through.

A few raindrops hit my face.

Sitah always believed that red and purple clouds were a reflection of the souls of unborn children—happy, but also mourning because they had not been allowed to be born. Is that what it felt like to be dead? Or did you feel nothing? Either way, I didn't think I would mind knowing that I was dying.

The rain had reached the camp and came down hard now. Soaked, I moved under the roof overhang of my barrack and listened for it to pass. Then hoping it would take my restless thoughts with it, I went inside.

The next morning, Mom gave me a solemn kiss on the cheek before we had our daily porridge and hard bread.

I was both surprised and suspicious. "What's wrong? What's that for?"

"Happy birthday, Sofia!" she said. "Let's hope the next one will be happier, and we will be somewhere other than a camp!"

And so it was. I had lost track of the weeks and months; I didn't realize it had been a year already. I didn't even know what day of the week it was. Each day was so much the same, going to the kitchen for food, hurrying to *koempoelan*, running for the latrine with belly aches, rushing to the gardens for *corvee,* and watching the little girls—and lately also Simon. Simon looked almost transparent these days. I was afraid I would look into his eyes one day and see the bones inside his head. And Emma-M was getting even sicker, evidenced by a moment last week when she had proudly showed me a long white worm that she had saved for me to see. She had pulled it out of her rectum, as she hadn't wanted to drop it in the latrine hole. I had laughed, though, because at least it was a break in the monotony. Emma-M could be a cool kid! We walked to the latrine, where, holding it between two fingers, she dropped it into a hole. As I watched, I knew that mine were somewhere in there too. Having worms didn't mean you were seriously ill, but it was far from normal and made your rectum really itchy.

Now, my pale brother was offering a birthday present. He had saved his banana from our meal three days ago. With tremendous effort, he had hidden his treasure, only sticking his tongue every now and then into the tiny hollow where the stem had been. Lying there, next to my bowl in its black peel, it smelled of overripe sweetness.

I looked at Mom, and she smiled. "Some willpower he has, Sofia. I don't think he could have held out much longer. He would have eaten it."

"No, I wouldn't!" Simon protested.

I looked at him then, at Simon my brother. I had known him all my life. His light eyes, his gentle face, and his quiet movements. Something warm and happy moved through me. I had been wrong all along. I didn't resent him; I respected him. Hell, I loved him just like Mom and Easabella and Emma-M did.

Wrapping my arms around him, I kissed his orange-red hair. "Thank you, Simon. You sure are my little brother!"

He pulled a face, because I had called him little, but then laughed. "And you are my big sister!"

I cut the banana into five pieces and we each had one on our slice of bread. It was the happiest breakfast we'd had in a long time.

Whenever two or more Japanese soldiers stormed through the gate, we knew they were after something: a notebook, a radio, or a thief. This time it was boys. Boys who had reached the age of eleven. They were considered men now and therefore had to move to an all-male camp to work.

The commander summoned Mrs. Frost and informed her that the boys were to move in two days. She then called all of the barrack leaders together, and told them to let the mothers know. The boys were allowed to bring only one bag and had to be ready to leave after the morning *koempoelan*. The mothers cried, as did most of the departing boys.

Jaap Martelaar also had to leave, but he didn't cry. He shrugged his shoulders.

"One camp or another, there's not much difference. We'll all still die and rot." There was no hope left in Jaap; he was indifferent to everything. He still lived in Nadine's barrack, where she kept an eye on him, but other than that, Jaap had no one to belong to and no one to care for. He did *corvee* duty and went for his own meals and that was it. So he had closed the door on everyone but Nadine.

When the time came two days later, we were standing in rows on the *koempoelan* square when they came running through the gate—four Japanese soldiers with harsh shouts and large rifles. One of them was the commander. They pushed the boys-turned-men to the front and shoved the mothers back as they reached out to attempt final hugs and kisses.

Then with closed faces and hating eyes, we watched as the boys were thrust into two rows and marched out of camp. There were no trucks waiting. They simply marched through the gate and into the forest, two by two and silent, not daring to look back for fear the whip would reach them. No waving, no last shouts. They just disappeared, leaving their mothers and friends in fear and doubt. They left empty spaces everywhere.

It made me anxious about Peter. He would be eleven later this year.

Looking over the stretch of bowed women and crouching children, the little commander had mounted a wooden box and was now standing on it, so that he could see it all. He was angry.

Just awhile before, Mrs. Frost, Nadine, and the kitchen supervisor had marched through the gate and demanded to speak to the commander, who spoke a bit of Indonesian. They had presented him with a long list of demands and complaints.

First on the list was the lack of food and medication. The food we were given was either of poor quality or smelled bad. Malaria, dysentery, beriberi, and festering sores needed attention and were not addressed by a qualified doctor.

The women were not strong enough anymore to do the garden work and the heavy *corvee* duties.

The children were severely undernourished and had a serious need for clothes. Almost none of them had shoes.

The list went on, but the commander hadn't even read it to the end before he had exploded in a fury. He had shoved the women out of his office and shouted something at the guards. Then the *koempoelan* bell had sounded, and here we were again, listening to the mad raving tyrant on the wooden box.

This time, he said, battering wasn't enough; severe punishment was in order. We had offended the *Tenno Heiko,* the God Emperor, and therefore, we were evil people. The God Emperor had been good to the prisoners—he had given food and water and protection for which we didn't have to pay. And see how he was rewarded—with rebellion and betrayal, with unrest and complaints! Evil people must be severely punished, so that they would not offend the *Teino Heiko* again.

Furiously hopping on his wooden box, the commander looked almost comical and all of us watched, fascinated. I was waiting anxiously to see him lose his balance, praying he would make that humiliating tumble. But, unfortunately, it didn't happen.

"Severe punishment," as it turned out, meant no food. So all of the supplies from the kitchen were removed, except for food that had already been cooked. Moving the heavy bags of rice to the gate required brute strength, so the guards sent in a group of *koelies*. These laborers carried the bags between them beyond the gate. Some of the bags split, and the rice spilled out and was left were it scattered. I looked at the spilled, dusty rice mixed with the webby grains that we had been eating for months. *No one*, I thought, *could do anything to deserve being so severely punished.* So maybe Nadine was right.

The crowd of prisoners watched in silence. After the last bags were removed from the kitchen, the gates closed with a loud bang, and the guards stood behind the fence, holding their rifles. They were watching the crowd of prisoners come closer.

We stood along the fence, a long line of dirty, shabbily dressed women and children, with hands clawed around the wire and with furious, hating eyes. And that is how we stood till the end of the day. Mute protest was our only way to fight back. We had one meal left.

Mom had some bread left over from the day before, however, and when I got back with our evening meal, she had broken it into small pieces. Simon and the little girls ate; Mom and I were not hungry. We saved our leftovers for the next day, together with the rest of the bread, when we could expect no food. I hoped it would rain during the night. It would make the temperature cooler, for in the tropics food would spoil fast, if not refrigerated. We went to bed early; there was not much else to do. Mom went to sleep quickly, probably happy to slip into her dreams, and she talked softly through the night. I couldn't sleep. I was scared. What would happen tomorrow with no food? After the lights went out, darkness was complete. Its somber stillness was rarely broken, and then only by a crying child, a whispered prayer, or the sound of hands slapping at mosquitoes. The night seemed endless.

It did rain during the night. Walking through the gate the next morning on our way to the gardens, I glanced at the food rations scattered on the clay. Soggy with rain, the food looked like a pile of garbage. The rice still in the jute bags would not be able to dry for a long time and would rot. And the salt and sugar bags had broken, and been melted by the rain into a gray layer of worthless sludge. There it sat for all of us to see, and we longed for it, despite it being ruined and covered in flies.

It wasn't until the end of the second day without food that the commander told those of us who had again gathered at the fence that the *Teino Heiko,* in his generosity and kindness, had taken pity on us; he was satisfied with two days of punishment.

There was no reaction. We waited for the rest of the announcement to follow, afraid to be too quickly relieved.

"You can take the food back," the commander finally announced generously. "You can carry the rice bags to the kitchen and have food tonight."

We were only allowed to cook as long as there was daylight, and by now, daylight would be gone in two hours—and the food was still outside the fence. To boot, two days without food had taken its toll on our strength, and now wet, the rice bags had become twice as heavy. We were able to drag in the salt and sugar, but it was a sloppy mess, and when Nadine tasted some, she said the soil had rendered it useless.

The guards watched, and I heard them joke among themselves. By now, they had learned broken Indonesian.

"Carry the bags yourselves, or leave them!" one shouted, and they laughed harder.

There we stood, hungry and weak, before the sneering guards, who had begun to repeatedly stamp their rifle butts on the ground, enjoying our grief. We were no impressive sight the way we stood there in a massive block, unmoving, uttering silent pleas for mercy. Painfully thin women and children with desperate eyes in colorless clothes over beriberi bellies. But we had something else too: stubborn defiance.

Mrs. Frost suddenly straightened up and turned back toward the camp, and as the guards stood watching, the rest of us followed suit. Together, we marched away from the gate, and then one voice rose in song and was instantly joined by the others. In seconds, we were all singing loud and hard:

> *Een karretje langs de zandweg reed,*
>> A little cart drove along the sandy road,
>
> *De maan scheen helder, de weg was breed,*
>> The moon was bright, the road was broad,
>
> *Het paardje liep met lusten*
>> The horse galloped happily
>
> *Ik wed dat het zelf de weg wel weet,*
>> I bet he knows the road himself,
>
> *De voerman lee te rusten.*
>> So the driver could dose off.
>
> *Ik wens je wel thuis me—vriend, me—vriend*
>> I wish you a good trip, my friend, my friend

> *Ik wens je wel thuis, me—vriend.*
> I wish you a good trip home, my friend.

We all knew this silly Dutch song. Every child learned it either in school or at home. It was an old, gentle folk melody, but we sang in a militant way, while marching off and leaving the soldiers gaping in silence. We stomped on, comforted by one another's courage and pride, until we had disappeared into the barracks, where we again faced everything we'd wanted to forget.

All through the night, kids cried and whined, restless with hunger. Some mothers were irritated while others sang soft lullabies. On our *tampat*, Emma-M moaned at times, and Simon was silent but awake. Easabella didn't cry at all, but I wished she would. I had not heard a sound from her in days, and she looked as bad now as she had before she'd left for the hospital at Lawe Sigalagala. Red spots, where she had scratched itchy mosquito bites, stood out on the pale skin of her face and arms, looking angry and infected. We all had bites, but Simon's and Easabella's seemed the worst. Mom had said it was because they were redheads and had sweet blood.

As usual, Mom stayed asleep the whole night, not letting anything interfere with her private peace. But when she woke up the next morning, she looked strange. Her face was puffy, and I could barely see her eyes. She ran her tongue over her dry lips again and again.

I gave her water, but her lips remained white and scaly, and she looked feverish.

"Which camp are we in, Sofia?" With her signature faraway gaze, she wiped her face with her sleeve. It was then that I noticed that she had slept in her dress, which she had never done before. At least she remembered my name.

"We are in Camp Belawan Estate, Mom." I wiped her face with a wet towel.

Easabella shrieked. Her crying had become painful and shrill to the ear.

Mom winced. "What is wrong with her? Why is she crying like that? Tell her to stop, Sofia!"

I picked up Easabella and looked at Simon.

"Don't you remember, Mom?" Simon went to her, but she looked beyond him at something none of us saw. "We are hungry. We have not eaten for days!" Then Simon started to cry.

Suddenly, Mom looked at him. It was as if seeing him upset had touched something deeply buried. "Why not?"

And Simon told her, because Mom did not remember the last few days. Perhaps, she had lost the last few weeks; Mom had been hiding a long time.

After that, Simon could not stop crying. I had never seen him like that before. He seemed to cry for everything he had gone through the last three years. For himself, his sisters, and his Mom. For everything he had lost and everything he hated and did not understand. For emptiness and longing and grief over losing all that was good and dear to him. He seemed to empty himself with a cry that was so touching and lonely that I couldn't stand hearing it. I put Easabella down and wrapped my arms around him. His body shuddered, and his crying became painful heaves of breathing, until slowly he calmed down.

Mom watched Simon until he was quiet. Then her eyes moved from Simon, over to Easabella and Emma-M, and finally to me. Suddenly, her hands moved. She grabbed her brush and started to stroke her hair vigorously away from her face. Once she had worked through the snags, she moved off the *tampat* and straightened her rumpled dress. Her feet felt for her sandals. (Mom still had sandals and never, ever walked on bare feet; it made her turn cold, imagining all kinds of little creatures waiting to nibble on them.) She walked briskly outside, and I followed her anxiously, Emma-M on my hip and Simon trailing me. Easabella stayed behind, uninterested.

Mom walked on, her back straight and purposeful, and I started to cry, lugging Emma-M from hip to hip. "Where are you going, Mom? What are you going to do?"

She didn't answer but just walked on with the determination of someone who knew what to do. She was such an unusual sight that people started to take notice and kids started running next to us. She marched past the barracks, past the kitchen, and straight to the gate. It was not yet eight o'clock in the morning, so the guards watched us, obviously suspicious. They pointed their guns.

I set Emma-M down, but she wouldn't walk, so I dragged her the rest of the way. My heart banged in my head. Suppose Mom had become *mataglap* (crazy) and tried to attack the guards—they would spear her with their bayonets! I was so terrified that my clothes felt wet, and I didn't care whether it was from sweat or urine.

Pulling her arm, I cried, "Don't, Mom, please don't! They'll kill you. Please come back with us!"

Mom shrugged me away and rattled the gate. "Open!" she shouted. "Open this gate!" Her voice sounded hard and hoarse, but her eyes were calm, as she rattled the gate without pause.

Several guards came down the steps of the guardhouse and they acted careful, not sure what to expect. Mom stopped rattling the gate and pointed at the pile of rice bags on the other side. One of the guards unlocked the gates, and she walked through. Then without saying more, she marched to the heap of sorry-looking rice bags.

Time stood still. People had gathered at the gate, but there was no sound. There was only fog hanging around us, somber and heavy, without the presence of the sun. My hands gripped the fence. Fear had paralyzed my body and mind, and I couldn't move when I saw Mom walking through the gates. What was she going to do? She was out there by herself, except for the two Japanese guards standing close by. Mom stopped at the rice bags. She looked at the soldiers and then at the gathered crowd of prisoners. Her eyes looked dazed, and she hesitated. Then she seemed to make up her mind. She must have thought back to what had happened in the barrack—about Simon's heart-breaking wailing for food and attention—and it must have struck her how thin and frail he had become.

She rose to her full height—in my eyes, taller than everyone else. Despite her hollow eyes, thin lips, and scrawny neck, she looked spectacular. She bent over, her large hands grabbed one of the jute bags, and then my mother began to pull. She pulled the bag through the gates, walking backward into the camp between the people who made way for her. She made a thin trail of raw, wet rice, which had escaped from the broken jute bags, all the way to the kitchen storeroom. There, she left the bag, marched back to the rice pile outside the gates, and did this three more times, before finally collapsing on top of the newly formed pile in the kitchen. She had found a solution for her hungry son and had, somewhere, found the strength to do something extraordinary.

All hell broke loose then. People shouted and sang, "Hooray, hooray, the food is back!" Other women, encouraged by what they saw, pulled and pushed more rice bags and brought in the rest. People were hopping around Mom, pushing each other to get close to her, and hands grabbed her and pulled at her arms, trying to help her up. I stayed back for fear of putting Emma-M and Simon in danger of being trampled by so many people.

When the horde started moving slowly toward our barrack, I figured Mom must be somewhere in the middle, so I followed, taking Simon and Emma-M with me. As we neared the barracks, people scattered. Mothers found their children and women hurried to the kitchen to prepare meals. By the time we reached our own barrack, there were only children still around us. I could now see Mies Miedema with Phaedra, standing close to their barrack. The excitement had really gotten to me now, and I felt wild.

"That was my mom!" I shouted at Mies. "My beautiful mom, who dragged four heavy rice bags on her own to the kitchen."

"When the need is highest," Mom had used to say, "salvation is near!" And today, she had brought this salvation about all by herself.

I felt so proud of her, I could scream. And scream I did, shouting for everyone to hear. "That was my mom, you know, that was my mom! Wasn't she wonderful? That was my Mom—my Mom!" I sang with happiness and cried with joy.

Then, I couldn't stop myself. I felt hysteria take over. Mies took me to her *tampat*. She tried to make me sit and calm down, and finally had to slap my face once really hard. That stopped the hysteria and emptied everything in me, except for the respect and admiration for my mom that I thought I had lost. Perhaps, I had never lost her, after all, but had just pushed her away too far. I decided never to forget what had happened that day.

That afternoon, we ate again. The soup smelled like fungus, but it was warm and filling after days of hunger. By that time, Mom had gone back inside herself, but I didn't mind. She had at least eaten, and life had returned to her eyes.

As the weeks passed, Mom didn't seem to remember her heroic day and slept whenever she wasn't at *corvee* or *koempoelan*. There were no more good days. There were either bad days or less-bad days. The bad days were filled with shivering fever, diarrhea, and farewells to dying friends. The less-bad days held less punishment, a little richer food, maybe even fruit for the children, and no death at all.

One day, as Simon and I were walking back from the kitchen with our ration of soup and beans, I remembered the chickens that Peter and I used to steal and the snails we used to hunt. At least that had been real meat and something to look forward to at mealtimes.

Avoiding the ever-present dirty puddles, I walked carefully with the hot soup, as it always sloshed easily over the edge. Carrying soup from the kitchen to the barrack was always my chore, because it was too dangerous for Simon, who carried bread and beans and sometimes *nassi tim* (soup with soft rice and mashed peas) for Easabella.

We passed Nadine's clinic and both glanced at two baskets next to the door.

"Dead people," Simon said, without emotion.

I nodded. We had seen enough of them that it felt no different from seeing live people; the dead were just colder. Death didn't frighten us anymore.

Nadine always said that dead people went to God. I didn't know much about God, except that he punished bad and rewarded good, and that when things were very bad, it usually was the devil's work. But that didn't make sense. Things were very bad for us, so where was God now? I decided that God had just forgotten us.

Mies had said once that God was in her, and that she could always find him when she needed to talk. When I asked her if she ever saw him, she smiled.

"I don't need to see him," she said. "I feel that he is inside me. Knowing he is there makes me strong. I am not afraid, because no one can harm me." I didn't understand that either, since she was probably hit more often than anyone by the Japanese soldiers.

When I questioned her about that, she said, "They can hurt my body, Sofia, they can break my skin—but they cannot break my spirit or take away my soul. This is what keeps me free."

"You are not free, Mies," I protested. "You are in a Japanese prison camp with guards and fences. You and all of us are locked up. You can't deny that!"

"They seem strong now, Sofia, but in reality, they are weak; they are lost in command and hysteria. They have lost free will and someone has gambled for their soul. They are the ones to be pitied."

Carrying the hot soup into our barrack, I thought about Mies's words. Had the devil gambled for the Japanese soldiers' souls? Could he gamble for mine?

Kids played in the narrow alleyway between the *tampats,* cluttering it with sticks and stones from which their imaginations had created bridges and cars. They made motor sounds, crouching and moving over one another. I stepped over them, careful to avoid the outstretched arms and feet, when suddenly my foot caught on a thin wire that had been stretched over the alleyway between two bamboo poles on either side. It had been nearly invisible against the clay ground.

Falling, my hands went up, still holding the precious hot soup. Then the pan toppled and flew out of my hands, and things happened all at once. The pan clattered onto the ground, and my ears stupidly followed the bouncing sound it made until it stopped. Kids jumped up and ran, some of them crying or screaming, then mothers came running, and someone let out a terribly high-pitched, never-ending scream that bounced off the barrack walls.

I looked down at my feet and something caught my attention. Some substance that I could not identify was stuck to my toes, and some of it also draped over the ground like a glassy sheet. Still puzzled, an excruciating pain started over my back and shoulders, and I realized that I was the one who had been screaming. I jumped away, the glassy stuff still sticking all over my toes. The hot soup had burned my shoulders and back raw, and my skin had melted off, draping around my feet and sticking to my toes. I had never felt such pain before, not even from Mom's belt or a soldier's whip. By now I was down on my knees, my flaming back arched.

Mom came running. She helped me up and to our *tampat,* which was close. She sent Simon to get Nadine, rolled me on my belly, and started to cut away my blouse with her little nail scissors. What followed was a haze of pain that would not lift even for a second. It was so severe that it was breaking even through my half-consciousness. I wished to be dead, to not feel that terrible pain any longer. There was pain everywhere.

Nadine came and tried to relieve me as much as possible. The hot soup had only burned my back and shoulders, but the burns were second degree and the blisters came up like mushrooms. Each touch was agony. She put wet gauze and Vaseline on the blisters and then crushed leaves between large, flat stones, preparing a mush to spread over my back. The leaves were herbs and would sooth the pain, she said, putting them on and removing them later only caused more agony. Exhaustion finally brought me to a state of half-sleep. I gratefully drowned in it.

Mom and Nadine took turns exchanging the cool compresses and herb mush every two hours through the night and the next day. I could sleep normally the second night, and started to feel better the day after. Even then, I couldn't even stand having clothes on my back so I moved around naked from the waist up, with my shorts pulled halfway down my butt.

I had everyone's attention. The story spread through the camp like wildfire, and all the kids came over to look at my back. They circled me like I was a zoo animal, with silent admiration on their faces. I didn't mind. For once, I was important enough to catch everyone's attention and respect. Actually, I felt great, despite the pain and discomfort that was very much present.

I especially enjoyed Mom's constant presence and attention. She had snapped out of her hiding place and actually looked at me. The worry and concern on her face warmed me, and the compassion in her voice almost made it worth the pain.

Even after Nadine let me leave the clinic, I had to stay out of the sun, as the heat made even the slightest pain feel like agony again. I was excused from *koempoelans* and garden work for awhile, but had to sweep the campgrounds instead, where I was protected by large shade trees. I didn't mind. It was much easier work than weeding.

Mom stayed with us after I burned my back. She started watching the little girls again, especially Easabella, who just couldn't muster enough energy. She seemed more content to lie down or lean against something, constantly sucking her thumb. She looked so pale that I often wondered if she had any blood left in her body. The rest of us were still sick all the time, too, but seemed to notice it less. We had forgotten how it was to feel well.

Over the following weeks, we lost track of time, until once again a sudden wave of rumor tension started, and then grew. Whispering women stood in huddles, bending in toward each other before dissolving and forming other groups somewhere else. As before, eyes became hopeful and people walked with a spring in their step.

And now, not only were the guards meaner than ever and still walking in pairs; they were also sometimes completely absent. This puzzled us most. Sometimes whole days would go by when no one showed on the veranda of the guardhouse, while two soldiers patrolled the camp without a break. What was going on? Could the rumors really be true this time?

Just before dark one day, Peter came to see me and we sat outside watching some little kids play. We hadn't seen much of each other lately, apart from when we worked together in the gardens. We were too tired to do more. Even talking was done in a few sentences or syllables.

I leaned forward, moving my still tender back away from the wall I'd been leaning on. We sat under the overhang of the roof, protected from a gentle rain. A fine mist sprayed down, wetting and cooling our bare feet, which stuck out from under the overhang.

"I love the dark," Peter said dreamily. "It hides everything ugly. And I love the wind, coming with the rain."

I nodded and leaned forward.

"Will we ever be free again, Sofia? The bastards have to lose the war one day, don't you think?" He looked at me. "Do you think the rumors going around are true this time? It has been so very long."

"I don't know, Pete. I am afraid to hope they might be. Each time, it is harder to hope. Perhaps, it would be better to wait and watch before hoping again."

Peter picked up a stick and poked around in the ground between his feet.

"Mom talked to Nadine the other day," I went on. "Nadine is more sure than ever that the war is about to end, but she's said that before and look what's happened. We are still here, and we are still hungry, dirty, sick, and rotting away. No one in the world seems to know we are here."

Peter pulled his feet out of the rain and started picking at his soles. His feet were the same as mine, calloused and dirty.

"Where are the birds?" he whispered.

"They must have found happier places to go to. Perhaps, they don't want to drink the water, since it is always dirty and colored. Yet the rain is always clear." I looked up at the sky. "Was the sun always so hot and bright?"

Peter didn't respond, but looked up at the sky too. He loved nature. He knew a lot about plants and animals and wanted to study marine biology when he grew up. But to find the right school he would have to leave Indonesia, which he didn't want to do. He had told his mother that he would never leave her and so would choose something else to study.

After tearing off a strip of skin from his foot, he looked at me.

It was dark now and even darker where he sat, in the shadow of the roof's overhang. I couldn't see his eyes, but his cheeks were wet. That's what I loved about Peter. He never said much, but felt a lot inside.

My arm touched his when I moved closer to him. "I can't help you, Pete, I don't know. I'm totally empty inside. All I know is tears and dirt, whippings and hunger, and death—dead people and dead hope. I can't believe in anything anymore. I don't trust tomorrow and I don't even care if I die."

We sat quiet for a long time, both lost in thought. Then Peter walked back to his barrack in the rain.

The next day, I didn't die. But Mies Miedema did.

The guards were all feared, one no more than the other, but when the commander showed up, we could expect big trouble. There were whispers of guards having found a notebook and pencils between the boards of some barracks while hunting for radios. It was assumed that any writing in notebooks was documentation of what was happening to us in the camps, and it was the thing the commander punished most severely.

He confronted us on the *koempoelan* square, as usual, screaming like a lunatic and waving his rifle wildly. He stomped through the rows of women and children, smacking his fist into faces, making sure every back was bent. He brought his rifle down whenever someone wasn't bowing deeply enough.

I had lost sight of Mom. I knew Emma-M and Easa would be with her somewhere on the square; she would protect them. I had seen Simon arrive earlier, but couldn't detect his red hair among the children hiding between their mothers. Most of the children were so scared, they were screaming, and some had even started to vomit and pee, which enraged the commander more. Women were on their knees, hovering over their children on the ground. There was little space around me, but I was one of the few still standing. I was trying to locate Simon when I saw the furious, stocky commander stumble between the masses toward me. When he was within arm's length, I felt the blow of his rifle on my head and almost went down.

Apparently still unsatisfied with the mountains of sobbing women, he continued to work himself between them, his hard boots kicking left and right, striking faces, heads, and bodies. He stumbled over arms and legs, and screamed in fury when he toppled and almost fell. After that, he used his rifle as a cane, putting its butt to the ground with every step, not seeming to care where it came down.

Because I was still halfway visible, he swayed his rifle in my direction and I went down, landing next to several other women who had fallen before me. As soon as I hit the square, someone fell on top of me, pushing me flat onto my stomach. Something wet came down on my ear.

While scaling the mountain of people I was in, the crazed Japanese commander stomped a black boot between me and the woman next to me, peeling one of the just healed blisters off my back. I screamed in pain, but was thankful his boot hadn't landed on my head.

After what seemed like endless hours of terror, suddenly the commander's screaming stopped. Only moaning and sobbing continued, noises of fear and misery. I heard his growled orders at the guards and the silence afterward. He must have disappeared in the guardhouse.

We never did learn why the sadist had exploded in such fury.

Slowly the women stood, many of them bruised and bleeding, looking for their children. Then upon finding them, they left, not waiting for the dismissal order of the guards and not caring. For the first time since we had been interned, the guards didn't order them back.

As my hands touched hard surface of the square, I realized that I must have ended up almost at the bottom of the pile. There was someone still pinned on top of me, and I couldn't get up. A woman next to me moaned. I tried to turn my head, but couldn't. I tried to move the person over me, but she was heavy. The moaning woman sounded as if she was having problems breathing; her breaths were strained and she coughed softly. When the woman over me finally moved off, I lifted my head and turned toward the labored breathing. I was looking straight into Mies's gray eyes. Her face was twisted oddly, and blood seeped steadily from her mouth. Scrambling up, I looked at her in horror. She tried to say something, but blood filled her mouth. Then someone's leg pulled out from under her face and her head came down hard on the asphalt. She had not been able to hold it up. The Japanese commander had somehow crushed her throat and neck, making it nearly impossible for her to breath.

I lifted her head and steadied it in my lap. Her mouth let go of everything in it: blood, teeth, and vomit. Her breathing became easier then, but was still ragged.

"Sofia, brave little girl." Mies could only whisper and then had to stop, her throat rattling a few times as she searched for air.

I started to cry, feeling myself break inside. Bringing my head down till I touched her face, I tried to speak, but couldn't.

"Sofia," Mies continued. "Don't stop feeling, Sofie. Without feeling, you are dead … "

My face rose to look at her, and she closed her beautiful gray eyes with their wondrous light.

"If you can't walk the road … with me … to Golgotha … " Her mouth filled up again. "You can't share my glory … " The words came hesitantly, in a painful whisper, almost a prayer.

Barely able to see her through my tears, I gently tipped her head to get rid of the blood again. The rattled breathing became softer and hope came flooding into me. Maybe she would make it. She would be all right. She had to be all right. She couldn't die—not Mies. Not Mies Miedema, who loved God. God would keep her safe!

Mies had told me about Golgotha. She had said that when God noticed how full of sin the world was, he had sent his son to teach everyone about God's love and forgiveness, and to rescue from sin anyone who was willing to follow him. He had had to die in a place called Golgotha on a cross of suffering, killed by and for men and women who couldn't believe in him. All God's son wanted, she told me, was for you to stay with him and do like he did, and when you did, he would let you share in the reward of his father.

Mies opened her eyes again and smiled, but not with her poor, bleeding, crushed mouth. The smile was in her eyes. "Watch Phaedra for me," she whispered.

I leaned closer and strained to hear more, but Mies stopped talking after that. And in the stillness of her suffering, the light left her eyes and I felt her go away. Yet long after the labored breathing had stopped, and long after the light had left, her eyes still looked at me.

She fell apart in my blurred vision. When the light in her eyes had gone, I had felt something else leaving me as well. She had taken with her any hope and youth, trust and faith left in me.

Looking at the sky, I searched for her and couldn't find her. The clouds had closed, and there was no light. There was no Mies and no spirit. Just an angry wind protesting what had happened. Just pain and regret and sorrow.

Memories crushed me. Karel and Baby Miedema, Jaap's grandmother and Mies, and all the others. They were forever lost.

My eyes cleared and there was Phaedra, her legs covered with blood. The blood was not hers, however, but her mother's. Startled, Phaedra had pulled her legs from under her mother's head when she had seen her terrible injuries. Now, she stared with empty eyes, sitting next to Mies whose head was still in my lap. She rested her hands on her mother's forehead. There was no sound, no movement in all of Phaedra.

We sat together, Phaedra and I, in the emptiness of life, in the total isolation of suffering, until Nadine came and carried Phaedra away. Phaedra didn't cry; she just closed her arms around Nadine's neck and rested her head against her mother's friend's face.

Alone with Mies, I wondered where Mom was and whether Simon and the girls were okay. But I wasn't worried enough about them to rush off and find out, leaving Mies in the dirt.

Flies came. Of course, flies came. I kept them at bay, as I buried Mies deep in a sacred place in my heart and memory. I loved her more than Mom or Dad, and more than anything else in the world, and I needed to keep her just where I could find her when I needed her for myself.

Looking down at Mies and her still and ruined face, I wished I were where she was.

Phaedra came to live with us for awhile. She had changed from a serious, confident girl into a rigid, terrified little child with a constant haunted look in her eyes. She couldn't speak anymore. Whenever she tried, her voice seemed to stop somewhere in her throat before she could form the words. She seemed to be faraway, in a land where I couldn't reach her.

Phaedra got lost in our family. Easa and Emma-M, too young to share so much grief, invited her to join in their quiet games, but Phaedra didn't play anymore. Mom had little time for her, as she was away all day on *corvee* duty. Simon, who never opened up easily, touched her with gentle hands, as if afraid to break her. She didn't even notice him. She was like a frail, pale statue. She was with us, yet far away; alive and moving, but lost inside. She was locked away in a terrible land.

What did Phaedra see? And what had she seen? I had not noticed her there when Mies had died. Had she been next to her mother when the Japanese commander had kicked her? She must have been. Mies had always kept Phaedra close, protecting her from blows and kicks, and catching them with her own body. Mies's head had rested on Phaedra's legs, coloring them red with her blood.

I held Phaedra close every night when I washed her face. I talked, but she never answered. I gave her part of my food, which she never ate. All through the night, she slept against me, her head under my chin, shaking and releasing the hurt through soft moans and gasps. Phaedra slept at night, but did not rest.

After a week, I took her to stay with Nadine. Nadine knew how Mies had died. She had carried Mies along with two other women to her own *tampat*. She had cleaned her face and closed her eyes and folded her fingers together. Later, she told me how Mies hadn't fit into the basket. They had used the longest there was, but her feet had stuck out. Nadine had tied them together and wrapped her own shawl around them. Mies had not been dragged over the path either. Instead, eight women had carried her and gently set her down at the gate, staying to hum the songs that Mies had taught them. Long after she was gone they stood there, humming her songs and saying good-bye, already suffering her absence. The basket Mies left in did not come back.

Listening to Nadine's story, I hadn't felt anything. I only thought about how I couldn't remember the words or melodies of Mies's songs.

"Watch over Phaedra for me, Sofia," Mies had asked me. I tried to. I went to see Phaedra every day. I took her little cold hands and rubbed them for awhile. I folded my hands around her stiff cheeks, trying to remove the terror from her eyes and bring a smile to her still lips. Nadine watched my efforts, and saw more than I saw.

"It will take a long time for Phaedra, Sofia. She has lost much more than her mother. You cannot reach her. She is in a place no one knows, a place where no one can hurt her anymore. Part of her will stay there forever. And perhaps part of her will be back, but we don't know."

I turned away. How could I watch over Phaedra if I didn't know where she was? Not being able to reach her and to relieve the pain inside of her made me feel guilty. I had fallen short. I couldn't do what Mies had asked me. I couldn't give back what Mies had given me all those horrible years. Worse, I couldn't keep my promise to a friend now gone.

I regretted not knowing how much I had loved and trusted Mies until I had lost her. She had been the only source of peace for me. She had seemed the only person who had really, really cared about me. And now, she was gone, dead. So much for God, who was supposed to help her and keep her safe! She had put her trust in him and he, too, had let her down. He had allowed that Japanese officer to kill her.

I resolved not to put trust in anyone—not in God, not in people. That was better. No trust meant no disappointment. No friends meant no farewell. No love meant no pain. It was much safer that way. It was the one thing about which Mies had been wrong. Very wrong. And now she would never know how wrong.

Every day when I came to see Phaedra, Nadine changed the dressing on my ankle. The ulcer hadn't gotten any better. It was deeper now and always hurt. The skin around it shined red and felt spongy. It stank too. Nadine tried to remove the puss every day, but didn't get very far, as it hurt so much that I'd pull my leg back and not let her do more. She put salt-water compresses on it and had told me to keep it wet with boiled water.

"What for?" I had asked her. "It rots through anyway, and will probably make my foot fall off!"

She looked at me with pity in her eyes. I hated pity. No need to feel sorry for me! I got up to leave.

"Sofia," Nadine said, stopping me. Her voice sounded sad, which made me angry. "You are changing, Sofia. Don't let the Japanese evil inside. Don't let it destroy you."

"I don't need Japanese evil inside," I snapped. "I already have a monkey!"

She looked puzzled. I walked away. Mies would have understood, and so would Hassan.

Nadine didn't give up. "Sofia!"

I turned at the doorway to look at her.

"Mies didn't die for nothing, Sofia. She wouldn't like you if she could see you now!"

I slammed the door. She shouldn't have said that. She shouldn't have mentioned her name. Mies was dead and wrong and gone.

Avoiding Peter was not easy, but I managed. Friends were dangerous; they would always go away and leave pain and empty places. I had had enough of those.

He'd come around like a stubborn puppy, puzzled, his eyes asking for what he couldn't say. He was patient, but finally broke under my silent indifference.

"What is wrong, Sofia?"

"Nothing, Peter."

I was not going to talk to him about Mies and Phaedra and the brokenness in my heart. I wanted to hide the grief and keep my memories of Mies all to myself. I didn't want to share them with anyone, even Peter.

I closed my eyes refusing to look at him.

"Talk to me, Sofia."

"What about, Peter?" I still wasn't looking at him, but I knew he wouldn't be easy to get rid of. We had been friends for too long and had shared too much.

It was one of those quiet, sticky afternoons, when even the flies didn't show themselves. My shirt felt hot and sticky, and Peter had already gotten rid of his. Even behind closed eyes, I knew how terribly thin he had become. Even after recovering from the dysentery, he could stand only soft food and had diarrhea every day, just without the cramps. He was so small and so frail that, from the moment he had moved out of Nadine's clinic, I had been very protective of him.

"Something is bothering you," he said.

"Nothing is bothering me."

His voice sounded desperate, so I finally looked at him. His eyes were dark; so dark that I had difficulty seeing his pupils. But they were wide open, entreating urgency. It seemed painful to him that he couldn't understand why I didn't want to talk, why my face was closed, and why I couldn't explain. But this didn't bother me. All I wanted was to get rid of him. Even if I did talk, he wouldn't be able to understand, not to mention follow me into the darkness of my emotions.

He kept pressing. "I can see it, Sofia."

I didn't answer, hoping my negligence would prompt him to leave me alone.

"I can feel it, Sofia," he said.

No answer.

"Talk to me, Sofia."

"I can't, Pete. Go away!" The tears started to come now and I felt my throat close. Peter was so persistent. Why wouldn't he go away! Why wouldn't he understand that I would never be able to talk to him about this?

"I'm your friend, Sofia!"

"Go away, Peter."

This time the silence lasted much longer. Maybe he would give up now and go away. Finally, I looked up from my seat among the dead leaves and saw him staring at me. Somehow he had moved without my hearing him. His face was pale and his eyes were like mine, full of tears.

"Don't you want me to come around?" His voice broke.

Why were there so many tears to be shed? Where were the sun, the light, the happiness, and the joy?

I didn't know what to say to Peter anymore. I felt drained and hollow. It was still quiet, but the heat had started to lift. The slight breeze ruffled his hair, making him look much younger than his years.

Crawling up from my sitting position I felt stiff. My legs were so swollen that they touched when I stood straight. My knees hurt almost always, and I couldn't run anymore because of the festering ulcer on my ankle. I wished I'd died with Mies.

"Go away, Pete, leave me alone!"

When Peter finally turned, I had one more piece of advice for him: "Don't wait for the birds to sing, Peter. Don't wait for the music to play again or for the water to clear. It never will. The war will last forever!"

Peter left then, not looking back. His narrow head was bent forward, and his hair was sticking out in plucks around a healing cut. His ears stuck out like panhandles. They always had, and I had often pulled them. I watched him go, till he disappeared around a barrack.

Better to lose him alive than dead, I thought while trying to push away the consuming loneliness in my heart.

Not long after that, the whole camp was loaded into trucks and driven out of Belawan Estate II. No one was excited, no one made a fuss, and no one hoped for better. We would be going to yet another camp with other Japanese guards and other fences. We knew what to expect; we had been through it before.

The trucks took us to a train station, where we stood and waited apathetically until we were loaded into the train. The mothers had lost the energy to scream at their children, and the children had lost the will to disobey. Mom and Simon captured two seats; Emma-M sat on Mom's lap and Easabella stood leaning between Mom and Simon. I had no seat, so I stood and hung my arm on a strap coming down from the ceiling.

The train rolled and stopped, rolled and stopped. When we were moving, if I bent down close to a window, I could see a little: a stretch of sky passing overhead, treetops coming and disappearing, misty mountains in the distance, and, once, a lonely turkey hawk sailing on spread wings, majestic and free. When we were stopped at the endless little train stations along the way, we had to stay in the hot train with too little space to be comfortable. No one was allowed out, so a bucket was used as a toilet.

After awhile, the heat in the wagons became unbearable, mixed with the stink of sweat and despair. There was no food. Though some people had brought bananas and water, no one shared, and it was all quickly gone.

Soon, the kids were having accidents. One of the mothers refused to let her daughter use the almost full bucket of urine. She carefully lifted the bucket to the open window and let go. Away it went. The wind took the smelly stuff and blew it back along the wagons behind us, and probably into their windows. I would have loved to hear the reactions to that! It didn't take long for the women to start begging the soldiers for a pee break. The soldiers pretended not to understand, until they finally relented. And at the next stop, we all ran out and did what we had to do.

Upon our return, counting became a nightmare. The soldiers couldn't agree on the number of people in each wagon, so we moved off the train again to be recounted, while they pushed and shoved and screamed. Finally satisfied, we went on, happy to have a bit of warm air flowing through the open windows. Although in a different wagon now, we still were together.

Easabella and Emma-M, who, so far, had been sitting up straight, now leaned into each other like lifeless dolls, and were slumped over Simon's seat. Simon had made room for them by sliding down onto his knees, so that he could rest his head on Mom's lap. I felt too restless to sit, and continued hanging on a ceiling strap. Twice I had a chance to squeeze myself through the people to the end of the wagon, where I could enjoy a bit of fresh air on the tiny balcony—though not for long, because everyone wanted a turn. At one place, I saw fruit, baked goods, and coconuts for sale, but then we traveled slowly past. We had no money anyway.

Finally, daylight faded into early evening and the air became less smothering. It was almost totally dark when the train stopped again. We had obviously arrived, for the soldiers were standing next to the train waving for everyone to get out.

A few *koelies* dragged our belongings out of the train and left them on the narrow cement strip, but by then, night had fallen and it was difficult to see. The little building in front of us had two lights up high, close to the roof. That was hardly enough to help us recognize our luggage, but it did illuminate a name on the side of the little building: AEK PAMINKE. The building was tiny, but it must have been the train station of a village—most likely an equally small village.

We looked around us, searching for more buildings, more people, perhaps some traffic. There was nothing. After finding our luggage, we began to understand that the rest of our trip would be on foot. The soldiers lit some lanterns, and we slowly followed them in a long, disorganized line.

The road we were following was difficult to see, but when the moon was visible, we could see how dangerous and uneven the road was. Tree roots and large stones caused the youngest children to stumble and lose whatever they were carrying; they often got up but never stopped crying. We passed shadows and dark shapes, which were only large trees but looked much more threatening. This scared Easa and Emma-M to no end. They walked in panic from one side of the road to the other, frequently falling and crying. They fell so often that even Simon lost his patience and started snapping at them.

Finally, we noticed a light in the distance, and this gave us strength to walk the last five hundred meters. At the end of the long road, we stood before a gate, looking without interest at yet another camp.

Nothing would be better, and yet nothing could be worse. As it was, we all had sores and ulcers. We all had diarrhea or dysentery, and were bloated and swollen with beriberi and starvation. Malaria was as much a part of our lives as sleeping. We all smelled dirty and looked every bit the prisoners we knew we were. Like cattle, we were yelled at and collected, counted and recounted. And like cattle, we were pushed or shoved, kicked or rolled, depending on how we had survived the voyage. Surely, the rest of the world had abandoned us.

AEK PAMINKE I

Our arrival the previous night was a vague memory of putting down sleeping pads on a few meters of open space somewhere in a barrack. No surprises there. We were surprised, however, when someone gave us warm tea and said to go for porridge in the kitchen if we were hungry. This gesture of welcome after the exhausting voyage seemed to break some tension inside each of us. We had forgotten how it felt to appreciate a simple gift of sweetness.

Cherishing the warm, welcome tea, Mom and I had looked at each other with tears in our eyes, and Simon went for the porridge. Easabella and Emma-M were too tired to eat, but they drank their tea before falling asleep. The porridge was tasteless, but we were hungry. And none of us expected more.

In the morning, Emma-M and Easabella woke up early and, with Simon, went on their first inspection of the new camp. Some while later, they woke us with hands full of large, shiny seeds. These were rubber pits.

Camp Aek Paminke was located amid a rubber plantation. Numerous rubber trees had been cut away to build the barracks, and huge heaps of tree trunks surrounded the perimeter of the camp. These trunks had to be cut into firewood for the kitchen. Simon told us that they'd seen *koelies* cutting the wood but that when he'd asked them questions, they wouldn't answer. I followed him outside and looked around, full of wonder.

The sun was shining and people were busy everywhere. Beyond the barbed-wire fence I saw trees—rows and rows of rubber trees. They gave me a feeling of space. The trees closest to the camp swayed their crowns gently over the fence, providing shade and dropping hundreds of the seeds that Easa and Emma-M had collected. Bare spots on the trunks showed where a little tin can had hung earlier to collect the latex, or rubber sap. The trees must have been dry now, as they were not being tapped anymore and all that was left hanging from the bark were little curly strings of dry latex.

Boys and girls were already working outside the wire in familiar gardens, growing vegetables for the Japanese soldiers first and our kitchen after. Other children were sitting with their feet in a narrow creek, which had rushing water and ran all through the camp. It came from some anonymous place outside the fence that we could only imagine, and then left the camp, traveling freely to some unknown destination. Sometimes the children, if they were fast enough, fished out things they saw floating by. They might end up with a banana, a lonely plant, a sweet potato, or just an old piece of paper. No one knew where these treasures came from, but they were all welcome.

Aek Paminke was also larger. There were a lot more barracks, and there must have been over a thousand women and children, all of whom had been gathered from various other camps. From the looks of it, the conditions in those other camps had been just as bad as ours, as they, too, were bald or had short, spiky hair, and some had bruises in different colors. The women all seemed suspicious about this; they wondered why they had all had to be gathered into one large camp.

With so many people, water was even more scarce, which meant we could take a shower only once every ten days, although we were still able to wash our faces and hands each morning in the washrooms, where we could also fill the bottles to *tjebok*. (wash after a bowel movement, since there was no toilet paper) The clinic also had enough water to regularly clean its patients.

The water for each person in the camp was measured and this was sufficient for personal use only. We used it for drinking, washing hands and faces after *corvee* duties, and most often for cold compresses when one of us had high fever, or pounding headaches. There was hardly water available for washing clothes, so lots of women washed clothes in the creek, as this was their only option, and with the total absence of soap, everyone's clothes looked grubby and drab.

Every day, an open lorry would leave the camp over a single, iron rail. It obviously had been used before, probably to transport rubber and supplies between the plantation and the train station, though neither the lorry nor the rail came close to train traffic. It was manned by one of the prisoners with a thick, strong pole, which was used like an oar in a rowing boat. Standing in the lorry, she would use the pole to push it smoothly over the rails and travel the three kilometers to the little train station to pick up rice, fruit, *sago*, and other supplies. Older girls or younger women usually did this, and they enjoyed the work. They felt free to be so far outside the barbed wire, and sometimes, if one of the bags split, they would put the spilled rice or beans in their pockets, using it later to supplement meals. I never found out how they prepared what they kept, though, since it was not possible to do private cooking. They never tried to escape or hide, for there was nowhere to go. All along the lorry rail was open terrain; *sawahs* (rice fields) and wetlands, with here and there stretched shallow water ponds. A soldier would check out the lorry in the morning before departure and again on arrival at the little train station. The same would happen on its trip back to the camp. There were constant warnings not to try anything foolish—punishment would be severe.

We had all of the same kinds of food here, although after a heavy rain, we could often find mushrooms or green vegetables growing in swampy areas, which had to go to the kitchen. The soup always tasted so much better with these extra vegetables.

Koempoelans became a nightmare, because there were now so many of us packed together on the square, standing for hours in the burning sun. Without exception, Japanese soldiers couldn't count, which meant that at the end of the *koempoelan* every day, the square had to be cleaned; no one could make it that long without going to the latrines.

Because there were no lights, and the evenings arrived early, there was nothing to do after dark but go to bed. I found these evening hours the most difficult; noises and voices could last till deep into the night. Conversations could be heard everywhere in the barrack, and they were often normal, but more often quarrelsome, with women fighting like hellcats, spanking and screaming at their kids for everything.

Mosquitoes were always present, too, and the *klamboes* gave little to no protection. Lice and fleas were just as common as mosquitoes, and were so numerous at Aek Paminke that real sleep became a luxury. Infections caused by scratching were the result, and were accompanied by fever. The nurses in the clinic couldn't do much but apply Vaseline to lessen the itching.

The clinic was now part of a small hospital building that sat outside the camp in an open area among the rubber trees. People loved to ask for clinic help, if only for the delicious feeling of a few minutes' freedom from the barbed wire. Nadine was there again with several other nurses, and there was much work to do, as more of us were sicker and weaker than ever.

I liked to sit outside in the dark, despite the mosquitoes. I never saw any local people apart from the *koelies*, but sometimes the wind brought music from *kampongs* (villages) far away. The music was of the *gamelan* sort (played on wooden instruments), which threw me back to the happiest time of my life—a time of freedom, which I never fully appreciated; a time of togetherness, which I never recognized; a time of peace, which I didn't dare believe in anymore, out of fear of losing it again.

The wind also brought in the faint odor of long-missed but never-forgotten Indonesian dishes. Their delicious spices could make a king's meal out of ordinary rice or noodles. When the smells came, I always went back into the barrack. Staying would have made me feel homesick, and my longing for Sitah, Hassan, Dad, and Mies would have swelled my throat with tears that I couldn't have stopped. And tears would not have brought them back.

Simon soon made new friends. He was almost nine now and particularly liked the boy who lived across from us in the barrack. His name was Bart and he had one older sister and one younger.

Bart's mother was usually the center of a group of women who were always together. They spent many hours of the night whispering and giggling and having secret conversations. Whenever I passed them, hoping to catch something of these conversations, they became silent or started talking about *corvee* work. They also had cigarettes, which they smoked outside in the dark. No one knew where the cigarettes came from or how the women got them, though there were rumors of smuggling with the *koelies*. These women were suspicious, though. They only trusted each other and wouldn't let on to anyone else.

There were other rumors around camp about some kind of plans these women had, but when I asked Mom about it, she refused to fill me in. She warned me to stay away from them and not to make it my business. Still, at night, I often watched them through the *klamboes*. They would walk to one person's *tampat*, where they spent the rest of the evening huddled in soft conversation around a small shaded candle, which was forbidden. I wondered when they ever slept.

I would peek through the biggest holes and try to hear snatches of conversation, wondering what all they knew and what it all meant. Bart's mother was one of the group's most active whisperers. Meanwhile, Mom would snore softly next to me, and usually snored me to sleep.

In addition to cigarettes and candles, Bart's mom had other things that I had not seen in a long time, like a button for a blouse, a few aspirins, and a pair of sandals with real straps. Once, she even got Mom a bra. Mom was so grateful, I thought she would fall on her knees and kiss her feet. Where did she get all these things?

She was not the only woman with such items, but she had a lot more than everyone else. The other women did not shun her for it, though. On the contrary, they seemed to take a liking to her for it. Maybe she was a spy.

When I asked Nadine how Bart's mom and some of the other women got extra things, she smiled and shook her head. "You don't need to know, Sofia. It's none of your concern."

Of course, Mom wouldn't even answer.

But Bart's mom was good to Simon; she gave him an old baseball cap without the flap. It looked like a Jewish skullcap on him. He was so happy with it, that he never took it off, not even in the bathhouse. He threw the water over his cap until it soaked his hair. It would keep his head cool, he said. Simon had a lot more pep since he had started hanging around with Bart.

One time when Bart's mom had cookies, Bart took two and gave one to Simon. Simon generously let Easabella and Emma-M each take a bite, but I refused. I told Simon it was because three bites would leave little to nothing for him, but that wasn't it. For some reason I couldn't identify, I felt uncomfortable around Bart's mom and just didn't want to taste her cookies. In fact, it bothered me so much that at night I dreamed the cookies changed into frogs and toads. They were growing and growing, and grew so fat, they burst, their pieces flying and sticking to my body. I had to spend the rest of the night picking the pieces off of my face.

We didn't see much of Simon during the day, as he roamed the camp with Bart, just like Peter and I did at one time. The boys spent a lot of time next to the little creek, where they often caught something. One day, Simon pulled a real little chicken out of the water. Although small, it was still a chicken. Simon pulled it onto the bank, soggy and scared. Bart then grabbed its legs, and together the boys came running to the barrack to show everyone.

Mom was at *corvee* and missed the spectacle. But I quickly arrived at the *tampat*, grabbed the chicken, and ran it outside with the boys, where I twisted its neck with a jerk. I had done it just as I had seen Peter do so often, and just for a moment, I wished I wouldn't miss him so much.

We now had a problem. To cook the chicken, we needed a pan and a little fire pit. I knew just where to go. I took the boys with me to the gate and told the guard that I needed my bandage changed in the clinic and that the boys needed to be checked for fevers. He looked suspicious but let us go. At the clinic, we got a pan and a little fire container for wood-burning from Nadine, which she used to boil water for patients. She watched as I cut the chicken with one of her sharp scalpels and removed the innards. Plucking the chicken didn't take long, and after that, the three of us sat around the fire, patiently watching the meat cook. We were behind the clinic, where the guard couldn't see us. And though he could have seen the smoke, fires were normal around the clinic since boiled water was always needed. The chicken was small and young and didn't take much time to cook.

Nadine kept the broth for her sick people, and then Bart and Simon split the chicken, each taking a half of it home. That night, Mom sat looking at

Simon with amazement and pride. He had delivered a fantastic meal for his family!

The next day we all had diarrhea, but we didn't care. The food had been worth it. For the rest of the week, Simon sat next to the little creek, patiently waiting to catch another bird, but no such luck.

Easabella and Emma-M also played outside all day, which was safer to do here since, although the camp stank, there were none of the shallow puddles filled with toxic dirt and garbage that we'd had at Belawan Estate. The girls collected fallen rubber pits from around the wire fence and once back in the barrack, they shined them up till they shone. They competed with each other to see who could make the shiniest pit, and in the process discovered that the harder they rubbed the pits, the hotter the pit became, until they were eventually too hot to touch. By then, they were beautiful—clean with dark and light stripes—and when you shook them, you could hear the seed moving inside.

As soon as Simon and Bart saw the polished pits, they went out and got their own. They picked only those pits without cracks or blemishes, and then while shining them, they discovered a new game. As soon as a pit was hot, one of them would touch a third boy with it. Of course, the third boy was not impressed. At first, it made him jump. But when all three of them saw the slight burn spot it made, and he felt the slight tenderness when touching it, this new game took off like wildfire. Now boys all over camp collected the rubber pits, rubbed them clean and hot, and burned each other. Simon and Bart came home each night with scads of little red circles on their arms and hands. They always laughed at it, even though it made Mom upset.

The next day, the spots had faded and the two boys set out to get more pits.

For the first time, Mom liked the *corvee* duty assigned to her, which was to help Nadine in the hospital. Now she didn't have to stick her hands in the stinking latrines that made her so nauseous, she often puked right over the filth. She hadn't liked kitchen work either. She'd come back from it hot and with her fingers black from soot or dirty pans; though her fingers cleaned up, she'd never gotten the black dirt out from under her nails. She hated to peel potatoes too. In fact, she hated a lot of chores. But nursing she found easy.

She washed sick people and fed them soup, or waved rattan fans over their heads to bring down high fevers and chase away the flies. And best of all, she was promised a nursing dress, which is something I knew she would fight, steal, even go on a hunger strike for, if she had to. She had not had a new dress since before the war started. Knowing Mom, I sensed how deeply depressing this was for her. At one time, she had owned so many dresses that she hadn't needed to wear the same one twice for a month.

Back then, the little Chinese shops would be filled to the brim with rolls and rolls of silk and cotton, velvet and flannelette. She would buy a few yards, along with ribbons and lining, and spend hours tracing patterns from fashion magazines sent to her from Holland. In two days, the dress would be ready, and then she would parade through the street as proud as a peacock. On her high heels, her back straight as a candle, she would say hello to everyone she met. She would pick up Dad from school, where he was the principal, just to show off her dress. (Although she told her friends that she liked to pick up Dad when he was done working, just for the pleasure of walking home with him.) Dad would always know the real reason, but he would smile and walk home with her, just as proud.

Mom really was a sight back then, I thought, and then felt very grown-up for guessing her real reason for liking the nursing job. She would take the vomiting, the diarrhea, the discomfort and the dying, and she would handle it well. For the new nursing dress, she would.

Great excitement exploded one early morning, when four airplanes flew overhead. The drone had started far away, as it had that time at Belawan Estate, but then it came nearer and nearer. It came so near that it drove everyone out of the barracks: women and children, healthy and sick. Even those in the bathhouses and latrines came running out, some dripping water and half-naked with towels around their waists or breasts. The planes were high, but we could see four brilliant streaks of silver and the faint khaki color below each of their wings.

Everyone yelled and screamed and hopped up and down. We laughed and cried, believing, yet afraid to believe.

"Did you see that?"

"Did you see them?"

"Did you see those planes?"

"Oh, God, they are ours!"

"They have seen us; they have come for us!"

Joy and excitement erupted like a volcano, flooding through the camp and staying with us long after the planes had disappeared. It stayed with us during the hot tropical nights, when doubt cropped up again and we needed to tell each other what we saw just to believe. It burned like a warm fire through days still filled with *koempoelans, corvee,* and cruel guards.

The guards seemed even more nervous, always shouting and quarreling amongst themselves, which delighted us even more.

Then newspapers were smuggled in. They were filled with reports about the losses of the Japanese Imperial Army and the successes of the Allied Forces, all of which lifted us in jubilant hope. Then there were the contradicting stories, which plunged us back into collective depression. Finally, one night, I decided that something big must have happened, since Bart's mom and the other women got together and read a newspaper in the light of the small, forbidden candle. None of them seemed surprised about what they read, but then Bart's mom spoke for a long time while the others listened. I found out later that she got her information, her newspapers, and even the stuff no one else had from the *koelies*—the same *koelies* who cut our firewood and wouldn't talk to us children, but at the time, I still thought she might be a spy.

Next morning, the newspaper had disappeared without a trace, but Bart's mom told my mom that it had been filled with pictures of burning ships, each with a red ball on the side. This news went through the camp like a storm, and suddenly all of the complaints and fights stopped. The absence of water and light, the filthy latrines, the insufficient meals, even the malaria attacks and painful dysentery cramps no longer seemed significant enough to prompt complaining; they were suffered in silence.

Hope had changed everything in just a few days. People started to sing softly. Mothers laughed more and spanked less. An atmosphere of expectation and excitement not only moved through the camp, but also couldn't be stopped. Whenever someone expressed fear or suggested something negative, the rest of the women protested loudly. There was no more room for worry or doubt; they had been crowded out by one thing: a consuming belief that this would be the end, that the war would be over, and that, finally, without a doubt, we would have a future. Life could become normal again.

Soon after, we were called to *koempoelan* at an unusual time, but instead of the Japanese commander or a soldier waiting for us, our camp leader was there. She was the camp leader from before we had even come, chosen by the people already here—I didn't even know her name.

Then, instead of being counted, we listened to her announce glorious news: She had been called to a meeting with the commander and big changes were ahead—namely, improvements in our conditions. Each barrack leader was to write down all of the complaints from her building, noting everything from urgent needs to mere wishes. This information would then be presented to the Japanese officer, who had already promised immediate action.

She also announced that counting on the *koempoelan* square would no longer be necessary. We listened, silent, unable to comprehend the news.

The next day, as promised, the camp leader presented the commander with list upon list of complaints and requests. We stood along the fence, deep rows of women and children, waiting for her to come out of the guardhouse.

Nearly an hour later, she came down the steps and I could see the tears in her eyes. She raised her arms in front of us and with a trembling voice started to sing the national anthem. Everyone joined in, and the melody rose proudly over the camp. I couldn't remember the words and watched Mom sing as she hadn't sung for years; her face was wet with tears. Looking around, I couldn't find a dry face.

After that she told us that the commander had listened with an expressionless face and had promised to begin changes the following day. I looked at Simon; he had his arm over Bart's shoulders.

Over the next days, we saw the *koelies* arrive and go to work. We saw lanterns and oil lamps go up. We saw the *atap* roofs get patched, and we received spray cans with which to kill mosquitoes, fleas, and lice. The latrines and barrack doors were repaired, and each barrack got its own clotheslines.

Best of all was the change in food. The rice was of better quality, without webs and little bugs and dust. And the lorries returning from the train station were loaded with sugar, salt, bread, soap, and fresh fruits and vegetables. Suddenly, we had eggs and live chickens, which we hadn't seen for a long time, and there was even milk for the children!

We finally dared believe that the rumors were true: the war was indeed over. And firm confirmation arrived soon after. The *koelies* who came to work brought stacks of newspapers with them, all announcing that Japan had surrendered and that the war was officially finished.

Still, somehow, several of us expected contradicting news to follow; we had forgotten how to feel free. What would happen now? Where would we go? We had been prisoners for three and a half years, and now we were afraid of freedom, for it brought with it too many questions.

A week later, a truck stopped in front of the gate. We never saw trucks, unless we were moving to another camp. This truck was covered. It stood there awhile before the driver got out, and went into the guardhouse for a long time. Finally, a guard came out, opened the gate, and shouted for the camp leader. Children ran to find her, calling her name, while the women at the gate started to whisper. What had happened? Were we going to be punished? Or, were we going to move again, to yet another camp?

The camp leader came running. She rushed through the gate and disappeared into the guardhouse. No sound was heard from behind the door, not even voices. Finally, the door opened again and the camp leader came out with two *koelies*. She waved her arms, laughing and motioning for us to gather around. The driver opened the back of the truck, and every one gazed at the glorious sight. There were stacks of Red Cross boxes and baskets.

A loud jubilant roar went up from the many women and children, who by now had gathered around the gate, as every person either laughed or shouted. The children ran back to the barracks to deliver the news.

There was no shortness of hands to carry things in. A few women even climbed in the truck to make sure not a single item was left. The British-Indian driver acted just as happy as we were. He laughed and smiled as we unloaded the parcels, and by the time the truck was empty, he had explained in half-English, half-Indonesian that now that the war was over, this was only the beginning of the change to come.

In the group of women surrounding him, listening, I stood next to Mom and had difficulty believing what he had said. Apparently, I wasn't the only one, however, as every one of us then fell silent.

When he saw our worried, somber expressions, his face became serious. "Believe me, ladies. The Japanese army has lost, the Allied Forces have taken over, and soon you will be free to return home. You all will become happy again.

"In the meantime, you should not leave the camp without an armed guard, since there is a lot of unrest and anger among the local people. The Indonesians are demanding their independence. They want to own their own country, and are resentful of all white people because they don't. Here and there are pockets of hate and unrest. Therefore, the Japanese soldiers will remain here, to guard the camp. Please stay safe, until your departure from the camp can be arranged."

The message about freedom and a return to a normal life made a deeper impression than the warning. Many women, including Mom, started to cry. They grabbed one another's hands and started to sing some patriotic tune.

I looked at the pile of boxes and the baskets of bread and fruit. Then I turned and fought my way out of the throng of happy, cheering people. I ran as fast as I could and ignored the heavy pain over my ankle. I didn't stop until my throat closed and I had no breath left. Going down on my knees, I heaved and tried to get air, but puked instead. It was sour and painful, and it closed off my nose, but I got air.

I closed my eyes as bitter regret filled my heart. One thought hammered in my head: too late for Mies. This all had come too late for Mies.

The Red Cross supplies had brought us more than food. They had brought hope and a desire to go on. Each day was exciting and brought curiosity and expectation. What would we eat today? Would we see more planes? Would we have news from the all-male camps?

Everyone made plans for the next day and the next week and the next month. Mom was talking about clothes and decent shoes. She hoped for makeup and a manicure, too, but said nail scissors and a pumice stone would be a start.

Some mothers worried about the school that kids had missed, but the children had no ears for that; they were too busy playing and running, showing bright eyes and more energy than they had had in a long time. They were eating more than ever and making new friends.

By now, Simon and Bart had a whole collection of polished rubber pits, which they used as marbles. Of course, after being used in this way, many of the pits cracked. One of the boys then opened one up, and they found a snow-white, fuzzy core. This gave them an idea: if the pits were roasted in the ashes of a dying fire, maybe their cores could be eaten. And sure enough, they could; they even tasted delicious.

From that point on, the boys got up extra early in the morning to gather the freshly fallen rubber pits. And after breakfast, when the cooking fires were out, they surrounded the fire pits and patiently sat waiting for their tasty, roasted snacks. As soon as they were ready, the boys ate them at once and took as many as they could. Simon thought they tasted better than peanuts.

Carla, Bart's little sister, liked them too. In fact, she liked them so much that she snuck the roasted pits away from the boys as often as she could.

The Red Cross supplies also included soap, shampoo, combs, brushes, toothbrushes and toothpaste, and much welcomed little bottles of *eau de cologne*. We finally felt clean again when we bathed. We untangled and washed our hair, and although it had lost its shine, and was either plucked or shorn, it smelled good again. The spray cans that had been provided to control lice were not sufficient for everyone, however, so women still sat around searching each other's scalps and killing the little bugs with delicious glee between their thumbs.

We had also now begun to receive regular supplies of good food, though Nadine constantly warned us not to eat or drink too much at once. Our starved bodies were not used to it, she said, and we could become very ill. But turning away perfectly good food after being deprived of it for so long was difficult at best, and as Nadine predicted, many did become ill, especially the children, who often ended up with severe cramps, diarrhea, and sometimes vomiting.

The soft bread we had for breakfast settled in my stomach like a stone, making me slow and lazy the rest of the day. Emma-M and Easabella loved the fresh white bread, though, and needed only margarine to call the slices cake. They couldn't get enough of the rich chocolate bars, so Mom had to hide them. Simon drank milk as much as he could. He loved to show his sisters the high, white moustache that formed on his upper lip and had stopped complaining about his gums. They were happy, really happy, for the first time in a very long stretch.

Women's laughter was heard throughout the barracks, since there were no more *corvees* and much of the housecleaning was done by *koelies* who came in every day from the nearby villages.

The *koelies* continued to be silent and unfriendly. They did not answer our questions, and their eyes were always downcast. Bart's mom had a special way with them, though. She waited till no one was around, asked a quick question, and got a short answer.

As a result, she knew more than anyone else what went on outside the fences. She told the camp leader that the *koelies* had confirmed what the British-Indian driver of the Red Cross truck had warned us for: the Indonesians resented the *blandas* so much that we had to remain in the camps for our protection. And even then, she said, the Indonesians could storm the camp if they were angry enough, and start killing. This made everyone nervous enough not to leave the area without a guard. Therefore, the Japanese soldiers guarding the camp still carried rifles.

After a few weeks the women became bored and restless and impatient. They wanted more. They wanted news. They wanted mail from their men and boys. They still laughed, but also started shouting and quarreling again. Often, hysteria remained just below the surface, ready to erupt, changing laughing into sudden sobbing. There was so much to feel and work through, so much to regret and long for. There was so much despair to get rid of without knowing how.

Mom, at least, had lost the emptiness in her eyes and was more interested in what was going on around her. Like many other women, she had kept one dress, which she hadn't worn during our time at the camps and probably had forgotten she had. She found it and hesitantly put it on after a fine bath and shampoo. We kids all looked at her in wonder, and I remembered Mom again, the way she was.

The dress hung loose around her; she had lost so much weight. But she was happy the dress had a belt to tie to hide her large belly, and the skirt would fall over her legs, which were swollen with edema.

She grabbed a cigarette to hide her discomfort under our admiring eyes. Cigarettes and matches had also come in the Red Cross parcels. Mom had accepted a pack, although I had never seen her smoke before. She lighted it between trembling fingers, brought it to her mouth, and inhaled the smoke deeply. Then she sat like a statue, still and straight, with closed eyes, until she finally let go of the smoke. She coughed for a whole minute, tears running over her face, her body racked with horrible, hoarse barking. When she recovered, she started all over with a new puff. I couldn't see the fun of it.

I started looking for Peter again one day, and when I caught his eye, he said nothing, but left his *tampat* quickly and joined me. We roamed the camp again and discussed the changes and excitement. We were just happy to be together again, and neither of us mentioned Mies or any of the awkwardness that had come between us over the past few weeks.

When evening came, before Peter veered to go to his barrack, he put his arm around my head and squeezed. "You were wrong, Sofia. The war has ended now and soon we will be free again. The birds are already back!"

He was right. We had seen birds in the rubber trees lately and heard the harsh cry of the magpies. Perhaps they had been there all along, just hiding from the grief.

"You are right, Peter," I said, ducking away from his arm. "The birds are back, we will be free soon, and there will be music again. I was wrong!"

Peter disappeared, and I continued walking to my barrack. Despite the enthusiasm I had just displayed, I didn't feel any different, from last month, or even last year. Why could I not be as happy as Peter? Why could I not feel anything?

Night followed evening quickly and it became difficult to see past the shadows. Walking past the kitchen supply room, I almost banged into the now empty Red Cross boxes piled against the outside wall. They would make nice little coffins, I thought. Better than the baskets, which would swiftly fall apart. Each box had had a beautiful silver lining when the truck had brought them. The lining was gone now, taken by many of the women and used for all different purposes. Nadine had used it to line her shelves in the little hospital, which were now clean and filled with various medications (also sent by the Red Cross), which she had sorted and organized with great pleasure. She had aspirin, quinine, liquids to stop diarrhea, and bottles with tablets to flush out the worms.

With ointments and powders for festering wounds, snow-white bandages and dressings, Band-Aids and tape, Nadine felt like a nurse again.

She had treated the ulcer on my ankle with her new powder and had dressed it tightly with a clean, long bandage. "It should hold for awhile, Sofia, but it needs more. We have to wait until a doctor is allowed to come."

I wondered what more a doctor could do. The inflammation was so deep that when walking, I could feel it sitting in there. But the powder took some of the pain off.

We had lights in the camp now, all around the main buildings as well as in the living quarters. Curfew was lifted, and people moved freely between the barracks at night to visit friends. No more soldiers hunted the grounds for hidden radios or notes, and open, lively talking and laughing replaced the forced silence.

I walked past the bathhouses and latrines, which didn't smell as bad now that the doors had been fixed and remained closed. Then as I followed along the little stream, I noticed four little kids crouched over a narrow part of it, with one leg on each side. One of them was Emma-M. She had all her attention focused on something between her legs, and coming nearer, I saw that all of them—three girls and a boy—were doing the same, seeming to study something on their bums.

Emma-M had mentioned once that she wouldn't sit over the holes in the latrines because there were too many yucky creatures down there. She preferred crouching over the stream to go, and then she could also use the water to wash herself. Smart kid! Maybe that's what they were doing now.

I stopped beside them. "What are you doing, Emma-M? Get off that creek. It is dark, and besides, the mosquitoes will come and bite your bum!"

"We were trying to see who has the longest rectum," she said, slowly coming up.

I laughed. "Get up you guys, it's dark. Go back to your barracks. Your moms will be worried."

They all jumped up, pulled up their pants, and ran away, shouting and laughing. They thought it was hilarious.

"Did you wash yourself, Emma-M?" I said, realizing now that she hadn't.

"I didn't have to go, Sofia. We only wanted to see who had the longest rectum. I think I won!"

I laughed and tussled her hair, and as we walked together back to the barrack, I wondered how far off we were from being normal again. Would it be a long time before rectums didn't come out anymore?

A few days later, the rubber pit excitement came to an end.

Bart, Simon, and the rest of their friends had gotten to the kitchen early, waiting patiently for the flaming wood to simmer down. When it was time, they dropped the pits and carefully covered them with the glowing, hot ash. Then instead of hanging around to wait for the seeds to roast, they left to look for more pits.

There were not many left now that all of the boys were hunting for them, so some of them sneaked outside the fence to find more. This was forbidden, but they risked it anyway. As soon as they got back, they found the rubber shells cracked in the hot ash, lifted out the pits, and ate the roasted centers, now warm and tasty. They were at it all afternoon, until they felt full. Of course, the mothers, seeing what they were doing, warned them not to eat too many for they would spoil their meals. But the children just laughed, promised to watch how many they ate, and took off to find some more. And somewhere in the mix of all these boys was Carla, asking to share the roasted seeds.

That night and the entire following day, Nadine and two other nurses had their hands full with the deadly ill children, suffering with extreme stomach cramps, constant vomiting, and seizures. The nurses guessed they were suffering from cyanide poisoning.

Nadine explained that most seeds contained a small amount of cyanide—too little to make people sick. But eating a large amount of seeds when you were underweight and not fully healthy could make you ill, and for children, the reaction would be even more severe. The children of Camp Aek Paminke, all undernourished and weak, were in serious danger.

Bart and Carla's mom stayed the night at the clinic and helped Nadine care for her two. Likewise, Mom didn't move from Simon's bedside. Simon didn't have the frightening seizures like many of the others, but he vomited till he became unconscious.

Carla was in her mother's arms when she died, one moment shaking violently and the next becoming slack and motionless. Her mother hadn't realized that her little daughter had passed; the body was still warm for awhile after, for Carla's fever had been very high. Her mother held her, walking with her through the room, until finally she sensed that life had moved away from her child. Then she cradled Carla tightly as if trying to share her own body heat, her own life, with her slowly cooling child. She made no sound, but tears ran freely over her thin cheeks, dropping on Carla's little face—until Nadine took her gently away.

Carla fit perfectly in one of the Red Cross boxes, and the lid closed tightly. Her mom, together with Johanna, her oldest daughter, carried the box to the gate, where a large group of friends silently waited. Then as Bart's mom and Johanna continued holding the little casket, one of the ladies read something from a Bible, after which they all sang a hymn. When they were done, Bart's mom refused to set Carla down. Gently, Johanna coaxed her mom to carry the casket to the little graveyard behind the camp, where so many more before her had been buried. They allowed the *koelies* to close the little grave.

Johanna had tied branches and flowers into a wreath, which she left on the raw soil that had been roughly shoveled atop the box. They walked back then, Johanna and her mom, arms around each other, mourning the little girl they had to leave behind. Such deep, unexpected grief ended the excitement of the past weeks. No one sang anymore in our barrack. People whispered whenever they talked to one another. And then one night, Bart's mom ended all that by praying a short prayer, followed by a funny little story about Carla when she was still very small. Everything went back to normal after that.

When the boys recovered, they brought flowers or green branches to Carla each day, and whenever rain leveled the little hill, they heaped it up higher. Simon did not mention her name ever, but Simon and Bart remained friends, drawn even closer by Carla's death.

Not all of the poisoned children recovered as soon as Simon and Bart did. Two of them still suffered from seizures, so Nadine requested their transfer to a hospital in Medan. They left in an ambulance the following day.

It took even the recovering children several weeks to completely get rid of the toxins in their bodies. The mothers watched their children closely after that, and many of them regularly swept the shady areas of the camp where the pits fell every day.

Mom received her nursing dress. It was a beautiful, soft-yellow dress made from silky parachute material. It had a belt and a shirt-like top, which closed with four large real buttons. She was immensely proud of it and was careful never to spill anything on it. Her skin looked slightly yellow, but the dress brought out her dark eyes, and ever since Bart's mom had gotten her a small mirror, she spent lots of time brushing her hair. She combed it up in an effort to hide the dull or bald places. Mom took better care of herself in general these days. Although she was still dreadfully thin, I could see in her the woman she had been before the war had started—before the Japanese soldiers had locked us away in camps, and long before Dad had been taken away and I had become a grown-up.

Mom also had started talking about Dad, and she was not the only one. Most women talked about their men and boys, making plans for when they'd all be together again and—though hesitantly at first, more confidently later—questioning whether they were even still alive. Not having answers put a shadow over the joy.

The Red Cross parcels kept coming and soon included clothes in all sizes and colors. The clothes often didn't fit right, but altering them was easy and saved the women from boredom. Sewing clubs popped up in every barrack, and the women paraded their tailored dresses and skirts for each other. The kids were just as happy trying on clothes, trading them with each other, and parading for their mothers. Easabella and Emma-M became little ladies, careful not to make their new clothes dirty.

We were still not allowed to venture outside the gate without a guard. It felt strange to think that the Japanese guards were now there to protect us, rather than to keep us prisoner. Indonesians in the nearby villages continued to rebel and assemble in dangerous groups, with weapons. We often heard fighting and yelling and sometimes a gunshot in the distance, but no one knew what was going on—who was fighting whom, or who was winning or losing.

Then one day an open jeep arrived with four British officers. They were tall men in impeccable uniforms. They got out of the jeep with fast, easy movements. The Japanese guards stood motionless, but then, to our big surprise, bent at the waist and made perfect bows for the officers, who ignored them and came through the gate. They walked around the camp, discussing what they saw and pointing things out to one another. Curious women and children followed them, and, occasionally, one of the officers would smile at a child or offer a cigarette to a woman. The officers then spent time with the camp leader, after which they left as quietly as they had come.

They were back the next morning with a small army truck, and the Japanese guards were handcuffed and shoved into the truck none too gently. We looked at the Japanese soldiers standing in the truck motionless, their faces closed. Then after another short meeting with the camp leader at the gate, the truck drove away, leaving four British soldiers in the guardhouse. They were loaded with chocolate and cigarettes, which they gave to those of us hanging around the gate. Then they just walked around the camp entrance a bit, making sure we were safe.

Koempoelans became necessary again, but just once a day, and there was no counting. Instead, we were briefed about what was going on outside the gates. We learned that there were two more women-and-children camps not far away, and that we were allowed to visit them when escorted by a guard. We were also told that an all-male camp was close by, which brought extra excitement. All of these other camps were on rubber plantations and in the same condition. We received newspapers and more news about the men and women in the other camps, and then we were told that a list of names from the all-male camp was expected to arrive any day.

The next morning, Nadine and two other nurses drove off in an army truck. They returned the next day with loads of medical supplies and a clean, large refrigerator. The refrigerator went into the guardhouse, which had been cleaned from top to bottom and became the nursing office, where the nurses would see incoming patients. People too sick to take care of themselves would remain in the clinic. Nadine also announced that a doctor from Medan would be coming that week or the next.

Mom was very busy at the clinic and got a second nursing dress—this time white. The material was a cool cotton. She unfolded it with careful hands, felt its softness, and held it in front of her for size. Of course, it was too big, but she didn't care. There was a belt with it, which she could use to pull the wide skirt together, making pleats around her waist. She looked at me, holding the dress over her breasts. She made a few dance steps and whirled around.

"It's dusty, Sofia," she said. "It has been in those army trucks and God knows where else. Wash it for me today, so I can wear it tomorrow. I'll use an iron at the clinic." Then she took off to the nursing office, which was now known as the polyclinic.

It was not difficult to wash Mom's dress. It was not really dirty, and we had soap now. I hung it over the clothesline next to the barrack and hung the belt beside it. It was a long belt and the ends nearly reached the ground. We had no clothespins and it was windy, so it wasn't easy to keep it on the line. I sat in the shade and watched it move in the wind for awhile. The wind felt cool on my face, which was still feverish from last night's malaria attack. I looked at the sky. There hadn't been much sun this morning; I knew rain would fall soon.

I closed my eyes and my mind took off. There had been news that large groups of men had been shipped to Burma and Thailand to build a railroad. Maybe Dad was there and that was the reason we still had no mail from him. I wondered if he would have been treated better there, since he'd be working at a railroad. Maybe he'd also have better food, since he'd be doing such hard work. Or, did any of that even make a difference? Maybe it didn't, because maybe we would never be together again. Mom must have wondered about the same things.

I loved the cool wind on my face and wished I could ride it. It would take me high and away from everything. I would feel weightless and without a body. Perhaps, somewhere up there I could find Mies. I could ask her how everything could turn out so wrong—how she could have been so mistaken. Perhaps, she would be with God. But most likely not. She would have found out there was no God at all. No God would have wanted anything to do with this hell. All she had told me was just a story to help me survive. And here, she wasn't able to survive herself.

I missed Mies Miedema. I missed her so badly that it had become a steady pain, always there—during the day and through the night; when people laughed; when I looked in Phaedra's eyes; when Mom talked about next month and next year.

The wind, much stronger now, flapped and clapped Mom's dress around the clothesline. *Rain would be coming soon*, I thought drowsily. A deep feeling of loss flooded my body and I scrambled up, unwilling to deal with it.

I went looking for Easabella and Emma-M; they would need to be inside when the rain came. The air changed, and the clouds passed dark and fast. I had to look a long time before I found the little girls at the gate, each licking a chocolate bar. A lot of kids were gathered around the British soldier, who entertained them by telling them a story in pantomime. He used his face, hands, and entire body. He said not a word, yet the kids followed his story in detail and only noticed the coming storm when the first raindrops hit.

The whole group scattered, shrieking and laughing. Taking each little sister by a hand, I ran, and we reached the nearest barrack just in time, half-wet and breathless. The tropical rainstorm drummed the roofs, the trees, and the grounds relentlessly. It changed the paths into mud, and then into streams that ran fast and dirty, taking garbage and wood debris on its way.

The storm stopped as suddenly as it had started. Kids came out and had a ball playing in the muddy mess, slipping and sliding until they looked like big chocolate dolls.

When Mom came home from the clinic, Easabella and Emma-M were waiting, tired and hungry, but clean. Then after supper, Mom asked me to see her dress. I froze. I had completely forgotten about it during the storm. I ran outside to find it hanging like a rag, whipped by wind and rain, mud spots at the seams and the collar. There was no sign of the belt.

Mom had followed me outside and she now stood there, taking in the scene: the crumpled, dirty rag that had once been a beautiful dress, the muddy ground around us as far as we could see, me frantically peeling the dress off the line. I shook it out, hoping to find the belt hidden between the wet crinkles. She had no problem guessing what had happened. Her eyes turned cold, as she looked at me.

"I'll wash it again, Mom," I said. "Again and again, until it is white." Then I spoke faster because her stony face scared me. "I'll look for the belt, don't worry—I'll find it! I promise I'll look until I find it!"

Mom said nothing. She just stood there, watching me squirm as I tried to wring the rainwater out of her dress, which really was a mess. It was so streaked and dirty, I would never get it white again! Her eyes were dark and angry.

Finally, she said, "You do that, Sofia. You wash that dress and get it white again. And you look for that belt till you find it. Until you do, don't come home. I will not talk to you again until this dress is complete and washed, ready for me to use in the clinic."

She turned and went inside.

I looked around me. Something seemed different, but nothing had changed. The same mud under my feet, the same wet dress in my hands, the same gray sky with patches of white and the sun at the edge of the clouds. I saw and heard and felt everything as usual, yet I knew something was very different. Mom had closed a door that I wouldn't be able to open again. A door that I unwittingly had kept open despite everything in Mom I didn't understand. Despite the fact that in her eyes I was less than Simon, despite my futile efforts to make her love me, despite the welts from Dad's belt, despite the total isolation she threw me into when she found it necessary, and despite her inability and unwillingness to try to know me, I had had hope. Until now, I had had hope that she would change—that she would see me and start to love me. Today, the door to my chamber of hope had shut, and she would never know how much I'd lost. I would never be the same again.

The dress was ruined, it would never again be nice and white, and with the belt missing it was useless.

I felt nothing. No pain, no regret. All I knew was guilt. I did understand her anger and disappointment. But she had expected too much and had not given me a chance to explain. Yet this cold feeling had nothing to do with Mom's cold eyes and bitter words; rather, it was that the dress seemed to have been more important to her than I.

If Mom didn't want to see me, that was fine. She wouldn't. And she didn't. I spent my days being with Peter, helping Simon and Bart collect flowers for Carla's grave, and sleeping at Nadine's clinic. She had a meal waiting for me every night after Mom left her job.

Talking to Nadine about the day I ruined Mom's dress needed time, which she gave me; she didn't ask. I needed to put my mind straight. Even Peter couldn't follow me when I tried to talk to him about it. He was my friend, but he was a boy and I had never told him much about Mom. I avoided Mom, which didn't feel so bad. I had no desire to see her. I felt unable to face what I knew for sure would happen—she would deliberately turn away. Her eyes would be everywhere but on me. I would be air; you couldn't see air. And the helpless, lonely feeling of rejection would be nothing new to me.

I missed Mies Miedema.

The day after the dress disaster, for the first time in my life, I saw Simon making his own choices. He had found me at the clinic helping Nadine. Simon was nine now. He had become wiser and had aged like I had, only his eyes remained solemn and serious. The rubber pit poisoning had left his skin transparent and pale, and his cropped red hair closed around his small face like a cap.

"Mom told me about the dress you lost," he said quietly.

I looked at him—at Mom's darling boy and the favorite among her children.

"What about it, Simon?" My voice sounded flat and indifferent. I couldn't care less, if Simon knew or not; it didn't change anything.

We sat on the steps of the stone building, the early evening falling around us. Simon drew figures in the soft ground, his thin frame bent over his knees. I looked at him. He was the same brother I always knew, and yet wasn't. He had gone through the same hell, the same abuse, and the same fear. Together, we had lost three and a half years of our youth, and I wondered if either one of us would ever be a normal child again. Sitting next to him, I felt a feeling of friendship grow in me, a fine, good understanding between two survivors of more than just prison camp.

"What about it, Simon?" I repeated, this time softer.

Simon stood. "I'm with you, Sofia," he said. Then he walked away.

Still sitting, I bent my head over my feet, not wanting my tears to show. He had scribbled my name in the sand. I wiped it away and looked up, feeling empty. I missed him.

There was water. A lot of light brown, unclean water through which I had to swim. Reaching the other side of the river had seemed easy, but wasn't. For the longer I swam, the farther away the other shore seemed. I got tired and stopped swimming, and my head disappeared under the water. I panicked, but my head just went deeper. Then I realized I was not alone. Large dark forms were floating with me. I pushed them away violently. One fell apart, and a body took its place.

They were baskets, and the dead bodies inside were bloated and had open eyes. One floating body touched me and slowly broke into pieces. No blood; just pieces. The pieces came at me, and they were many. Knees, feet, eyes, hands, and heads, they all kept coming. I jerked and fought, struggling to avoid the body parts, until Nadine woke me. Drenched in sweat, but crying with relief, I realized it had only been a dream. Even with Nadine's arms around me, I didn't dare to go back to sleep.

She changed the dressing on my ankle. I had kicked the bed poles in my sleep and opened up the sore. Blood now stained the clean white bandage, which she removed and threw out.

"I'll wash that bandage for you tomorrow, Nadine," I said, but I could only whisper. "Don't throw it out; we can use it again."

I became very cold after my fight in the water.

Nadine smiled. "When the doctor comes later this week, we'll have this ulcer taken care of, Sofia, once and for all. Go to sleep now. I'll watch you for awhile."

It was a long time later that I watched her quietly leave my side.

After I had stayed at the clinic for a week, Nadine talked to Mom. I never found out what they discussed and I didn't care. Nothing Nadine said to Mom would make any difference. She did, however, give Mom another white nursing dress, and sent me to sleep at home the next night.

Although the new dress was not as nice as the ruined one, Mom seemed happy with it. She washed it herself. It took weeks before she talked to me like before, and even then we were both silent with each other most of the time. We had nothing to discuss, and the door remained closed.

Pieces of new information arrived in the camp as the days went on. We learned that American airplanes had dropped bombs on two Japanese cities, and the *Tenno Heiko* had surrendered. The gate had remained open all the time, but we were still warned not to leave the camp without an escort. An Indonesian man named Soekarno had declared the independence of Indonesia just a few days after the emperor Hirohito had surrendered, resulting in a lot of shooting and killing. The fighting had increased, and guerilla troops roamed everywhere.

Twice a week, a doctor came to see patients. Most of his time was spent cutting into festering sores and swollen tropical ulcers. When people were too sick or their ulcers too deep, however, they were lifted into an ambulance and transported to a hospital in Medan.

As Nadine had promised, the doctor took care of my ulcer once and for all. He was Dutch and himself a free man only a few months. He was thin and looked tired when he entered the camp in the morning and exhausted when he left at night. He had gentle hands and a soft voice, but Nadine did most of the talking. She explained the history of all the patients who had to see him.

When I came, she told him how I'd gotten my tropical ulcer and how long it had been festering. He removed the bandage, inspected the spongy flesh around the ulcer, and then nodded to Nadine. No words were exchanged, but the silent communication between them gave me an uneasy feeling. Something was going to happen and I wouldn't like it. I was right. Nadine told me to brace myself; it would hurt. And she was right.

I had promised myself not to cry or scream. No matter how bad the pain, I could handle it. I wasn't a kid anymore and I had become used to pain. *This couldn't possibly be any worse than the* koempoelan *beatings*, I thought. And it couldn't possibly be worse than the pain of having the boiling soup burn my back. But when Nadine strapped my wrists to bamboo poles, I became scared.

Nadine explained that when the doctor handled ulcers on kids, he needed to be protected from kicking and hitting. In so much pain, the patient would reflexively hit the doctor's working hands, causing more damage and pain. During the first several of these procedures, it had taken four people to handle a child, so Nadine had decided to strap the children down.

There was no anesthesia available in the clinic, as operations were not done in the camps. So when an area had to be anesthetized, the doctor used an ether cap, which Nadine would put over someone's nose. Then the doctor would give an injection to numb the area to be treated.

As Nadine put my wrists and healthy leg in straps, I tried to see what the doctor was doing. He rubbed something very cold over my entire foot and ankle, which I recognized as ether. I had smelled it before in the clinic. A coat of iodine followed, and then I felt the sting of a needle. I came up in a hurry. What was he doing?

Nadine pushed me down again, and a second sting didn't seem to hurt as much.

"Relax, Sofia," Nadine said in a crisp, professional voice and looked at me. "It'll be over soon. Let the doctor do his job and try not to move. I'll hold onto your leg."

I must have looked terrified, for she promised to put a little ether cap over my nose, if I found the pain too bad. "Although I know you will not like the smell of ether," she added.

I had always pinched my nose when I'd smelled it in the clinic. It smelled strong and sharp, and the odor crept up in my nose and made me sneeze.

I missed the sign she gave the doctor and the pain began. I screamed and forgot my determination to be brave. I screamed so hard, I forgot to swallow and almost choked. It felt like he was chopping off my foot. Was I going to have only one foot from now on? Why hadn't Nadine told me about this?

When Mom came later, Nadine told her that the ulcer was so deep that it had festered close to the bone. The doctor had had no choice but to cut it all away and then spoon it out. She showed me the little spoon tool he used, and I shuddered, reliving the horrible pain. *Perhaps*, I thought, *I should have chosen the ether cap.*

The hole in my ankle had been filled with a yellowish powder and dressed with extra pads. Nadine kept me in the clinic two days, with my foot high on a pillow. I wasn't allowed to walk for a week after and never felt so bored. The wound healed nicely, though it felt sunken and hollow underneath the scarred skin. Nadine explained that time would fill the hollow a bit, but that the scar would always be visible. It would forever be a long, elevated, white ribbon where the knife had gone in, surrounded by a large white circle as wide as the ulcer had been. It would be a memento of my brutal years in the camps. But at least there would be no more pain.

When I could walk normally again, I needed only a large bandage over my ankle. Then I went to the gate every day to watch men, and boys almost as tall as men, come and go. They were the men and boys now living in the all-male camp close by, who had gone through the same misery as we had, and been separated from their families, just like us.

Would it not be something wonderful and fantastic if I saw Dad just come in? Just out of nowhere? I knew this would not happen, but for a moment, I let myself drift into the dream. It could be possible, couldn't it? Why should I have seen other fathers come walking through the gate and not mine?

They pushed in hurriedly, shouting and asking and searching for the faces they'd been longing to see. Some had already found their wives and heartbreaking hugs and tears followed. Couples couldn't let go of each other, and between the men and women, children squeezed, trying to get attention from their fathers.

Other men kept on searching for cherished faces and wouldn't find them. And there were women who asked the visiting men whether they had known their husbands, whether they might have been transported somewhere else, and, with hesitation, whether they had perhaps died.

Mom did this. She never tired of asking and remained hopeful. "No news is good news!" she would say.

But I was afraid we would never see him again if he was not still in Sumatra, because among the happy women and children, there were others who had only now heard that their men and fathers had died. There were also children who had found their fathers and had had to tell them that their moms had died.

Emma-M and Easabella stood watching these unusual scenes with big eyes. They looked at the happy, laughing women, and then they looked at the women standing together, holding onto each other, and sharing their grief.

Emma-M asked what Dad looked like. Easabella tried to explain but got stuck because it was difficult for her to remember as well, let alone describe him. Simon said he was looking for a man with red hair.

Mom frowned at him. "It is not red hair, Simon, it is a red beard!" Then she added softly, "His hair will probably be gray by now."

As the weeks passed, more and more men visited the women-and-children camps, and vice-versa. Information was exchanged and questions were answered. Men and women listened to each other's stories of loneliness and pain.

We learned that thousands of women and children had been collected into three Aik Paminke camps in close proximity of each other, and that more than two thousand men and boys from camps all over Sumatra had been transported to Camp Si Rengo Rengo. There remained one unanswered question: how long would this continue?

Men also brought the news that the emperor of Japan had surrendered on August 15, but that we hadn't been informed of the end of the war until ten days later. It seemed odd to be aware again of months and dates.

One day during the last week of that wonderful August month, we all stood outside around our barracks and welcomed Allied airplanes with waving hands, jubilant voices, and happy tears. They flew over the Aek Paminke camps and dropped more food and goodies.

Right after that, in the first week of September, a small Allied reconnaissance unit arrived at the gate. They had been close by for weeks, hiding in the jungle.

The days were filled with surprises. Mail came in at least once a week, sometimes more. We could take baths more often, and the entire camp had lights. Nadine and two other nurses had started a vaccination program, whereby first the children and later the adults could be immunized from a number of diseases. Easabella and Emma-M refused to go, until Simon and Bart called them sissies, and then they changed their minds. For awhile after getting the shots, we walked around with painful swollen arms and low fevers. For malaria, we now had a regime of pills to be taken weekly. And the worms had stopped dropping in the latrines.

Life had become much easier, except that we still didn't know where Dad was. Mom had gone to the other camps in the area and asked the men there the same questions: Did they know Dad? Had he been in any of the same camps with them? Did they know whether he had been transported somewhere else? The only thing she learned was that she wasn't the only one among many in the Aek Paminke camps without news about her husband, and this gave her more hope. She thought that all of these missing husbands must have been transported away together.

Shortly before the Aek Paminke camps were to be emptied and we were to be transported to Medan, Mom received the message that long lists of POWs were available in the city for the women to search. This message was sufficient for her. She stopped scouting the other camps for information and focused on the hope that, indeed, Dad's name would be on one of those lists.

Leaving Aek Paminke happened in stages. There were so many of us, it would take weeks to move everyone from the four camps to Medan. We left in groups, and when it was our turn, we were ready. It was now October, more than two months after we'd been told that Japan had surrendered.

We did not have much to take. And we left most of what we did have, since little of it was worth anything and we would be given new possessions in Medan. There were still many uncertainties about our arrival in the city. Mom was talking about living in a real house, which in the beginning we might have to share with another family. I had forgotten how it felt to live in a house like free people, making our own choices and going wherever we wanted. We could play and walk and go to school. We would recover from all suffering and illness. We would again live a life that we thought would no longer be possible. And we would wait till Dad came.

I looked back at the camp as we drove through the gate of Aek Paminke I. The same gate we'd gone in and out of so many times over the past weeks, we were now leaving for the last time. I gazed upon the almost empty barracks and searched for the little graveyard hidden behind the rubber trees. It had been the best camp of them all, but like the others, it had taken things from all of us. Together, the three Aik Paminke camps had buried many, many women and children amid the multiple rubber trees. We could go now, but there, behind the trees, were the graves we had to leave behind.

The camps and the Japanese guards had pillaged and plundered, emptying us piece by piece until there was nothing left. They had stripped us of values, decency, and health. They had robbed us of youth, joy, unity, and future. They had left us with nothing. No strength with which to rebuild, no vision, no security. Would we ever feel safe again?

With ridicule and torture, they had damaged, if not killed, goodness and truth; they had destroyed the core that separated people from animals. They had killed what was dearest to us: fathers, mothers, and children. And yet, here we were, the ones who had survived these dark years. Despite our damage, despite our bloated bodies and fearful minds, despite bowing and bending and falling and standing, we were still here. We had survived. Did that mean something? Should we not all be proud for persevering? If we should, I didn't know how.

I looked at Mom. She sat straight in her seat, with Simon next to her. Her eyes were clear and without confusion. She had washed and combed her dark hair, and although the wave had not returned, it seemed fuller and had a bit of the old shine. Her dress, a present from the Red Cross, was clean, stylish, and the right size. Mom's legs, belly and face were bloated with edema, her nails were short and unmanicured, and her body was frightfully thin, but she seemed determined to be Mom again—a mother of children and responsible for them.

We had all survived. Emma-M and Easabella had been babies when we'd left Langsa and there was nothing left of their playful happiness and silly behavior. They were almost six and seven now, and had never been to school. Their faces were serious, although they looked around with excitement. They looked forward to new and better things.

Simon was different. He was nine now, the same age I had been when this mess had all started. His eyes were always watchful and a constant wariness leaned over his narrow shoulders. Although his friendship with Bart had toughened him up, he seemed to expect nothing good of the things that lie ahead.

And then there was me. I sat away from my family, far in the back of the bus. This was my choice. I didn't want to have to answer Emma-M's endless questions or listen to Mom's orders when one of the girls did something wrong. I wanted to be alone with my thoughts.

I had said good-bye to Peter when he had left before us, and he had promised to hunt me down in Medan. I wondered about that. I couldn't explain my feelings, but I wouldn't have been disconsolate if we didn't find each other. I would just bury him in my heart like all the others. I almost expected it. After Mies's death, I had grown away from Peter, outgrown Peter, and had felt guilty about it; he had been my best friend since we had started school together. But I had gone to a place where Peter couldn't follow, and, perhaps, I didn't want him to follow. All I had left from Mies were memories, and I didn't want to share them with anybody. Not even Peter.

I looked around me. It was quiet in the bus. Many dozed, their bodies following the bus's movements over the rough road. We had arrived in Aik Paminke in trucks, shoved together like cattle. We had been pushed and counted, hit and yelled at. We had been sick, hungry, and totally depleted, without any expectation for something different or better than we'd had the last three years. Now in busses, each of us had a seat, comfortable and roomy—all except the weakest and sickest, who traveled before us in ambulances, arrived in Medan, and got the care they needed.

All I felt was indifference, an aloof acceptance of more pain, grief, and loneliness, should that be what our future held. I realized that was wrong, but didn't know how to change it and whether it was worth trying to change. I had forgotten how to look forward to change and future and beauty.

Evening was falling. The sun hung low and I thought about its last rays softly slipping over the small graveyard we left behind. Its markers would soon disappear in the shadows of the rubber trees. Carla would be left behind, forever sleeping under the little hill that Simon and Bart had dressed with flowers this morning for the final time.

They all came back to my mind. Karel, Baby Miedema, old Mrs. Hansen, Jaap's grandmother, Carla. And Mies. And the many others who were nameless to me who had died and left the camp in baskets, to be buried in graves now left behind, without names or markers that would, too, soon disappear.

Why did they have to die without dignity, without seeing the faces of their husbands or fathers a final time? Why did they have to die without the chance to say good-bye?

Herman and Trudy Sanders were still in the camp. They would follow a few days later. Phaedra would leave with Nadine in the last group. What would happen to Phaedra? Nadine had promised to take care of her and take her home. Where was home for Phaedra? Would Nadine bring Phaedra to her family in Holland? Would Phaedra ever laugh and live again?

What would happen to us if we got to Medan and learned Dad had died long ago? It was safer not to hope. Then there would be no despair, and we could go on living the way we had for so long now—without him.

The road was quiet. Our bus was the only vehicle around. The evening had arrived and brought with it the peace of day's end. The doors of houses along the road were closed and their oil lamps burned softly.

We found the train with clean wagons waiting for us at the little station. Everyone found a place to sit, and no families had to fight to stay together. The toilets were clean and they had water and toilet paper. We would travel through the night, which Mom found wonderful. Emma-M and Easabella could sleep comfortably and be surprised in the morning when they awoke to discover that Medan was nearby.

The train would be under surveillance, and our protection from Indonesian rebels ensured. They had become more powerful and dangerous now, and many of them in Medan carried weapons that they didn't hesitate to use.

In Medan, Mom would be able to find a list with the name of men sent to Burma and Thailand in 1942 and 1943. There would also be a list of men who drowned when their ship was bombed by Japanese airplanes. The Japanese pilots hadn't known that the ship was filled with prisoners on their way to build a railroad for Japan.

What would happen to us if Dad's name was on that list? It would mean he'd have been dead for years.

There were too many thoughts and too much fear. The future felt like a very long, very dark tunnel, and I didn't know what was waiting at the end.

I felt more afraid than I ever had been in the camps.

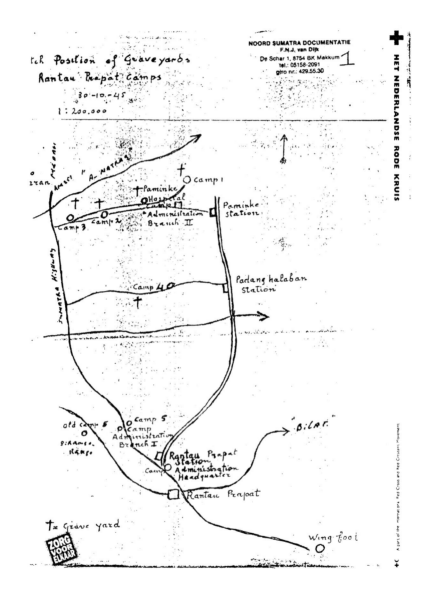

MEDAN

November 1945

In Medan, we were assigned to a house with another family. An entire house, with bathroom and running water and many bedrooms. There were even two extra rooms in which to play, eat, or just sit around. There were chairs and there were two tables where we were supposed to sit when eating or speaking to each other.

Easabella and Emma-M couldn't remember how it was to live in a house, and didn't realize that doing so had been normal before the war. They didn't know how to sit on a toilet and both slipped into the bowl a few times before doing it right. Flushing was an adventure for them, as they pulled the chord against the wall and heard water coming down from somewhere high. When the water came and flushed everything away to an invisible place, they looked around the bowl to try to see where it went. And when they couldn't find water, they pulled the chord again. They did this endlessly and found it all hilarious.

Finally, Simon stopped them and called them wasteful little snots who did not deserve to live in a nice house. They didn't speak to him for a few days, pretending he was air.

"Just like Mom," explained Easabella.

The other family living with us had only one kid, but the father was already there. His wife called him Johan. He was very thin and looked sick. He coughed constantly and spent all day outside, swaying in a hammock, spitting out whatever the coughing had brought up. Simon called him a dirty old man.

Whenever he slept in his hammock, Easabella and Emma-M thought he was dead, but they walked on their toes in case he wasn't dead but was actually

179

asleep. They definitely did not want to wake him. And they had to be careful to avoid the spit in the grass.

Even when he was awake, I thought he looked dead. He moved and spoke, but didn't want to be bothered, especially by the kids. We were all happy that he preferred to spend the day outside.

Mom had finally found Dad's name on a list of men who were shipped to Burma to do railroad work. Not much more was known, except that he was alive and that transport of the surviving men in Burma would be arranged as soon as possible; they would return by airplane instead of by ship.

I had expected Mom to be happier after hearing this, but instead, she became more nervous. Waiting was difficult for her and made her smoke all the time.

Simon didn't like the smell of her clothes, and said she smelled like a campfire. But Mom couldn't care less. She continued to smoke because she said she needed it.

She said she wished she could go for walks, but because of the unrest all around us, we'd gotten strict orders to stay off the streets—and in fact, not to leave the house at all. The environment in the area outside Medan was definitely unsafe, but we had been told that shootings, abductions, and murders were also regular inside the city. There was no heavy organized fighting, but groups of young Indonesian men were rumored to roam the city streets, swinging their spears and swords, screaming "*Merdeka*! (Freedom!)" with loud, militant voices.

So Mom stayed in and around the house, trying to find things to do. She did those things that Sitah and Hassan had done for her so long ago, but she didn't seem to mind. We didn't have many possessions to take care of anyway, and it made the wait for Dad easier.

She particularly loved to cook, which she had learned from Sitah. She sometimes baked *pisang goring* for us in the kitchen, even though Johan always complained for days about the greasy odor in the house. To this, Simon again had an answer. He told Johan that we loved *pisang goreng* and that if it bothered him, he could always go outside.

Lately, Simon spoke up a lot; he had spent too much time with Bart. But I liked this new Simon, and thought it was funny, since he'd never spoken up before.

We lived a strange life those first months in Medan. We took baths twice a day, just to enjoy the delicious feeling of cold, clean water over our shoulders. We didn't like the scratchy feeling of toilet paper, so we quickly went back to cleaning ourselves with water from a bottle. We had to unlearn eating with our hands and learn how to eat less greedily; hoarding the leftovers was not necessary anymore as they could be refrigerated and saved. Throwing off clothes when the heat became unbearable wasn't done anymore and shoes were worn always. We had enough to wear and enough to eat. We were never hungry. We went for medical exams and dental check-ups. And though the clinic was close by, we still had to take a bus to get there. It became an outing for us.

One day, we had to go to one of the several clinics provided for the survivors of the Japanese internment camps for more worm and malaria pills, and when we got there, we found Nadine. Mom and Nadine couldn't stop talking; they had so much to tell each other. Nadine told Mom that she had a supervisory function in Medan, and was now responsible for supplying all of the clinics with necessities.

It seemed every hour of the day was spent trying to get things back to normal. I had looked for Peter everywhere but, so far, could not find him. Peter's father was a KNIL sergeant before the war started. He was Indonesian—his mother was Dutch, which made Peter an Indo (mixed race). It didn't help that, because of the *"Merdeka"* (Freedom) dangers, there were large areas of the city where we *blandas* were not even allowed. I hoped that he was looking for me as well, as he had promised. And that one day, we would just meet each other.

Schooling proved a special problem. There were teachers ready to start, but having gone four years without school, the children all had to be tested for knowledge, and age didn't count. I was twelve now and should have been ready for high school. Simon was nine and supposed to be in grade four. Instead, he was placed in a fast-forward grade one class. He should have gone to grade one back in 1942.

Further, the camp children were not used to the discipline of going to school on time every morning. They had difficulty concentrating on material that they were not interested in or not fit enough yet to follow. School necessities were almost nonexistent and organization was poor. It was easier not to go to school at all. Besides, many students were either lethargic or rebellious. Like all the other mothers must have done, Mom sent us to school each morning. But we often came home halfway through the day, for one reason or another.

On one very hot day, I refused to go to school. I sat listlessly on the veranda steps of our house, watching the traffic on the street, which was mostly just pedestrians, bicycles, and *betjaks* (two-wheeled carts pulled by men), but there were a few cars. Then three large covered trucks turned slowly around the corner, and when they passed me, I saw the Japanese soldiers. They were standing in the trucks, dressed in drab uniforms that looked all the same. These uniforms, though, had no shiny buttons, ribbons, or decorations. The

Japanese soldiers stood in the truck without their caps, their shiny black boots, and their rifles, and were being guarded by British soldiers with guns.

I knew they were going to an area outside Medan to work in the fields, because a week before, a school bus had taken us to a dentist office, and on the way there, we had seen the soldiers working. Their heads were bent over their shovels, and they had closed faces and expressionless eyes. When a British soldier passed, they all bowed toward him instead of in the direction of Japan, to greet their God Emperor Hirohito. Was he not anymore that godly person, now that he had surrendered?

They now bowed for foreign soldiers the way they had made us bow, without mercy, to them. I wondered what was going through their heads, whether they felt sorry in any way for what they had done. As I saw them pass, I remembered the numerous times that I had in the beginning, without thinking, automatically bowed for the British soldiers who had replaced the Japanese guards. I couldn't help feeling ridiculous afterward, hurrying to stand straight again, and the humiliation angered me even more. At least, I hadn't been the only one. We'd all had to unlearn bowing and always feeling so degraded and enslaved.

It reminded me of one day in the polyclinic at Camp Aek Paminke. I'd been there helping, when a nervous woman came in, talking nonstop about the misery of the past years. The doctor was there, but Nadine was not, and I didn't know the nurse who was helping him.

The doctor had asked her for her reason for being there, but she had been nervous and seemed to want to talk only about what she went through in the camps. The doctor listened, not saying much, but he put his hand up to silence her when she started her story again from the beginning.

He sternly explained, "The Japanese soldier is filled with contempt for all prisoners. Becoming a prisoner to him means shame and lost honor, and he would prefer death over both those things. Not choosing death is seen as shameful and deserving of punishment. Also, the Japanese soldier feels a part of our shame, since he is forced to guard us. He blames the prisoners for his disgrace, and so works himself out on them with fury and cruelty.

"He is used to being in Japan, also, where women are to serve. Holding her head up high and looking a man in the face is seen as a sign of pride and arrogance. A Japanese soldier feels offended when a woman doesn't cast her eyes down humbly, but keeps on staring. He feels this is deserving of punishment."

The patient had looked at him with angry eyes, her face pale and hard. "They have reduced people to lower than animals. They have killed numerous men, women, and children without reason. They have taken away trust, hope, and identity. They have taken away more than they will ever be able to repair. They had no right! This will be forever remembered by all of us!"

The doctor had been silent after that.

I didn't quite understand his answer. Was he defending the Japanese occupiers? Was he agreeing with their behavior and excusing the sadistic games they'd played? I had the same feelings as the woman and would have added to her list of accusations.

I talked to Nadine later about this conversation. Nadine, gentle and understanding as always, smoothed over the doctor's attempt to help the woman understand the Japanese culture. Nadine thought that all he had been trying to do was to explain that Japanese men were this way because they were products of their culture and they had never known any different.

"It will take generations to change this way of thinking and it will only come about if there is more contact with other cultures," she said.

I couldn't figure out if I agreed or disagreed with Nadine.

Sitting on the veranda, watching more passing trucks loaded with Japanese soldiers, I still didn't feel anything. I wanted to hate them and despise them. I longed to feel something, anything, just to recognize an emotion inside me. But there was nothing. No feeling, no interest, no hope, no expectations—no answers.

I had difficulty sleeping now. Every night, I lay in bed, my experiences of the past years traveling through my mind like a film in slow motion. For weeks, I wondered about the *koempoelan* square, empty now, but blotched with dark stains left by blood, waste, and vomit, footprints forever molded in the soft tar from our standing in the sickening heat or cold rain, hour after hour. These were the stains and imprints of humiliation, abuse, and sadistic punishment.

When I finally did sleep I'd hear the dull sounds of gun butts striking bodies and the specific crack of a breaking bone, in exhausting dreams, accompanied by screams and shouts or whistling whips. Then the haunting of Mies's suffering and death broke through and changed my sleeping into crying.

Dad came back to Sumatra from Burma on a cloudy afternoon.

He was to arrive by plane with other male survivors of the Burma-Siam railroad project. Mom was informed of his arrival two days before, and did nothing after but pace the house. She started projects, attempting to pass the time, but didn't finish them. She smoked nonstop and became so hyped up, that I went to the clinic just to get away. I was lucky to find Nadine there, who held me tight for awhile without explaining why. I told her about Mom, and she gave me a sleeping pill for her.

When the time came to go to the landing strip, Mom couldn't do it. She was trembling. "Go, Sofia, go with Simon," she said. "I'll wait here. It is much better if someone waits at home to welcome him. Look for his red beard—you'll know him right away."

Simon and I walked and were almost too late. We had expected to see the plane somewhere high in the sky, but before we even reached the airstrip, we saw it swooping in over the houses with its landing gear out. I ran ahead of Simon, afraid we'd miss the first men emerging from the big plane door.

Among the throngs of people on the airstrip, it would be hard for Simon to find me, but I didn't want to miss Dad, and we would find Simon soon enough. Out of breath, standing behind the roped-off path, I searched the faces. All of the men looked the same. They all were thin with stooped shoulders and short hair: blond, brown, and black, and lots of gray, with some white. What about red? A red beard and black hair! What if he had not come?

I stretched my neck up as far as I could and saw them pass, one by one. There were so many. Their eyes were searching the waiting women and children, who screamed and shouted. It was hard to see who belonged where or to whom. Lots of people around us cried silently, as women and men embraced, clinging to each other. But many men were still searching, all of them with fear on their faces.

Then Dad came down the steps. My heart jumped and I felt my throat close; I hadn't seen him for so long. But he had filled my mind so often that I didn't need the red beard or the black hair to tell me it was him. They weren't there anymore, anyway. Just like Mom had said, his red beard was now streaked with gray—much gray. His hair wasn't black anymore either, and was much thinner. Dad was never a tall man, but now he looked smaller than I ever remembered.

Perhaps because I had grown, I thought.

Taken up by the immense excitement around me, I jumped high and yelled, "Dad, here we are! Look here, Dad!"

So many were shouting the same thing. How could he see or hear us in that mass of people! I slipped away to stand in the back, so that he would see me for sure, after he had worked his way through the crowd. I still couldn't see Simon anywhere.

Here Dad came pushing forward, slowly shoved by the men behind him. He came closer still, but was too far away to touch. Then I caught his eye, and waved and laughed and called, "Here Dad! I am here, Daddy!"

I saw him look. His eyes looked straight into mine for a moment and then wandered to the next face, searching for the familiar one.

Dad had not recognized me.

I did not go further to find Dad and explain. I did not look anymore for Simon. Instead, I drifted aimlessly through the streets of Medan, wondering, my head full of questions and my heart empty.

I wondered what happened after I left the airstrip. Had Dad's eyes continued to search the crowds until they came to rest on the red-haired lanky boy? Had he then looked into Simon's gray-blue eyes and known that at least his only son had survived the lonely, grim years?

I wondered if Simon would refuse to leave the airstrip with Dad until they'd found me. Or maybe they would leave, but not finding me at home, Simon would return to look for me. I hoped Simon would return to look for me.

I wondered about Mom, what she would do when she saw Dad coming and they found each other. Two people who had gone through hell and were once again together, with too much, or perhaps not enough, to share. I didn't expect Mom to miss me until evening. And perhaps not even then.

I wondered about Easabella and Emma-M, the little girls who were not so little anymore. They would be together when Dad arrived, finding comfort and support in each other as they looked at this man they did not remember and did not know. A man whom they would see all the time now and whom they should call Dad. I wondered if they would look for me; if they would ask this new man whether he had seen me.

And I wondered about myself. But I didn't know where to start. Where would I go from here? Where did I belong? Where would I find all of those things that I had lost before I'd even known they were there?

When Karel de Boer had died, Nadine had said, "Karel traded peace for conflict." I had wondered what she meant then, but knew she could say the same of me now.

Would the rest of my life be conflict? Fears and scars and frozen hate? Would I continue to struggle through lakes of loneliness and closed doors? What would it take for me to find peace? Why did you have to die, Mies?

EPILOGUE

At the end, large groups of survivors from the many camps on Sumatra were gathered in the Aek Paminke Camps I, II, and III and in the all-male camp, Si Rengo Rengo, where they were belatedly informed of Japan's surrender on August 24, 1945.

In November, trucks, busses, and airplanes to the cities of Medan, Palembang, Padang, and Singapore transported the surviving ex-internees and POWs, none of whom had been aware of the ultimate elimination plan waiting to be put into action.

At the occupation of Indonesia, the Japanese troops and their partners had received orders from the top brass to humiliate, starve and eventually execute all Dutch people. The mass graves were dug, the machineguns stood loaded and the waiting was for the order to execute. Because of the two atom bombs on Hiroshima and Nagasaki and the following fast collapse of the Japanese government, the order to the commanders was never delivered. The terrible atom death of more than 100,000 Japanese civilians saved the lives of the Dutch people and many others in Asia.[1]

—J. F. van Wagtendonk
Secretary Stichting Japanse Ereschulden

---

1   From the foreword of the book *Ooggetuigen van oorlog* (*Witnesses of War*), published in 2003 by the Stichting Japanse Ereschulden (Foundation of Japanese Debts of Honor). *Witnesses of War* contains sixty personal stories written by WWII survivors and their children. The foreword, titled "Getuigenissen van de Japanse bezetting in Nederlands-Indië" ("Witness Declarations of the Japanese Occupation in the Dutch Indies"), was written by the secretary of the Stichting Japanse Ereschulden (Foundation of the Japanese Debts of Honor).

Lightning Source UK Ltd.
Milton Keynes UK
UKOW04f0734170215

246352UK00001BB/416/P